Twenty-Five Years of Research into
KOREAN SHAMANISM

Twenty-Five Years of Research into

KOREAN
SHAMANISM

Hyun-key Kim Hogarth, PhD

To contact Customer Sevice, email customer service: sihwaeum@gmail.com, call 82-10-9519-3232

For information:
Sihwaeum Publication Co.
No. 1412, 6, Sapyeong-daero 58-gil, Seocho-gu, Seoul 06611 Republic of Korea

Printed in Seoul, Republic of Korea

ISBN 979-11-966840-6-8

Library of Congress Cataloging in Publication Data

Hogarth, Hyun-key Kim
Korean Shamanism/Hyun-key Kim Hogarth
Description: First edition./ Seoul: Sihwaeum, [2021] Korean Culture Series No.1
Subjets: Korean Shamanism

....

Korean Shamanism
초판인쇄 2021년 9월 15일
초판발행 2021년 9월 21일
지은이 : 김현기
펴낸이 : 연기영
펴낸곳 : 시화음
등 록 : 2018년 11월 21일(제2018-000240호)
주 소 : 서울특별시 서초구 사평대로58길 6 1412호(서초동)
전 화 : 02)534-6726 E-mail : sihwaeum@gmail.com
ISBN 979-11-966840-6-8   정가 30,000원
....

Contents

Preface

It has been twenty-eight years since I first conducted my intensive academic fieldwork among the Korean shamans, generally referred to as *mudang*. There is a Korean saying that in ten years even mountains and rivers change, and it is interesting to see what changes Korean shamanism has undergone in nearly triple that time. What is remarkable is that the principles and the basic formats of the Korean shamanistic practices have stayed more or less the same, although the practitioners, both *mudang* and their associates including administrators, have changed. Many people who kindly helped me so much for no financial rewards during my fieldwork have retired or died, and new faces have emerged, but I have managed to retain many friends among them. It is largely thanks to Mr. Choe Sujin, the late second President of Daehan Gyeongsin Yeonhaphoe (The Republic of Korea Spirit Worshippers' Association) and a son of the late first President Choe Nameok, its founder.

Shamanism is a highly fluid religious phenomenon, which adapts itself readily to the social changes. Therefore it is interesting, but not surprising to see that the name of the largest *mudang* society, originally called Daehan Seunggong Gyoengsin Yeonhaphoe (The Republic of Korea Spirit Worshippers' Association for Victory Over Communism) was changed to Daehan Gyeongsin Yeonhaphoe (DGY) in 1997, without "Seunggong (Victory over Communism)," and its new name was officially registered in 2000. It was deemed necessary, since the inclusion of "Seunggong" was politically incorrect against the backdrop of the gradual opening of the dialogues between the two Koreas. Since the economic crisis of North Korea and President Kim Dae Jung's Sunshine Policy,[1] communication between the two Koreas has somewhat improved, despite

---

1 For an anthropological analysis of the Sunshine Policy, see Hogarth (2012).

the continued deadlock in talks about the reunification and incidents caused by North Korea's belligerence.

Accordingly the objective of DGY has also altered. In the 2005 members' handbook, it was specified as:

> The goal of this association is to instil historical national consciousness through mutual communication (with North Korea) in preparation for the age of reunification, and to preserve, nurture and develop Korean folk culture.

In the 2012 version, the wording was slightly changed to:

> Now that we have entered the age of the reunification (of the two Koreas), the objective of this association is to instil the (common) national historical view, and to preserve, nurture and develop the indigenous demand culture of the Korean nation though mutual communication.

The society's motto, i.e. 'harmony, understanding and creativity,' remains the same, since it reflects the essence of shamanism.

In 2003 DGY's website was first launched, and now there are many websites concerned with the activities of *mudang* and their associates. Anybody interested in DGY's activities can now follow them through www.kyungsin.co.kr and also through other related links, such as www.*mudang*.org/kyungsin/gs_jo.php. In the website, it is specified that as of 2003 DGY had 199 branches nationwide with 200,000 registered members, and according to the elder Mr. Choe the number of the registered members has been steadily growing. In 2013, the number of *mudang* is shown as 300,000. However, I have often been told that some members drop out and work freelance, which is more in keeping with the general nature of shamans. I have also often noticed that *mudang* prefer to form their own small groups with like-minded people and work with them. So I am keenly aware that the activities of DGY only partially represent all the shamanistic practices in Korea.

In recent years, many South Koreans have visited North Korea, albeit under supervision, the most popular places being Geumgang-san (the Diamond Mountains) which are renowned for their supreme natural beauty, and Mt. Baekdu which has long been a symbol of Korean nationalism.[2] DGY have organized tours to Geumgang-san on many occasions[3]

---

2 Mt. Baekdu is so popular as a tourist spot that people apparently say jokingly, "If you want to see someone you have not seen for a long time, go to Mt. Baekdu."

3 400 times according to Mr. Choe Nameok, although it sounds like an exaggeration.

for their members, who offered sacrifices to the Mountain Spirit there with their president as the chief officiator. Their first visit to Mt. Baekdu as a group took place between 22 August and 27 August 2005, with just over 100 members of DGY participating. They offered sacrifices and prayers to Cheonsin (the Heavenly God) at the summit, while there.

I last saw President Choe Nameok in the DGY offices on 26 July 2005 with Prof. Ilmari Vesterinen, a professor of cultural anthropology from Finland. President Choe had been incapacitated for some time after suffering a stroke, and he could neither move without help nor speak coherently. I had to get answers to my questions through his son Mr. Choe Sujin, who was then general manager of DGY and the editor of their newspaper, *Minsok sinmun* (The Folklore Newspaper), and subsequently took over as new President after his father's death. Sadly Mr. Choe Sujin himself died on 25 March, 2016. Mr Choe Nameok told us that although shamanism had been wiped out by the Communist regime, some North Korean people were said to offer prayers to the spirits in private in front of a lighted candle. He also heard people say that they remembered their mothers praying to the spirits in the old days. When I asked him whether there were practising *mudang* in North Korea, he answered that nobody knew, but it was fairly safe to assume that they virtually did not exist. It will be interesting to see whether Korean shamanism, which seems to have totally disappeared, will return to North Korean society some day. One of the tasks of future researchers of Korean shamanism is to find out whether it has indeed gone underground, being kept alive covertly by some die-hard traditionalists.

Another interesting change that has taken place is in the researchers of Korean shamanism. Until recently most research was done by academics or other interested non-*mudang* spectators who were mostly highly educated. *mudang* and their associates performed *gut* and other activities as they had done for generations, and helped the researchers as informants. They were unaware of, or disinterested in any complicated theories that the researchers were formulating, such as "possession/ trance," "shamanism and religion" and "*musok* and shamanism." They were merely interested in improving their techniques through hands-on teaching and practice. However, today it would seem that many *mudang* themselves are keen to study and discuss many different aspects of Korean shamanism. Mr. Choe Sujin, the late second President of DGY, was very keen to promote education of *mudang*, and often contributed articles to *Minsok sinmun*, concerning various theoretical aspects of *musok*. He set up scholarship funds in his late father's name for furthering the education of *mudang*'s children. He was also interested in the psychotherapeutic effects of *gut*, and launched a course on psychotherapy and *musok*. Those who successfully complete the course are presented with a certificate.

This book is a collection of the papers on Korean shamanism that I presented at international conferences and public lectures during the past two and half decades. Some of them have evolved into full-length books, but this book will give insights into various aspects of Korean shamanism to those interested who do not have time to read them all. The papers contained in this book discuss various theories which the academics are concerned with, such as "possession and trance," whether shamanism can be called a religion, and whether *musok* is a form of shamanism or not. The fist paper, "Korean Shamanism and Cultural Nationalism" deals with those questions as well as gives an introduction to shamanism, Korean shamanism and its history. More detailed discussions on "possession and trance" can be found in Paper 6, "Trance and Trance-Possession" and paper 10, "Drumbeats in the Korean Shamanistic Ritual: 'Musical Magic' or 'Magic of Music'?"

The papers are arranged chronologically according to the year they were first presented.

1. 'Korean Shamanism and Cultural Nationalism' was presented at the Royal Asiatic Society lecture on 23 March 1994, and published in *Transactions*, Vol. 69, No 2, 1994, Seoul: The Royal Asiatic Society, Korea Branch. It is a shortened version of my MA dissertation, submitted to the University of Kent at Canterbury in 1992. It was expanded and published by Jimoondang Publishing Co, Seoul, as a full-length book in 1999.

2. 'The Importance of Shamanism in Understanding Ancient Korean Culture' was the lecture given at the McDonald Institute, the University of Cambridge on 10 May 1995.

3. 'Reciprocity, Status and the Korean Shamanistic Ritual,' first delivered at a lecture on 25 May 1995 at the Nissan Institute, the University of Oxford, was based on my PhD thesis submitted later that year at the University of Kent at Canterbury. It was published as *Kut, Happiness through Reciprocity* in 1998

by Akadémiai Kiadó, Budapest, Hungary. It is the result of my intensive fieldwork during 1993 preceded by extensive library research, and gives a good introduction to shamanism and Korean shamanism as practised today.

4. 'The Power Structure between Buddhism and Shamanism in Contemporary Korean Society' was presented at the International Society for Shamanistic Research Conference at the University of Paris on 3 September 1997. It was published in (2000) Denise Aigle, Bénédicte Brac de la Perrière, & Jean-Pierre Chaumeil (eds), *La Politique des Esprits: Chamanismes et Religions Universalistes*. Naterre. Paris: Société d'Éthnologie.

5. 'Rationality, Practicality and Modernity: Buddhism, Shamanism and Christianity in Korean Society' was an article published in *Transactions*, Vol 73, 1998, Seoul: The Royal Asiatic Society, Korea Branch.

6. 'Trance and Possession Trance' was published in Keith Howard (ed), 1998, *Korean Shamanism: revivals, survivals and change*, Seoul: The Royal Asiatic Society, Korea Branch.

7. 'The Gangneung Danoje Festival: the Folklorization of the Korean Shamanistic Heritage' was publish in *Korea Journal*, Vol. 41, No 3, Autumn 2001, Seoul: Korean National Commission for UNESCO.

8. 'The Dan-gun Myth as an Invention of Tradition, and its Significance in Korean Shamanism' was presented at the Keimyung International Conference on Korean Studies (KICKS) conference on 17 September 2001.

9. 'Inspiration or Instruction? Shaman-training Institutes in Contemporary Korea,' was published in *Shaman, Vol 11, No 1-2*, 2003, Budapest: Molnar & KelemanOriental Publishers.

10. 'Drumbeats in the Korean Shamanistic Ritual: "Musical Magic" or "Magic of Noise"?' was presented at the Keimyung Internatioanl Conference on Korea Studies (KICKS) on 19 May 2004.

11. 'Eschatology and Folk Religions in Korean Society' was presented at the Joint Asian Studies Conference at the University

of Leeds on 6 September 2004, and was published in (2005) *Papers of the British Association for Korean Studies, Vol. 10.*

12. 'Buddhist Elements in Korean Shamanism' is the lecture on 9 February 2005 at the Sigur Centre, George Washington University, Washington DC, USA.

13. 'Transvestism in Shamanism: a Reflection of Female Hegemony in the Primeval Era?' was presented at the Women's Worlds 2005: 9th International Interdisciplinary Congress on Women at Ewha Women's University, Seoul, Korea, on 24 June 2005.

14. 'Geomancy and Korean Shamanism' is an unpublished paper, written in 2006.

15. 'The Korean Shamanistic Ritual and Psychoanalysis' was presented at the International Society for Shamanistic Research (ISSR) conference at the University of Alaska Anchorage, "Traditional Belief and Healing Systems in a Changing World: an Interdisciplinary Approach" on 28 May 2009. It was published in *Shaman Vol. 11 No. 1-2*, Budapest: The International Society for Shamanistic Research.

16. 'Redefining the Korean identity through the Revival of Once-Lost Cultural Heritage: from Subversion to Cultural Nationalism' was delivered at the 17th Hahn Moo-Sook Colloquium, "Representing Korea's Visual Cultural Heritage: Defining Identity through the Aesthetic Qualities of Korean Art" at the George Washington University, Washington, DC, USA, on 17 October 2009.

Because this book is a collection of papers delivered as lectures and presentations, there are inevitably repetitions, for which I apologize to the readers.

As always my gratitude goes to the two late Presidents of DGY and my *mudang* friends for their support of my research. Last but not least I thank Dr. Hoagy Kim, Director of the Hahn Moo-Sook Foundation, for sponsoring the publication of this book, and President Kee-Young Yeun and Dr. Myongsook Koo for publishing it.

Hyun-key Kim Hogarth
2021, in Canterbury, England

Notes on the Stylistic Conventions

The following conventions are observed throughout this book:

1. Korean is Romanized mainly according to the new Korean government system introduced by the Ministry of Culture and Tourism in July 2000. Where a Korean scholar uses a personal Romanization of his/her name, it is used, if known with the new Romanization in brackets.

2. Chinese names were shown in Korean pronunciation with the Chinese characters in brackets.

3. The ages shown are reckoned in the Korean way, i.e. when a baby is born, it is one. A person adds another year to his/her age on New Year's Day. Thus a baby born in December becomes two, a month later. 'The Korean age' is to be distinguished from 'the western age.' When someone says he/she is ten, it does not mean that he/she is ten years old, but means that he/she is in the tenth year of his/her life. This way of reckoning age is widely used in Korea, not only for a person's age, but for all other events. I use 'the Korean age' in this thesis, because of the various folk beliefs connected with a person's age. To avoid confusion, I show a person's year of birth, whenever possible.

4. Surnames precede given names in Korean names, which most often consist of three syllables. Thus the first syllable of any Korean name appearing in this thesis is the surname.

5. Foreign expressions, including Romanized Korean words, are

italicized, except for proper nouns, which are capitalized and in normal script. The names of the shamanistic gods (e.g. San-shin), rituals (or parts in a ritual) dedicated to specific gods/people (e.g. Dan-gunje, Seokjeonje, Bulsa Geori), and holidays (e.g. Chuseok) are treated as proper nouns. However, the names of sundry 'ghosts' are not treated as proper nouns (e.g. *dongbeop*, *yeongsan*). The titles of the books written in Korean or other foreign languages are italicized.

6. Inverted commas are used to denote the special meaning of a word (e.g. 'family,' 'ancestor,' etc.), for the titles of the books cited in the text (but not in Bibliography), and for quotations within quotation.

7. Plurals are not usually used in Korean; the plural suffix, *-deul*, is only occasionally employed, mainly for emphasis. Therefore, plurals for Korean words are used without -s (e.g. *Mudang* are...). A group of spirits consisting of more than one, such as Obang Shinjang (the Five Directional General), Chilseong (the Seven Stars Spirit), is treated as one.

8. A Korean woman keeps her maiden name after marriage. Hence, it would be wrong to translate a married woman's name into English as Mrs. So-and-so, as is usually done. I have therefore used Ms. as a title for a married woman's name.

9. When discussing money, 'W,' signifying won, is used , e.g. W10,000.

10. Figures under ten are spelled out, and those over (and including) ten are written in Arabic numerals. Figures over (and including) 1,000,000 are represented as 1 million, 10 million, etc.

The Two Systems
of Romanization of Korean

Consonants

Korean	McCune-Reischauer	New Korean Government System
ㄱ	k-, -g-, -k	g, -k
ㄲ	kk	gg
ㄴ	n	n
ㄷ	t-, -d-, -t	d, -t
ㄸ	tt	dd
ㄹ	r, -l	r, -l
ㅁ	m	m
ㅂ	p-, -b-, -p	b, -p
ㅃ	pp	bb
ㅅ	s, -t	s, -t
ㅆ	ss, -t	ss, -t
ㅇ	( )-, -ng	( )-, -ng
ㅈ	ch-, -j-j, -t	j, -t
ㅉ	tch	jj
ㅊ	ch'-, -t	ch-, -t
ㅋ	k'-, -k	k, -k
ㅌ	t'-, -t	t, -t
ㅍ	p'-, -p	p, -p
ㅎ	h	h

Twenty-Five Years of Research into Korean Shamanism

Part 1

KOREAN SHAMANISM AND
CULTURAL NATIONALISM

Introduction

My fascination with shamanism began in 1987, when I came into direct contact with its practices, on returning to my native Korea after an absence of nearly twenty years. I only vaguely remembered the shamanistic ritual, called *gut,* which used to be held by women, mainly in the countryside, as noisy, colourful, and strangely eerie events. I was surprised, however, to find that *gut* was often performed by university students, and was sometimes presented in a well attended theatre by a famous shaman, called *mudang,* who has been declared a "human cultural treasure" by the government. I was also intrigued to notice that shamanism was an object of serious academic research by various scholars, as well as being protected by the government as a cultural heritage to be cherished. Why, then is shamanism, which has suffered centuries of official persecution for being the undesirable "primitive" element in Korean society, enjoying a revival among some educated elites whose religious affiliations are Christianity, Buddhism, etc, as well as managing to survive so persistently among people in rapidly industrializing modern Korea? To find the answer, it is necessary to study Korean shamanism in detail and its influence on the lives of the Korean people in the past as well as the present.

Definitions of the shaman and shamanism

The various aspects and manifestations of shamanism itself are still shrouded in considerable ambiguity and controversy, despite comprehensive studies spanning over two centuries and a large number of publications on it. At one extreme, the concept of shamanism itself is sceptically viewed; Geertz mentions shamanism among the "desiccated" and "insipid" categories "by means of which ethnographers of religion devitalize their data," and Spencer (1968) questions even the existence of such a phenomenon as shamanism. At the other extreme, La Barre (1970) claims that shamanism is the "basis of all religion," since the construct god is based on the shamanistic man-god.

Shamanism is notoriously difficult to define, since the term tends to be used in a wide variety of senses. Shamanism is best defined in terms of who and what the shaman is. Some scholars, for example, most British anthropologists, are extremely reluctant to use the term, while some others tend to abuse it without inhibition to refer to any practitioner of non-western religious phenomenon which is beyond their comprehension. It is, therefore, important to present working definitions of the shaman. Shamans have been known as "medicine men," "witch doctors," "exorcists," "magicians," "visionaries," "mediums," "sorcerers," "rainmakers," "necromancers," "oracles," to name but a few, and at times all these "religious specialists" have indiscriminately been called "shamans." Since the term "shaman" is generally thought to have come from the Tungusian (Evenki) *saman* (Shirokogoroff 1935), North Asia seems to be a logical place to look for a definition of it. According to the Tungus (Evenks), shamans are capable of having direct contact with the spirit world through ecstasy, controlling spirits and using their power for helping other people who suffer illnesses or misfortune, attributed to the influence of malignant spirits. Shamans have the recognized abilities to achieve ecstasy, summon their guardian spirits, and with their help, ascend to heaven or descend to hell, to bring back the lost soul, or fight with and win over evil spirits, which cause illnesses or misfortune, and thus obtain the cure. They have ritual codes and paraphernalia, which are socially sanctioned and enjoy a privileged social status.

One of the most important features of shamans is their will and control, being able "to transcend the human conditions and pass freely back and forth through different cosmological planes (Furst 1972)." Most of all, they can will themselves into ecstasy and in the midst of such a radical transformation, are simultaneously aware of the ordinary reality (Harner 1980). Hence a somewhat comic situation described by Kendall (1985), in which a possessed Korean shamaness asks for her rubber shoes before going outside during a *gut,* becomes perfectly understandable. This is what differentiates shamans from spirit mediums; the former are fully aware of what transpires in the altered state of consciousness, whereas the latter have no recollection of their visionary episodes afterwards, having merely acted as passive channels for the received revelations.

Shamans are especially healers, but they also engage in divination, making use of their abilities to see into the present, past, and future. Hence shamans are clairvoyants, but not all seers are shamans, since divination is only one of the many aspects of shamanism.

Shamans are empiricists, in the sense that they "act on observation or experiment, not on theory," and "regard sense-data as valid information (Oxford English Dictionary)." They depend primarily on firsthand experience of the senses to acquire knowledge.

Shamans are people of action as well as knowledge. They serve the community by moving into and out of the hidden reality when asked for help. Thus they are highly sensitive to social needs and can improvise ritual procedures as the need arises. Harvey (1979), who studied the socialization of six Korean shamanesses, also remarks on their "above average capacity for creative improvisation."

Shamans are highly social people, being the central figures in rituals, which are an integral part of shamanism. Thus their priestly function is important, and for that reason shamanistic vocation is often followed by years of training and initiation. Thus some people cannot become shamans, despite possession sickness, through a lack of funds for training, and remain as mostly individual spiritual specialists, such as fortune-tellers, exorcists or spirit mediums (Akiba 1957; Yu 1975).

Last but not least, shamans are largely altruistic people who guard the welfare of their clients close at heart, although in some tribes, e.g. the Buryat, there exist "black" shamans, practitioners of sorcery. Shamanistic vocation is often received with extreme reluctance even by shamans who enjoy a special social position. It is attributed to mankind's ambivalent attitude towards the sacred (Park 1938; Eliade 1951). In Korean society, where *mudang*'s status is traditionally very low, becoming a *mudang* involves a great self-sacrifice for the initiate, particularly if she/he is of good social class. Their self-sacrifice calls forth a commensurate

emotional commitment from their patients, a sense of obligation to struggle. Most *mudang* that I have met are warm, caring people. As Harner
(1980) aptly puts it, "caring and curing go hand in hand."

Thus Lebra's definition (cited in Harvey 1979) has a more universal value: shamans wield recognized supernatural powers for socially
approved ends and have the capacity to enter culturally acknowledged
trance states at will.

Possession sickness and psychopathology

There are two methods of recruiting shamans: hereditary transmission
and spontaneous vocation ("call" or "election") (Eliade 1951). Lowie
(1963) argues that a shaman acquires his status only by divine inspiration, not by heredity or learned skills. Heredity, however, is not absolute;
even in the case of hereditary shamans, divine intervention plays a part.
Among the Buryat, for example, although both methods of recruit-
ment are in force, in either case, the shaman's vocation is manifested by
dreams and convulsions, both provoked by ancestral spirits, who choose
a young man in the family. Among the Altaians, where the shamanic gift
is generally hereditary, a child who is to become a shaman proves to be
sickly, withdrawn, and contemplative. Akiba (1957), in discussing shamanism in Korea, also remarks that the shamanistic predisposition seems
to be hereditary. In Korea, this predisposition is called "*buri*" or "root,"
which is supposed to exist both patrilaterally and matrilaterally and in
the case of a female, also in her husband's family. Thus the distinction
between spontaneous vocation and hereditary transmission gets somewhat blurred, although there are broadly two different types of shamans
in Korea, i.e., god-descended shamans and hereditary ones.

According to a shaman, Mr. Bak Ino, Vice-president of Daehan
Seunggong Gyeongsin Yeonhaphoe (the Korean Spirit Worshippers'
Association for Victory Over Communism) and the director of the
musokbojon-hoe (*Musok* Preservation Society), a shaman training institute, there are three different ways in which spirits descend on people.
The First and the most common is through sickness, the second through
financial ruin, and the third and the most feared, through deaths of loved
ones, called *indari,* meaning the "human bridge." Sometimes all three
can happen in turn. In the midst of these extreme sufferings, the first sign
of a "choice" from above manifests itself in what is commonly called
"possession sickness (*sinbyeong* in Korean)," which has been likened

to acute schizophrenia (Silverman 1967), and other forms of mental illnesses, because of a remarkable similarity between people suffering from
it and psychopaths. They get meditative and dreamy, seek solitude, seem
absent-minded, and have prophetic visions and sometimes seizures that
make them unconscious. They lose appetite and sleep, and often wander
off alone to the mountain or forest. They occasionally find shamanic
objects buried by shamans who died without leaving successors (Eliade
1951; Akiba 1957).

Many of my numerous shaman-informants have told me their life
experiences of possession sickness before becoming shamans. Let us
consider a few cases:

1) Mr. Bang Changhwan (b.1943), one of the most successful
male shamans today, first experienced possession sickness at
the age of 19. He was locked away in a mental asylum three
times, and attempted suicide innumerable times. As a result of
the shock, his father died. On the third night after his father's
death, at around 1 a.m. he had a vision in which his father's
tomb split open, and his father, carrying an octagonal table in
his left hand and a staff in his right hand came out of it. He
came down the mountain and said, "Get up quickly and take
this table." He took it, and taking off all his clothes, he dashed
out into the snow-covered garden. He poured a bowl of icy
water all over his naked body, murmuring, "Filthy, dirty, and
disgusting!" He got a job at a trading company at 29, but was
unable to continue with his career, since the spirits started
building *indari* around him, i.e. his close relatives started dying. The following year, he had an initiation rite, by *Pama
Mansin* (Perm Shaman), becoming her spirit son.

2) Another successful male shaman, Mr. Jo Jaryong (real name:
Jo Yongjin: b.1946), as a child often had visions of his grandfather who had covertly practised the shamanistic profession.
He tried to commit suicide at the age of 13, but survived. A
year after his marriage at the age of 26, he was given a death
sentence by his doctor, after his condition was diagnosed as
blood cancer. As a last resort, he asked a *mudang*, who said
that it was caused by the spirit descent. After various experiences with the spirits, he had a series of *naerim gut* (initiation

rite), after which he was cured. He has had no serious health problems since then.

3) A first-class performer of the Seoul area *gut,* Bang Chunja (b.1939), experienced the spirit descent at the age of 14, as a result of which her father threw her out with only a tram ticket. She was trained under extremely difficult circumstances by her spirit mother until the age of 21, when, disguising her vocation, she was married off to a Christian. She immediately got sick, and nearly died. The spirits told her to resume her shamanistic career, or she would die, which obliged her to start "serving the spirits again." Her husband's violent objections broke up her marriage. She tried to be independent, trying her hand at various businesses, none of which was successful. After suffering a succession of misfortunes, which included losing all her money and an attempted suicide, she decided to accept the spirits. Since then, she has prospered, becoming a most successful shaman.

Those above and over 100 other cases I have collected all fit Eliade's traditional schema of the future shaman's vocation: suffering, death, and resurrection. The Siberian shamans' first ecstatic visionary experience almost always include one or more of the following themes: the dismemberment of their own bodies, their blood sucked by "devils," followed by a renewal of the internal organs, ascent to the sky and dialogue with the spirits, and descent to the underworld and conversations with spirits and the souls of dead shamans about various secrets of the shamanic profession (Eliade 1951). The Korean shamans I have talked to all have undergone similar experience: suffering and death or near death, visions of the spirits, followed by the cure.

A shamanic vocation, be it hereditary or by divine election, is obligatory: one cannot refuse it. A person who receives the call suffers a mysterious illness or the above-mentioned misfortune until she/he obeys it and becomes a shaman. However, she/he cannot become a shaman without several years of training and being initiated at an initiation rite, called *naerim gut. Naerim gut* is a rite of passage for the shaman, in which the "psychopath" dies and is reborn as a consecrated shaman by demonstrating her/his mystical capacities. From then on, the teacher shaman is called the spirit father or spirit mother. On becoming a fully-fledged shaman, the person recovers completely from the illness or other misfortunes, which recur if she/he stops shamanizing. Here lies the main difference between a shaman and a psychopath, i.e. a shaman is a sick person who has cured her/himself and is prepared to cure others suffering from similar or other ailments.

Characteristics of Korean *musok*

The equivalent of the shaman in Korean is *mu*, which is based on the visually explanatory Chinese character, *mu* (巫). It represents the linking heaven (⁻) and earth (_) through two humans (人人) dancing in the air. The existence of a great number of words referring to the *mu* bears witness to the extent to which shamanism has pervaded Korean society throughout its long history. The most generally used word for "shaman" is *mudang*, although it usually refers to shamanesses, who predominate in number. The male shaman is called, most commonly, *baksu*, or *baksu mudang*. The female and male are collectively called, *muggyeok* (巫覡), *mu* (巫) meaning the former and *gyeok* (覡), the latter. The regional and other variations are:

> Female: ***mudang, bosal, mansin, munyeo, danggol, seon-gwan, myeongdo***, etc.
> Male: ***baksu, beopsa, dosa, boksa, jaein, hwarang/hwaraengi, sinjang, simbang***, etc.

The terms reveal the extensive syncretism of Korean *musok* with foreign religions; for example, *bosal* and *beopsa* came from Buddhism, while *dosa* and *seon-gwan* are Taoist terms. *mudang* is generally believed to have the same origin as the Mongolian *udagan*, the Buryat *udayan*, the Yakut *udoyan*, which all mean shamanesses. The influence of the Chinese character "*mu*" may have given the initial sound "m," making it *mudang* (Akiba 1957; Yu 1975; Gim Inhoe 1987). The most commonly used term for a male *mu*, *baksu*, likewise can be linked with the Tungustic *baksi*, the Mongolian *baksi* or *balsi*, the Goldi *paksi*, the Manchu *faksi*, the Orochon *paktjine* (Akiba 1957) and also the Kazak Kirgiz *baqca* (Eliade 1951), which all refer to a male shaman.

Shamanism in Korea is usually referred to as *musok*, which literally means "popular mu practice," or even *mugyo* (*mu* religion) by some scholars (Yu 1975; Cho 1984, 1990) who argue that Korean *musok* is a religion. Although it fits in with Tylor's broadest definition of religion, "belief in spiritual beings," it cannot be called a religion for various reasons. First of all, although there exist the priest (*mudang*) and the ritual (*gut*), there is no written scripture (scanty records of the ritual procedures for instruction of shamans do exist, but they can hardly be called a scripture), thus the ritual and even ideologies are somewhat fluid, since they are passed on mostly verbally. Secondly, it is only concerned with the profane and this worldliness, the spirits being merely used to achieve the aims of the living. The gods do not enter people's consciousness until a disaster strikes them, and as soon as the crisis is over, they are equally quickly forgotten; thus a shaman shrine is not believed to be inhabited by a particular spirit to which it is dedicated, but a place to which it descends, only when invoked. Thirdly, there is no focal figure, such as the founder, as in the great religions of the world. The spirits themselves are numerous and highly fluid in character. The polite term of address for a shamaness, *mansin* (literally ten thousand spirits) implies that she controls all the spirits, which number "ten thousand (literally a myriad)" a number which is used to mean "innumerable." Many culture heroes in Korean history appear as gods; gods are invented as a need arises, and stop existing when they have served their useful purposes. A feared disease is believed to be the responsibility of a specific god, as in the case of *mama shin* (Smallpox God). When an epidemic of smallpox, which was introduced in the 15th century from abroad, ravaged the Korean population, *mama gut* was one of the most important and frequently performed *gut*. Today the eradication of the once-dreaded disease means the disappearance of *mama gut*, which only remains in sketchy records, and according to Mr. Sim Useong, a folklorist and folk dramatist, in a few regional community *gut*. Finally, but perhaps most significantly, shamanism can and is practised alongside another religions, in the way no two other religions can.

In *musok*, gods are not worshipped metaphysically, but used as a means to obtain this wordly goals. Thus a *gut* is less a sacred exercise, and more a very profane "strategic party," in which spirits participate as honoured guests, enjoying food, drink, lively conversation, drama and other entertainment provided by man. Humans hope that spirits will reciprocate by granting them their wishes. In other words, gods and humans communicate freely with one another on equal terms in *gut*, where the latter obligate the former to reciprocate by means of various gifts.

Thus the most fundamental difference between Siberian and Korean shamanisms lies in the fact that in a Siberian shamanistic séance, the shaman makes a journey into heaven or descends into hell aided by his helping spirits, whereas in *gut* the shaman, entering into ecstasy through frenzied dancing, invites the spirits to descend and join the human gatherings. Yu (1975) attributes the difference to the different lifestyles of the Siberian and Korean peoples. Thus the Siberians, pastoral nomads, actively travel to seek spirits, while the latter, settled agrarians, stay put, passively inviting and receiving spirits as guests.

The above hypothesis, however, does not fit in many other similar situations. For example. Potter (in Wolf ed 1974) describes how a Cantonese shamaness makes an upward journey into the Heavenly Flower Garden, possessed and helped by her "familiar" spirits, meeting the souls of the assembled crowd's deceased relatives and neighbours, who speak through her. Cantonese society is also a settled agrarian one, so if the above hypothesis worked, the Cantonese shamaness would also invite the spirits down, instead of making a journey herself. Therefore Yu's explanation is purely one scholar's conjectural interpretation, which lacks universality.

A more probable explanation may be the influence of the ancient Korean belief, according to which, singing, dancing, eating and drinking make spirits appear (Hyeon 1986). The Korean word for "to get excited, elated or ecstatic" is *sinnada*, which literally means "spirits have appeared." Thus the rhythmic drumbeat and frenzied dancing that send the shaman into ecstasy cause the spirits to descend on the scene, possessing the shaman in her state of trance and speaking through her.

Another way of making gods descend is singing long biographical epic songs about them, based on the principle, "Talk of the devil, and he will appear (Hyeon 1986)." What is interesting is that *taryeong*, mostly frequently rendered in Chinese characters, 打令 (meaning "striking an order"), which refers to all ballads, can literally mean, "compromising with spirits (妥靈)."

The shamanic costumes and paraphernalia are also vital, since it is believed that spirits recognize their own clothes and objects, and descend on them. Thus a great *mansin* possesses a huge collection of various costumes, which are often donated by her clients, called *danggol/sindo* (regulars/believers). Only a few of these costumes are used at an ordinary *gut*, the whole collection only being displayed and worn at her own *gut*, called *jinjeok gut*.

In appreciation for their appearance, and by way of supplication, the spirits are then regally entertained with food, drink, song, dance, and drama. Sometimes clothes and money are given to them to curry their favour. Thus "entertainment" is one of the most important aspects of Korean shamanism, which distinguishes it from other shamanisms of the world. When a *gut* is in progress in the neighbourhood, the noise can be heard miles away, and food and drink are given to anyone who happens to be nearby or passing by. That even applies to *japgwi* (sundry ghosts), which are always fed at the end, as part of the ritual procedure, called *dwitjeon*.

Another distinguishing feature of Korean *musok* is the existence of hereditary "priests" called *seseummu*, alongside god-descended shamans called *gangsinmu*, who are all called by the same name, *mudang*. Although they share basically the same functions, the most important of which is performing *gut*, there is an essential difference between them. *Gangsinmu*, the god-descended type, get possessed by spirits and practise *gongsu* (spirits speaking through the shaman) during a *gut*, whereas spirit possession, thus *gongsu*, is absent in *seseummu*. The god-descended ones are the accepted norm north of the Han River, while the hereditary ones predominate to the south of the Han River and along the east coast of Korea, and at one time nationally outnumbered the real shamans (Akiba 1957).

The hereditary *mudang* also have regional variations. Those in the southern counties of Honam and Yeongnam are mostly female; in the former areas they are called *danggol* (regulars), and in the latter *mudang* or *mudang gakssi* (*mudang* bride). Although the lineage is patrilineal, the profession is often passed down from mother-in-law to daughter-in-law; a *mudang*'s daughter marries another *mudang*'s son, thus learning her trade from her mother-in-law. The husband, who is called *gongin* in the Honam area and *yangjung* or *hwraengi* in the Yeongdong area, and *hwaraengi* or *sani* in the Gyeonggi area, south of the Han River, works as her assistant, usually playing the hourglass-shaped drums called *janggu*. On the east coast of Korea male and female *mudang* co-exist; the females are called *mudang* or *mudang gakssi*, and the male *yangjung*, *hwaraengi* or *baraji*. Unlike those in the Honam area, who have a territory of regular customers, they form a group, usually by blood or marriage, get together only when there is a *gut* to perform, and normally live in different areas. Unlike *danggol mudang* in the south, who are settled in one place, those on the east coast are highly mobile; thus even their hourglass drums are smaller in size than those in other areas, and are collapsible for ease of transportation. The ritual song, dance and paraphernalia are supposed to keep to the ancient form which is rare elsewhere. In Jejudo, the island county off the southwest coast, the two types of *mudang* co-exist.

In view of the existence of these hereditary *mudang* and other differences, opinions are divided among the Korean scholars who have studied *musok* as to whether it can be termed shamanism or not. First Im Seokjae (1971) argues that it is an indigenous religious phenomenon, totally different from Siberian shamanism in terms of rituals, shamanic costumes, paraphernalia, dance and music, and thus should not be called shamanism. Secondly, Choe Gilseong (1969) maintains that only the central and northern variety is shamanism, the southern variety being a residue of the indigenous primitive beliefs. Thirdly, Gim Taegon (1969) suggests that all forms of Korean *musok* are essentially a kind of shamanism, though it has undergone a certain metamorphosis in the south owing to the cultural differences between the north and the south. He applies Weber's theory of "routinization of charisma" to explain the differences between the two types of *mudang*.

To begin with, to say that *musok* is a totally different religious phenomenon from Siberian shamanism, there are too many parallels between the two, for example, the similar terms, symbols used and ritual gestures, as well as the basic principles. Even the paraphernalia used in the rituals, such as the important drum, rattles/bells, are remarkably similar. The superficial differences, such as the costumes, can be accounted for by the extremely fluid nature of shamanism itself, which is highly adaptable to the society in which it occurs.

Some anthropologists, such as Laurel Kendall (1985) refer to *seseummu* as "priests," totally avoiding the term "shaman." Many scholars of shamanism (Weiss in Harner ed 1973; Lowie 1954) make a clear distinction between the shaman and the priest. The shaman obtains his powers primarily from direct contact with spirits, operates independently, often on a part-time basis, deals mainly with individuals, particularly for purposes of curing, and is associated with activities characterized by possession, trance/ecstasy, and frenzy. On the other hand, the priest achieves his status through special training, is a member of an organization consisting of full-time specialists, leads group activities of a ceremonial nature, and conducts routine propitiatory acts of adoration, prayer, and offering (Shirokogoroff 1923; Lowie 1940; Norbeck 1961; cited in Weiss in Harner ed 1973). Viewed from this perspective, *seseumu* cannot be called "priests" either, being closer to shamans. They are mostly part-time practitioners with special abilities to control spirits, which are often used for the benefit of individuals, particularly for purposes of healing, both therapeutic and prophylactic, and their activities are also character-ized by frenzy. The only important element missing is possession. If we endorse Eliade's argument that spirit possession is not essential in sha-manism, we could argue that *seseummu* can also be considered "quasi-shamans." Then, it becomes perfectly understandable why the general Korean public call them both by the same name, *mudang*.

I, therefore, support the third view that Korean *musok* is a type of shamanism. Whilst agreeing that any spiritual specialist should not indiscriminately be called a "shaman," I consider the extreme reluctance to use the term, even when one should do so, a "constipated attitude," as Lewis (1984) rightly points out. Shamanism is a term adopted by Eng-lish to refer to a certain socio-religious phenomenon, which happened to be first spotted among the Tungus in the late 17th century, although it had existed for a long time prior to that. A similar phenomenon, *mutatis mutandis,* can be found not only in Siberia, but also in such culturally diverse areas as North America, Mexico, South America, Australia, In-donesia and Malaysia, and east and north Asia (Drury 1989). Thus the term "shamanism" no longer refers only to the religious phenomenon of the Tungus and other Siberian tribes. The fact that the functions and the contents of the *gut*, performed by both types, are identical, and *ses-eummu* "act out" the voices of the spirits or the sentiments of the dead souls, and sometimes simulate *gangsinmu*'s magical acts, supports the view that even the southern variety is a form of shamanism, although it may be said to be a relatively later development. What seems to confirm this view further is the fact that with the abolishment of the rigid social stratification, *seseummu* have been fast disappearing, particularly in the southern counties. Today the god-descended shamans overwhelmingly outnumber hereditary ones (Hwang 1988), whose number once exceeded that of the former nationwide (Akiba 1950), signifying that without the artificial social constraint, Korean *musok* is reverting to its original form.

The variety and the structure of *gut*

The *gut* is a comprehensive shamanistic ritual in which *mudang* invite the spirits by entering into ecstasy, (in the case of *seseummu*, by means of frenzied dance and music or borrowing the body and mouth of a member of the audience with psychic powers), and through entertaining them propitiate spirits with unresolved grudges, or *han*, which are believed to be the cause of misfortune and illnesses, send off the dead to the other world, or merely seek the health, happiness and prosperity of a village or of an individual family.

Unlike many Korean words, *gut* does not have an equivalent Chinese character. Yi (1927) interprets *gut* as based on a pure Korean word, *gutta*, which means "nasty, foul or unfortunate," as in *gujeun-nal* (a rainy day), or *gujeun-il* (a nasty affair, i.e. a bereavement). Thus a *gut* is concerned with resolving the problems of misfortune, particularly illness and death. That is why *gut* is also sometimes called *puri* (solving or "dispelling"). Ramstedt (1949) traces the origin of *gut* to the Tungustic *gutu*, the Mongolian *qutug*, and the Turkish *qut*, which all mean "happiness" or "good fortune." Thus the purpose of a *gut* is to bring about happiness and good fortune. Combining Yi's and Ramstedt's interpretations, a *gut* is a ritual which aims to dispel unexpected disasters and bring about good fortune.

Gut is inseparable from the *mudang*, since depending on the officiating *mudang*, the form of the *gut* can also change. In the central and northern variety, the *mudang* (i.e. the shaman) not only evokes the spirits, but also gets possessed by them. Therefore, their costumes and paraphernalia tend to be more elaborate, since the shamans incarnate the descending spirits with them. They also perform magical acts, such as standing barefoot on sharp blades, and carrying a huge bucket filled with water with their lower lips, which get stuck to the rim of the bucket, standing a whole carcass of a pig on a trident, etc. These are supposed to be the signs of the powers of the possessing spirits.

The hereditary *mudang* perform the same function, i.e. masterminding rituals and getting in touch with the spirits. They have highly developed dancing and singing skills, by which means they evoke the spirits and entertain them. Although possession never occurs, they act out the speech and the actions of the dead spirits. Apart from the absence of *gongsu*, or speaking in tongues, the contents, structure, and function of the *gut*, performed by both types of *mudang* are fundamentally identical.

A *gut* basically consists of 12 *geori*, each *geori* being a small independent *gut* dedicated to a specific spirit. 12 does not always represent the exact number of parts inside a *gut*, but a number symbolizing "a whole" or "completeness," as twelve months complete a year (Yu 1975). The contents and the number of *geori* can vary slightly according to the officiating *mudang*, but the basic structure of the *gut*, i.e. 1) the evocation 2) entertainment, and 3) finally, the sending off of the spirits, remain unchanged.

Gut can be broadly classified into four kinds;

1) *gut*, performed for the dead, called *jinogi gut* (Seoul and Gyeonggi-do), *ssitgim gut* (Jeolla and Chungcheong provinces), *ogu gut* (the East Coast), *siwang maji* (Jeju-do), etc.

2) healing *gut*, called *byeong gut*, *uhwan gut*, *michin gut*, etc.

3) *gut* performed for *mudang*, i.e. the initiation *gut*, called *naerim gut* or *sin gut*, and the offerings to the shaman's tutelary spirits, called *jinjeok gut* or *harabeoji gut* (Grandfather *gut*).

4) *gut* to pray for good fortune, which can be sub-divided into a) the private *gut*, and b) the community *gut*.

The most commonly performed private *gut* are called *jaesu gut* (good luck *gut*), but also include *dosin gut*, *jeolgi gut* (season *gut*), *seongju maji gut* (for the housesite spirit at the construction of a new house), *honin yetam gut* (pre-wedding *gut*), etc. Community *gut* are performed every two to nine years to offer sacrifices to the village tutelary spirits, who are believed to bring good fortune, health, and prosperity to all the inhabitants. The names vary regionally, from *daedong gut*, *byeolsin gut*, *bugun je*, *dodang gut*, *seonang gut*, *dangsan gut*, *yeongdong gut*, to name but a few. These *gut* are performed on a grand scale, involving and sponsored by everybody in the village, and sometimes neighbouring villages, creating an atmosphere of great festivity, as well as consolidating unity and solidarity among the villagers. They reflect the quintessence of Korean "culture" and national identity, being a residue of the national scale shamanistic festivals of earlier ages. This is the very reason why the colonial Japanese government tried to eradicate all forms of *gut*s, under the pretext of superstition, particularly those performed en masse (Cho 1990; et al.).

The Korean shamanistic pantheon

Innumerable gods and spirits occupy the Korean shamanistic pantheon, which is reflected in a polite term of address for a shamaness, mansin, meaning literally "ten thousand spirits." It implies that a competent shaman is capable of controlling all the spirits, which number "ten thousand," a number often used in the sense of 'countless' in Korean in the same way "a myriad" does in English. It is, therefore, impossible to discuss them in such a short space of time, so I shall present the ten most popular spirits. In Korean, the distinction between singular and plural is sometimes blurred, so a group of more than one spirit is considered as one, for example, Chilseongsin (Seven Stars Spirit), although there are seven figures, is treated as one.

1) Heavenly God/Lord (Cheonsin): is depicted as a white haired man, often wearing a crown, and controls life.

2) Mountain Spirit (Sansin): is shown as an old man always accompanied by a tiger. He is responsible for procuring descendants, national security, and rain.

3) Seven Stars Spirit (Chilseongsin): has been derived from the Big Dipper, or Ursa Major, and gives long life and general good fortune, including easier childbirth, healthier babyhood, wealth, prosperity, and virility.

4) The Dragon King (Yongwang): is depicted as an old man is royal robes and a crown, seen with a dragon, and is in control of the storms at sea and the rain.

5) Five-directional General (Obang Sinjang): is responsible for the changes in one's life, usually for the better. When the shaman is possessed by this spirit, she carries five differently-coloured flags, which represent: 1) white-heaven 2) red-Mountain Spirit 3) blue-generals 4) yellow-ancestors 5) green-originally black, but since traditionally Koreans do not like black, has been replaced with green-sundry ghosts. She asks the sponsor to pick a flag, after rolling all five up together. White and red ones are supposed to be lucky, whereas a green flag signals trouble, and the sponsor is often asked to pick again. Blue and yellow ones seem to be indifferent.

6) Three Buddhas (Sambul, or Sambul Jeseok): are shown as triplets wearing Buddhist monk's costumes of peaked white hats and grey robes. They are deities of birth and fertility, as well as good luck.

7) Abandoned Princess (Bari Gongju): The Ballad of Princess Bari the abandoned seventh daughter of a king, who eventually revives her already-dead parents, is recited at a mortuary *gut*. A personification of filial piety, one of the most important virtues in traditional Korean society, she is an ideal deity to guide the dead parent to the other world.

8) High Government Official (Daegam): is a bringer of luck, in exchange for wine, food, and money which he especially likes. The shaman demands a lot of money while playing this spirit, wearing ten thousand won notes stuck on her/his brow, and around the hat strings. Daegam-nori ("playing" Daegam) is often a part very entertaining for the shaman and the other participants of the *gut*, since it includes cheerful banter, catchy songs and dance.

9) A group of deified tragic kings (Byeolsang): are ironically responsible for welfare and good luck.

10) A group of deified war heroes (Gunung): which include foreign (mainly Chinese), and Korean generals, are believed to help drive away the evil spirits, which cause disease and misfortune.

A brief history of Korean shamanism

Many Korean scholars who study shamanism trace its beginning to the famous and ancient myth of origin, known as the Dan-gun Myth. According to it, Hwanung, an illegitimate son of Hwanin, the Heavenly Lord, came down to Taebaek Mountain through a sacred tree, bearing the Three Heavenly Seals. At that time, there lived a bear and a tiger, who prayed to him to transform them into humans. They were ordered to eat only some sacred mugwort and garlic, and not to see light for 100 days. Both tried, but the tiger could not endure the ordeal, while the bear succeeded in becoming a woman after 21 days. The bear woman eventually became Hwanung's "wife" and gave birth to a son, named Dan-gun, who founded the first Korean nation in 2333 B.C. He eventually became the Mountain Spirit at 1,908 years of age.

This myth, which is known to all Koreans, contains many elements which are also found in Siberian shamanism. First of all, the name Dan-gun is reminiscent of *tengri* of the Mongols, *tengeri* of the Buryat, *tan-*

gere of the Volga Tartars, *tingir* of the Beltirs, *tangara* of the Yagut, etc., which all mean "sky" or "heaven." The tree, as the cosmic axis which links heaven and earth, is a common concept in many Siberian tribes.

The transformation of the bear into a woman is effected only after a prescribed term of eating ritual food, and avoiding light which symbolizes life. In other words, the bear's ordeal is similar to a Siberian shaman's initiation experience of symbolic death and resurrection. It is interesting to note that mugwort is also considered sacred by other tribes of the world, for example, the Chumash call it the "dream herb" and use it as a hallucinogen (Drury 1989). In Korea, even today, mugwort rice cake forms an indispensable part of the food offered to the spirits.

The union of gods and earthly women and the zoomorphic character of the shaman's guardian spirits originating from totemism, are also common themes in Siberian shamanism. The Evenki shaman's cult of the bear, which, according to Anisimov (1958, cited in Basilov, in Hoppal ed 1984) originates from a totemic source, is an interesting coincidence. Also among the Yagut, an animal mother is considered the most important (Hultkrantz in Hoppal, ed 1978). A remarkable parallel can be found in the existence of a zoomorphic guardian spirit in the form of a bear-mother in the Dan-gun myth. Hultkrantz (1978 ibid) claims that "shamanism cannot be spoken of without the belief in helping spirits and the ecstatic who attains the other world without the help of his guardian spirits is certainly no shaman." Dan-gun with his powerful bear-mother as his guardian spirit can be said to be an archetypal shaman. The Dan-gun Myth first appeared in *Samguk yusa* (The Anecdotal History of the Three Kingdoms), compiled by the Monk Iryeon in the late 13th century, when the then Goryeo Kingdom was under Mongolian rule. It was a period of national submission and humiliation; the kings were forced to marry Mongolian princesses, and their culture, with its distinctive costumes and hairstyles, was avidly adopted by the fashionable elites. The Dan-gun Myth was a sort of "invention of tradition" by Iryeon, based on the orally transmitted ancient myth, to boost the national morale and instil a sense of national identity and nationalism in times of national crisis. Since then the Koreans have prided themselves as the chosen people who have a divine origin, and their country a holy place specially chosen by God for his own son. Thus Koreans often proudly refer to themselves as "we, Dan-gun's descendants." For centuries the Dan-gun Myth, in which the central figure may well have been a shaman king, has provided the

Korean people with the rationale for national identity and its sustainment.

There has been a theory among some Korean historians that Dan-gun was a historical figure; the North Koreans have recently claimed that they have actually found Dan-gun's bones. Dan-gun, whether he existed historically or not, plays a significant role in Korean shamanism, as one of the most popular tutelary spirits of the shamans. His picture invariably decorates the shaman's private shrine, together with a Korean flag and often with a vase of pink artificial hibiscus, the Korean national flower. In the tenth month of the lunar calendar, when he is supposed to have come down to earth, a sacrificial offering is made by shamans on mountains everywhere, one of the main sites being Mani-san in Ganghwado.

Apart from the Dan-gun myth, various historical documents contain evidence that shamans were mostly men, who had political and jural, as well as ritual, power. For example, the second king of the Shilla Kingdom was called Namhae Chachaung (4-23 A.D.), and according to Dr. Ross King of the SOAS, "*chachaung* (次次雄)" are the Chinese characters used to transcribe a pure Korean word, *seuseung*, meaning "teacher," but in the Hamgyeongdo area a male shaman was also called "*seuseung* (teacher)." (Akamatsu & Akiba 1938)

Another piece of evidence that the early Korean kings may have fulfilled the shamanistic role is the royal regalia, excavated inside the royal tomb in Gyeongju, the capital of Silla (Yu 1975; Grayson 1989; et al.). The regalia, which consists of a gold crown, a gold belt, and shoes, bear a remarkable resemblance to the modern Siberian shaman's costume. The crowns have wings, made of beaten gold in the shape of feathers, which also decorate the Siberian shaman's headgear; the claw-shaped jade pieces, which hang from the crown and the belt, are reminiscent of the bear or tiger claws, with which they decorate their clothing in the belief that they may obtain the power of those animals. The royal tomb, in which a set of these regalia was found, called Cheonmachong (the Tomb of the Heavenly Horse; 4th-5th century A.D.) also contains a mural of a flying horse painted on birchbark. It is another piece of evidence to suggest that the early Silla kings, before the adoption of Buddhism as the national religion, may have been shamanistic rulers, since the cosmic tree in the form of a white birch, and magical flights to heaven are classic concepts in Siberian shamanism.

The degeneration of shamanism from the central cult to a marginal cult is generally believed to have begun with the introduction of

Buddhism from China in the fourth century A.D (Yu 1975; Gim Taegon 1987). However, although Buddhism was adopted officially as the central morality religion, extensive syncretism of Buddhism with shamanism meant that shamanism survived alongside it.

A full-scale persecution of shamanism began with the adoption of Confucianism by the Joseon dynasty (1392-1910) as the national guiding ideology. *mudang* of all descriptions were cast into the lowest social class, from which there was no escape. Moreover, special taxes were levied heavily on all *mudang* to discourage their practices (Yi 1927). However, shamanism continued to thrive among the down-trodden mass belonging to the lower strata of society and women of all classes, providing cathartic release from oppressive patriarchy and social hierarchy.

Under Japanese colonial rule, shamanism was practised in defiance of the government ban, as a way of expressing cultural nationalism (Robinson 1988). After liberation, successive governmentsP movements for Korea's modernization, particularly during President Park Jung-hee (Bak Jeonghi)'s Third (1961- 1972) and Fourth (1972-1979) Republics, meant a further setback for shamanism. By 1968, the year I left Korea, *gut* was rarely performed in the centre of Seoul, at least not in public places, which accounts for my then scanty knowledge of it.

During my long absence, towards the end of President Park's Third Republic, a revival of the traditional cultural movement was effected; Daehan Seunggong Gyeongsin Yeonhaphoe (The Spirit Worshippers' Association for Victory Over Communism) was officially formed in 1971 by Mr. Choe Nameok. However, ironically *gut* performances were banned at private homes because of the noise, and confined only to designated places. As part of The New Village Movement which included the abolition of superstitions, many shamanistic village shrines were destroyed. While many religious leaders, mostly Buddhists and Christians enjoyed powerful political connections, shamans continued to survive on the periphery of Korean society.

During the Fifth Republic (1980-1987, 8), the government's main concern was with security and stability, and was particularly obsessed with globalism, which culminated in the 1988 Seoul Olympic Games, hence its motto, "Korea to the World, and the world to Korea."

Korean shamanism and cultural nationalism

I returned to Korea in May, 1987. With rapid modernization and industrialization, traditional Korean culture was fast disappearing, particularly in large cities, where American culture, symbolized by hamburgers and Coca-Cola, dominated. In Seoul in particular, with wide roads and ubiquitous MacDonald's, Wendy's, and Kentucky Fried Chicken restaurants, it was sometimes difficult to know where one was exactly. Against this background, Korean shamanism, which had been deprecated and persecuted as tangible evidence of Korea's backwardness, was enjoying a revival as "something uniquely Korean."

Anthropologists studying rapidly modernizing, or more specifically westernizing societies, have often remarked on the revival of ancient or traditional rituals or customs by the people, including sometimes the sophisticated elites of the society, as a way of asserting their national identity and expressing their nationalistic feelings (Bloch 1984; Smith 1981; Lan 1985).

Ecstatic cults, in various forms, have suffered gravely by the introduction of Christianity, which deprecates them as "demonic" as testified by numerous missionaries' accounts (e.g. Bishop 1898). During the colonial periods, they remained largely in the "primitive" backwaters of the society, kept alive by the "ignorant" rural community. However, in the 1960s and 1970s, among the Xezuru in Southern Rhodesia, the ZANLA were legitimized as the returning ancestors by traditional spirit mediums, by observing the ritual rules set out by them (Lan 1985) In a less deliberate and self-conscious way, among the Kaffa of south-western Ethiopia, the *ego* (spirit) cult serves as a vehicle for Kaffa cultural nationalism (Lewis 1971).

Likewise in Korea, *musok*, which has never ceased to play an important part in the peoples' lives despite a long history of severe persecution, is being reappraised as a uniquely Korean religio-cultural heritage. Prof. Gim Taegon (1972) goes as far as to maintain that shamanism is "the source of the Korean people's spiritual energy." I would argue that this renewed interest in hitherto disgraced shamanism is directly linked to the revival of the national identity, which has always been strongly present throughout Korea's long turbulent history, and cultural nationalism. There is a sense in which Korean shamanism is revived as a protest and protection against cultural "colonialism" by the West, particularly America, and a reaction against pan-global cultural homogenization.

Part 2

THE IMPORTANCE OF SHAMANISM
IN UNDERSTANDING
ANCIENT KOREAN CULTURE

Introduction

Shamanism is a belief system which can be found in many parts of the world such as Asia, Africa, aboriginal Americas, and northern Eurasia. Shamanism premises that there exist people with special abilities to mediate between the spirits and humans, called "the shaman." Shamans make contact with the spirit world in the altered state of consciousness, generally referred to as "trance," which they can enter into at will with the aid of drums and other noise-inducing instruments, frantic dance, etc. Shamans in certain parts of the world, e.g. North and South Americas, are also known to enter the state of trance by taking hallucinogens. Their supernatural powers are socially recognized and used in a ritual, which is performed for a specific purpose, such as healing of the body/mind, keeping misfortunes at bay by chasing away evil spirits that are believed to cause them, and bringing about good fortune.

It is often said that shamanism was first introduced to the West after the Russian travellers to Siberia discovered its practices among the Tungus (Evenks) of Siberia in the 17th century. The word "shaman" itself is from a Tungusian (Evenki) word, "saman." However, shamanism has been in existence from the dawn of human civilization as evidenced by ancient petroglyphs and cave paintings that still remain in different parts of the world. [1]

Ancient cave painting and petroglyphs (Figure 2.1-2.5)

Fig. 2.1: A cave painting in colour, popularly called "The Shaman in the Cave," thought to date back to the Palaeolithic Age . It was found in Les Trois Frères in the French Pyrenées.

Fig. 2.2: Rock carvings (petroglyphs) of an anthropo-morphic figure with a bear-head mask dating back to 4000-3000 B.C., found in Maya, Yakut Autonomous Region, SSR (Okladnikov-Mazin 1979: 126).

Fig. 2.3: Petroglyphs of human figures with horned headdresses, thought to be shamans in action, found in Central Asia (Sher 1980: 192).

Fig. 2.4: Siberian petroglyphs depicting a shaman with his helping spirits, 15-18 A.D in Mohsobolloo-Haya, Yakut ASSR (Okladnikov 1949).

Fig. 2.5: Shamans with drums, dating back to around 18-20 A.D., found in the Khakas Autonomous Region (Kyzlasov-Leotiev 1980: 117).

---

1 Figures 1, 2, 3, 32, 45, 55, 56, 66 & 67 are my drawings based on various sources including the Internet. Figures 4, 5, 6, 14, 15, 16, 17, 18, 19, 20, 21,22, 23, 24, 25, 26, 46, 52, 53, 60, 61, 62, 63 & 64 are copies of the drawings and photographs in various books, reproduced with the permission of Mihály Hoppál. All the other figures are the photographs I took during my fieldwork.

Ancient Korean culture was so imbued with shamanistic elements that it is important to know what shamanism is to understand it. This lecture is to give you some of the examples through analyzing documental records and material relics from ancient Korea.

The following table shows the archaeological classification of the prehistoric age, and the social organization of the ancient world, based on various scholars' theories.

Table 2.1: The Social Organization in the Prehistoric Age

Christian Thomsen's (b.1788-d.1865) Archaeological classification	Sir John Lubbock (1865/2005)	Hodder Westropp (1865[2]), and other scholars	Friedrich Engels (1884/1972)	Elman Service (1962/1971)	Ancient Korea (Yun Naehyeon 1986)	Ancient China (張光直 1969[3])
Stone Age	Palaeolithic Age	Palaeolithic Age	Primitive community	band	*muri sahoe* (band society)	游團社會
		Mesolithic Age				
	Neolithic Age	Early Neolithic Age		tribe	*maeul sahoe* (village society) (8,000 BC)	村落社會 (3,500 BC)
		Late Neolithic Age		chiefdom	*goeul nara* (district country) (4,000 BC)	村群社會 (3,500 BC)
Bronze Age	Bronze Age	Bronze Age	state	state	*gukga*: Go-Joseon (state 國家:古朝鮮) (2,333 BC)	國家:夏商周 (2,200 BC)
Iron Age	Iron Age	Iron Age				春秋戰國時代 (770 BC)

Dan-gun Myth and the Foundation of the Korean Nation

There remain many artefacts suggesting human habitation in Korea from the Palaeolithic Age, such as flint stone arrow heads and other tools, but extant Korean written history only dates back to the Three Kingdoms

---

2 In a paper given at the Anthropological Society of London.

3 Cited in Yun 1986: 122-138.

Period (18 B.C.-668 A.D.[4]). So for ancient Korean history before that period, we have to rely on the scanty information contained in ancient Chinese chronicles.

However, almost all Koreans trace the origin of their nation to the mythological progenitor, Dan-gun, who is believed to have founded the first Korean kingdom of Go-Joseon ("Old Joseon") in 2333 BC. The story of Dan-gun first appears in the Monk Iryeon's *Samguk yusa* (*Memorabilia of the Three Kingdoms*) written in the 12th century. It was during the period when Korea's existence was under threat after the Mongol invasions, and has held a special significance to all Koreans. Iryeon writes:

> It is written in **Wiseo** (魏書) that two thousand years ago, there was a man called Dan-gun Wanggeom who set up the capital at Asadal and founded a nation called Joseon. This was in the time of Chinese Emperor Ko (高) of the Yo (堯) dynasty.
>
> It is written in **Gogi** (古記: the Old Chronicles) that in ancient times, Hwanin (this refers to Jeseok), had a son ("*seoja*"[5]) called Hwanung, who had an ambition to descend onto the earth, and to rule over humans. His father, realizing his intentions, chose Taebaek-san (Mt. Taebaek) among three great mountains, for him to descend upon, deciding that it is a befitting place from which to benefit mankind. He gave Hwanung three **Cheonbuin** (the Three Heavenly Seals)[6] and allowed him to go and rule over mankind.
>
> Accompanied by three thousand followers, Hwanung descended upon the peak of Taebaek-san through the Sacred Tree. That area was called the City of God and he was known as Hwanung

---

4 "Traditional" dates—from the founding of Baekje (18 B.C.) to the unification of the Three Kingdoms by Silla (668 A.D.).

5 *Seoja* is known as an "illegitimate son" by the general Korean public. However, in Korean academe, it seems to have a multiplicity of meaning. To the Korean historians at the Academy of Korean Studies in traditional Korea it referred to any son other than the eldest son who had the primary inheritance. Thus they included secondary and subsequent sons of the primary wife, and sons of concubines. Illegitimate sons issuing from casual relationships were called "*eolja.*" Together they were called "*seo-eol.*"

6 *Cheonbuin* is an object, which symbolizes the powers of God. No record of what this object exactly is, remains, but it is believed that there are three such objects, namely a knife, a mirror, and bells (*Samguk yusa*, 1987: 4). Interestingly they are still used as paraphernalia in the contemporary Korean shamanic ritual.

Cheonwang (Heavenly King). Together with his ministers of Pungbaek (Wind), Usa (Rain), and Unsa (Cloud), Hwanung instructed and enlightened mankind about some three hundred and sixty kinds of work, including agriculture, preserving long life, curing disease, punishments, and distinguishing between the right and the wrong.

At that time, there was a bear and a tiger which lived together in a cave. They prayed incessantly to Hwanung to transform them into humans. He gave them some sacred mugwort and twenty pieces of garlic and said, 'If you eat this and do not see light for one hundred days, you will turn into humans.' The bear persevered, becoming a woman at the end of three times seven days. The tiger, which could not endure the ordeal, did not become a human.

As there was no one whom the woman Ungnyeo (Bear Woman) could marry, she went constantly to the base of the Sacred Tree to pray for a child. Hwanung temporarily changed his form and married her. She gave birth to a son who was called Dan-gun Wanggeom. In the fiftieth year of Emperor Danggo (唐高)[7]'s reign, in the year *Gyeongin* (庚寅年)[8], Dan-gun set up the capital at Pyeongyang and called the nation Joseon. He later moved the capital to Asadal on Baegak-san which was also known as Gunghol-san or Gummidal. He governed the nation for 1,500 years. In the year of the coronation of King Ho (Hu:虎) of the Chou (周) dynasty[9], the king (Dan-gun) abdicated in favour of Gija. Dan-gun then relocated to Jangdanggyeong. Later, he returned to Asadal and hid himself, eventually becoming the Mountain Spirit, at 1,908 years of age.

(***Samguk yusa***, Book 1, Part 1: my translation)

The historical authenticity of the above myth, which is literally accepted by the Korean people in general, including most scholars, is beyond the scope of this lecture, and will be dealt with elsewhere.

What is relevant is that it is imbued with shamanistic themes and

---

7   Refers to a king of Yo (堯) in China.

8   Traditional date, 2333 B.C.

9   Traditional date, 1122 B.C.

motifs. First of all, the name Dan-gun is reminiscent of *tengri* of the Mongols, *tengeri* of the Buryat, *tangere* of the Volga Tartars, *tingir* of the Beltirs, *tangara* of the Yakut, etc., which all mean "sky" or "heaven."

Second, the concept of *axis mundi,* which links the human world to the sky or the realm of the gods and spirits, is a common motif in shamanism. The Siberian shamans are believed to ascend to the sky or descend to the underground hell, through the *axis mundi*, which is often represented as a pole or a tree. The cosmic mountain linking the earth and the sky is also a prevalent concept. In the Dan-gun Myth, both trees and mountains feature prominently; for example, he descended upon a mountain through a sacred tree.

Third, one of the most important features of shamanism is the existence of the shaman's guardian and helping spirits without which he/she cannot function properly. Hwanung's ministers of wind, rain and cloud, and 3,000 followers can be paralleled to the shaman's helpers. Also his ministers of' "wind, rain and cloud" suggest that his chief function was to ensure plenty of rainfall, which is the main requisite for agriculture. It is an interesting co-incidence that one of the most important functions of the shaman everywhere is to bring rain. Hwanung's 360 kinds of work is similar to what modern Korean *mudang* attempt to do, i.e. curing disease, preserving long life, ensuring a good harvest, punishment where it is due, distinguishing right from wrong, etc.

Fig. 2.6: Blackfoot Indian shaman wearing a bear skin costume (early 19th century).

The zoomorphic character of the shaman's guardian spirits originating from totemism is a common feature of Siberian shamanism.[10] The Evenki shaman's cult of the bear, which, according to Anisimov (1958), originates from the toemic source, is an interesting co-incidence. Apparently Evenki shamans are prohibited to hunt the bear or eat its meat, since for a totemist, totemic animals are his blood relations. Among the Tuvans, of all the guardian spirits the bear spirit was considered the strongest, and only a 'powerful' shaman

---

10 Basilov in Hoppal (ed) (1984).

could own it. The bear is also considered to be a powerful shaman's helper by some American Indians.

Also among the Yakut and Dolgan, the "animal mother" is considered the most important. The shaman has an *ie-kyla* (animal mother), a sort of mythical image of an animal helper. A powerful shaman has a bear or an eagle as his animal mother. A remarkable parallel can be found in the existence of a zoomorphic guardian spirit in the form of a bear-mother in the Dan-gun Myth. Guardian spirits are so fundamental in shamanism that "without the belief in helping spirits shamanism cannot be spoken of (Vajda 1964: 72)," and "the ecstatic who attains the other world without the help of his guardian spirits is certainly no shaman (Hultkrantz 1978/96: 14)." Then Dan-gun with his powerful bear-mother as his guardian spirit can be said to be an archetypal shaman.

Fourth, the importance of the number "three" in shamanism has been observed by many scholars.8 What is significant is that "three" also features strongly in the Dan-gun Myth; Hwanin, Hwanung and Dan-gun form the Trinity; Hwanin gave Hwanung three heavenly seals; Hwanung descended on Earth accompanied by 3,000 followers; he had three ministers; he taught humans 360 (multiples of three) kinds of work; and the bear became a woman after three times seven days (Note it is not written 21 days).

Fifth, there is an interesting parallel between the process of the bear's metamorphosis into a woman and the making of the shaman. The former was accomplished only through adhering to the ritual restrictions, which involved eating prescribed ritual food and avoiding light. Light is generally thought to symbolize life. The prescribed food, i.e. 20 pieces of garlic and some bitter mugwort for such a long period of time, is tantamount to a starvation diet. In other words, the bear's trial is similar to a Siberian shaman's initiation experiences of the symbolic death and resurrection. Incidentally it is interesting to note that mugwort is also considered sacred by other peoples of the world. For example, among the Chumash it is called the 'dream herb, ' and the shamans use it as a hallucinogen to enter trance states. In contemporary Korean *musok*, rice cake made of mugwort (*ssuk ddeok*) is an indispensable item for the *gut* table.

Sixth, the union of gods and earthly women is also a common theme in Siberian shamanism. According to Sternberg's (1924: 476 ft.) [11]interpretation, the nature of the relationship between the spirits and the

---

11 Cited in Eliade (1951/1964: 73-75).

shaman is primarily sexual. He presents various evidence to support his argument. Shirokogoroff (1935) reports that a shamaness experienced sexual feelings during her initiation ritual; the Goldi shaman's ritual dance also had sexual connotations; in the Yakut folklore studied by Troschansky,[12] there is constant reference to young celestial spirits descending to earth and marrying mortal women. The union of Hwanung and the bear woman is a familiar shamanistic theme.

Dan-gun: the mythological progenitor of the Korean nation (Figure 2.7-2.12)

Fig. 2.7: one of the oldest known Dan-gun portraits.

Fig. 2.8: Guksadang (shaman hall in Seoul) where it is kept.

Fig. 2.9: Jeong Wonhae (b 1932) at her shrine, with a modern replica of the Dan-gun portrait inside Guksadang.

Fig. 2.10: Another version of Dan-gun portrait at Gim Geumhwa's private shrine.

---

12 Cited in Eliade (1951/1964: 73).

Dan-gun ritual held by Daehan Seunggong Gyeongsin Yeonhaphoe
at Mani-san on 11 November 1993.

Fig. 2.11: Members are queuing to enter
the shrine to pay their respects to Dan-
gun.

Fig. 2.12 : Inside the shrine with a Dan-
gun statue and sacrificial offerings.

"*Dan-gi* (The Dan-gun Calendar)," which calculates its first year as 2333 B.C. based on Iryeon's Dan-gun Myth, was officially adopted by the newly-independent Korean government in 1948 and used until 1961. In 1949 the government proclaimed the third of October (by the western calendar) an official holiday to celebrate Gaecheonjeol (National Foundation Day: literally meaning "Heaven Opening Day"). On that day and also all throughout October, sacrifices to Dan-gun are offered on famous mountains nation-wide to this day.

When I was at school in Korea, we learned all our historical dates in *dan-gi*, which sometimes posed a problem on the world stage. For example, the famous dates that most people know by heart such as 1066 (the Battle of Hastings/the Norman Conquest), 1776 (the American Independence), 1789 (the French Revolution) were taught to us Korean children as Dan-gi 3399, 4099 and 4122, respectively! It caused a great inconvenience as Korea advanced to the world stage bit by bit. So when Park Chung Hee came to power after his military *coup d'etat* in 16 May 1961, as one of his "reform measures," he abolished it adopting "*seogi* (the western calendar)."

Prehistoric Korean states

Apart from the "traditional" date shown in the Dan-gun Myth, the period that this lecture covers is from around the time of the formation of the

Three Kingdoms to the end of the Three Kingdoms period. The rough time scale is shown in the following:

<The North>

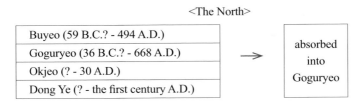

Buyeo (59 B.C.? - 494 A.D.)	
Goguryeo (36 B.C.? - 668 A.D.)	absorbed into Goguryeo
Okjeo (? - 30 A.D.)	
Dong Ye (? - the first century A.D.)	

<The South> Samhan (Three Hans)

Mahan	→	absorbed into Baekje
Jinhan	→	absorbed into Silla
Byeonhan	→ Gaya →	absorbed into Silla

<The Three Kingdoms Period>

Goguryeo	高句麗	37 BC ?– 668 AD
Baekje	百濟	18 BC ? – 660 AD
Silla	新羅	57 BC ?– 935 AD

* The question marks in the above denote "traditional" dates or dates unknown.

Shamanistic festivals in ancient Korea

For written history of Korea, the earliest sources by Korean historians available to us is the Monk Iryeon's *Samguk yusa* (*The Memorabilia of the Three Kingdoms*) and Gim Busik's *Samguk sagi* (*History of the Three Kingdoms*), both of which were compiled and written in Chinese characters several hundred years later, in the 12th century. So for ancient Korean history we have to turn to the scanty information contained in ancient Chinese historical documents under the heading of "The Eastern Barbarians (東夷傳)." There are two documents which deal with the Eastern Barbarians, namely, *Samgukji* (*History of the Three Kingdoms*, 三國志) and *Hu Hanseo* (*The Later Han Chronicles*, 後漢書=後書 for short). Although they describe the locations, sizes, customs of several tribal societies and early kingdoms of ancient Korea, these documents only describe three "religious" festivals, namely *yeonggo-je* of Buyeo, *dongmaeng* of Goguryeo and *mucheon* of (Eastern) Ye (Choe Gwangsik 1994: 143).

 Yeonggo-je of Buyeo is described in both *Samgukji* and *Hu Hanseo*. Since it was held in the 12th lunar month which has no relevance to the agricultural calendar, it would appear that it was closely connected with hunting (Choe Gwansik 1994: 145). It is said that they offered sacrifices to Heaven in a national scale ritual/festival, which lasted for days and during which they ate, drank and danced. The name "*yeonggo*" (迎鼓), which means "welcoming with drums," indicates that it was a shamanistic ritual, and the fact it was held as a national festival suggests that the shaman may have occupied the central position in Buyeo society. An immolation of an ox is said to have taken place during the ritual, to predict the outcome of a war or other future events. Interestingly an ox is occasionally immolated on a large-scale *gut* in contemporary Korea.

Yeonggo-je "Welcoming the spirits with drums"): Indispensable drums for shamans (Figure 2.13-2.21)

(from left to right)
Fig. 2.13: Mongol shaman. / Fig. 2.14: Gilyak shaman. /
Fig. 2.15: Ostyak shaman's séance.

(from left to right)
Fig. 2.16: Krasnoyarsk region shaman. / Fig. 2.17: Altai region shaman. /
Fig. 2.18: Otsir böö (Bajangol district) shaman.

(from left to right)
Fig. 19: Samoyd shaman. / Fig. 20: Sojot shaman. / Fig. 21: Lebed Tartar shaman.

Yeonggo-je **("Welcoming the spirits with drums"):**
Indispensable drums: Siberian shamans' drums (Figure 2.22-2.26)

(from left to right)
Fig. 2.22: shaman drum – ex Ivanov 1954: 594, fig. 43 (Khakas).
Fig. 2.23: Shaman drum – ex Ivanov 1954: 642 fig. 84 (Altaic Turk).

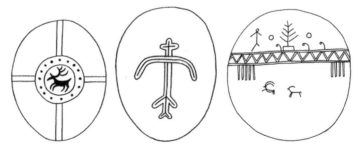

(from left to right)
Fig. 2.24: Shaman drum – ex Ivanov 1954: 104, fig. 6.3 (Dolgan).
Fig. 2.25: Shaman drum – ex Ivanov 1954: fig. 67.1 (Evenki).
Fig. 2.26: Shaman drum – ex Harva 1938: fig. 30 (Altaic Turk).

Janggo/janggu: Korean shamans' indispensable hour-glass drums
(Figure 2.27-2.30)

(from left to right)

Fig. 2.27: Seo Jeonghwa recites the Ballad of the Abandoned Princess at a *jinogi* (mortuary) *gut*, playing the janggo at the same time.

Fig. 2.28: Bak Ino gets possessed by Five Directional General with one of his spirit daughters playing the *janggo*.

(from left to right)

Fig. 2.29: Han Guksan (real name: Jeong Munseon) gets possessed by his guardian spirit with his spirit mother playing the *janggo*.

Fig. 2.30: Won Gannan invites the spirits down while playing the *janggo*.

Hunting for sacrificial animals (Figure 2.31-2.34)

(from left to right)
Fig. 2.31 & 2.32: A mural of a hunting scene in Muyongchong ("Tomb of Dancers") a Goguryeo tomb. *Samguk sagi* states that hunting for animals to offer to Heaven was an important national event.

Hunting scenes are often enacted by modern Korean *mudang*.
(from left to right)
Fig. 2.33: Bang Chunja emulates a hunting scene in her *jinjeok gut* held on 7 March 1994.
Fig. 2.34: A similar performance by one of Gim Geumhwa's spirit daughters in a *gut* held on 4 December 1993.

Offering an ox to the spirits (Figure 2.35-2.36)

Fig. 2.35: Jo Jaryong (real name: Jo Yongjin) immolates an ox during his *jinjeok gut* held on 5 April 1994.

Fig. 2.36: The immolated ox is offered to the spirits, after which it is barbecued and consumed by the participants.

Dongmaeng of Goguryeo, whose name may have derived from its founder Dongmyeong, also appears to have been a shamanistic ritual/festival. According to the Chinese chronicles, they welcomed the spirits, set up a spirit tree and offered sacrifices to the spirits.

The spirit tree linking the human and spirit worlds (Figure 2.37-2.39)

Fig. 2.37: Goguryeo tomb mural in Muyongchong (Tomb of Dancers).

Fig. 2.38: Tree as an important prop in Gim Geumhwa's *gut* held on 4 December 1993.

Fig. 2.39: The sacred tree through which the spirits descend at Gangneung Dano-je festival.

Mucheon of (Eastern) Ye, is also described in the Chinese chronicles. Like *dongmaeng* of Goguryeo, it was held in the 10th lunar month. As the name "mucheon (舞天 which means dancing to Heaven) indicates, people ate, drank, sang and danced for several days. It is interesting to note that tigers were worshipped as gods. In contemporary Korean shamanism, one of the most important gods, the Mountain Spirit (Sansin) is usually depicted accompanied by a tiger. In the Dan-gun Myth, Dan-gun himself is said to have become the Mountain Spirit.

Mucheon ("Dancing to Heaven) ritual/festival of Ye: Dancing, eating and drinking in *gut* in Korea today (Figure 2.40-2.43)

Fig. 2.40: A mural in Muyongchong, a Goguryeo tomb.

Fig. 2.41: Food is served to everybody present in *gut*. Gim Geumhwa's *jinjeok gut* on 17 November 1993.

Fig. 2.42: Clients and other participants in *gut* enjoy themselves, drinking, eating and dancing. Bang Chunja's *jineok gut* on 7 March 1994.

Fig. 2.43: In Ye society, tigers were worshipped as gods. In contemporary Korean shamanism, Mountain Spirit , one of the most important gods, is usually accompanied by, and also occasionally depicted, as tigers.

The Four Seasons Rituals in the Three Hans are not described in the Chinese chronicles, although the Three Han tribes are mentioned. But according to *Samguk sagi*, they were held in the fifth lunar month after planting seeds and again in the tenth lunar month after harvest. Sacrifices are said to have been offered not to *cheonsin* (天神: Heavenly Spirit), but to *gwisin* (鬼神: ghosts). In *sodo* (the towns in the Three Hans), large trees were erected on which were hung rattles and drums, through which the ghosts descended and served. It is exactly what happens in shamanistic festivals such as Gangneung Dano-je in contemporary Korea.

Shamanism seemed to continue to play an important social role, judging from the material relics from the Three Kingdoms Period that are imbued with shamanistic elements. As well as those mentioned earlier, the ornithological theme is an integral part of shamanism, since birds soar into the sky where the spirits are thought to dwell. Apart from the birds, flying animals, such as horses and mythological animals with human faces and animal bodies with wings also appear in tomb murals from the Goguryeo period.

Ornithological theme (Figure 2.44-2.54)

(from left to right)
Fig. 2.44: Sun God: Goguryeo tomb mural.
Fig. 2.45: Three-footed/winged crow motif inside the circle over the Sun God's head which symbolizes the sun.
Fig. 2.46: a shaman drum with a similar motif – ex Ivanov 1954: fig. 67.1 (Evenki).

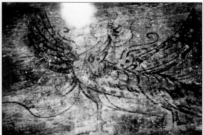

(from left to right)
Fig. 2.47: Goguryeo tomb mural; a flying horse.
Fig. 2.48: Goguryeo tomb mural; a mythological flying animal with a human head.

(from left to right)
Fig. 2.49: Goguryeo tomb mural depicting a man flying on a crane.
Fig. 2.50: One of Gim Geumhwa's shamanistic painting, showing a female god riding over the clouds on a crane.

(from left to right)
Fig. 2.51: Birchbark painting of a "Heavenly Horse," from the Heavenly Horse Tomb of ancient Silla. The suggestion of four extra legs gives it the magical power.
Fig. 2.52: Mother corn. The decorated ear, carried on the Pawnee ceremony of adoption, has the tip painted blue to symbolize the heaven, dwelling of the Powers. Four blue lines coming from it are the paths by which the Powers visit man. From the Annual Report, Bureau of American Ethnology, No.22, Part 2.

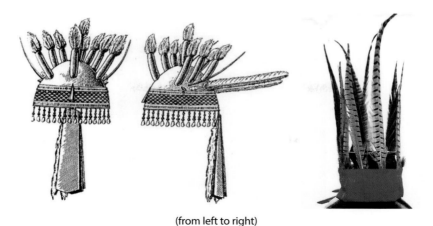
(from left to right)
Fig. 2.53: Tuba shaman's headdress decorated with feathers.
Fig. 2.54: Han Guksan (Jeong Munseon)'s hat decorated with pheasant feathers.

Heaven worship in Korean shamanism also means the worship of everything in it, such as the sun, the moon and the stars, which frequently appear in ancient tomb murals. In Korean shamanism they are personified as deities. One of the most important gods in Korean shamanism today is Chilseongsin (the Seven Stars Spirit), which usually appears before any other spirits in contemporary *gut*.

Sun, moon and stars (Figure 2.55-2.58)

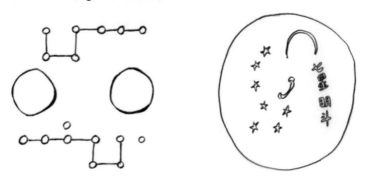
(from left to right)
Fig. 2.55: The painting of the sun, the moon and the Seven Starts (the Big Dipper) in an ancient Goguryeo tomb, Jangcheon No 1 Tomb).
Fig. 2.56: Back of a modern *mudang*'s *myeongdu* (brass mirror).

Fig. 2.57: Gim Geumhwa's *musindo* (Shamanistic spirit painting) of the Seven Stars Spirit.

Fig. 2.58: Bang Chanaghwan possessed by the Seven Stars Spirit in the *jinogi gut* held on 24 February 1994.

Korean shamans make contact with the stars by being possessed by the spirits representing them, giving their blessings to their clients, or predict the future events, etc. Cheomseongdae, which is known as the oldest astronomical observatory in Korea may well have been used for shamanistic rituals. It has been said that the narrow opening at the top is not suitable for studying the stars and other celestial entities. What is interesting is that its shape closely resembles the tents used by some Native American Indians for shamanistic purposes.

Cheomseongdae: The world's oldest astronomical "observatory" Studying stars through direct contact? (Figure 2.59-2.61)

Fig. 2.59: Cheomseongdae: Built during the reign of Queen Seondeok (r. 632-647) of Silla. Thought to be the oldest astronomical observatory in the world. Designated National Treasure No. 31 on 20 December 1962. Made of 381 stone bricks, weighing 264 tons, and measuring height 9.17 metres, base diameter 4.93m, top diameter 2.85m. It consists of 27 layers, and is filled with earth and stones up to the 12th level, where there is a square window/entrance facing south. There are traces of ladders having been placed at the window.

Typical aboriginal American conjuring lodges in which a shaman receives his spirits and questions them. (from left to right)
Fig. 2.60: (from an imaginative drawing by J. C. Tidball, in Schoolcraft, Part I, p 428) It is constructed of birch bark strips made by the Ojibwa Indians.
Fig. 2.61: (a drawing by Lucien M. Turner, from "Ethnology of the Ungava District, Hudson Bay Territory" in Eleventh Annual Report of the Bureau of Ethnology(1889, 1890), fig. 85, p. 274, made of skins by Eskimos of Hudson Bay.) The lodges are placed over the shamans; there is no opening at the top, where the spirits enter, often shaking the tent.

Although Silla's architectural techniques were much more advanced than those of the American Indians, and therefore Cheomseongdae is a much more solidly built stone structure, and much larger, there is a remarkable similarity in shape between the two. The Native American Indian shaman's headgear made of bird feathers in the picture below also revokes the image of a Silla king wearing a gold crown. It has also been pointed out that the Silla gold crown was not suitable for prolonged wear, being very heavy and does not fit the head securely. So it may not be too farfetched to hypothesize that Silla kings, who may also have been shamans may have worn the gold crowns and performed shamanistic rituals inside Cheomseongdae. The window is the only entrance to Cheomseongdae, and it has been generally accepted that they used ladders to climb up to the window to gain entry into the structure, which was filled with earth and stones up to that level. Could it be that the shaman king himself was the only one to be allowed into the hallowed place where he communed with the spirits? It is only a hypothesis and deserves further research.

Silla gold crowns and Siberian Shamans' headgear (Figure 2.62-2.67)

Fig. 2.62: A Siberian shaman's headgear; the most important part of the costume.

(from left to right)
Fig. 2.63: Tungus shaman (Witzen 1672).
Fig. 2.64: A shaman hat decorated with trees, birds and antelopes.

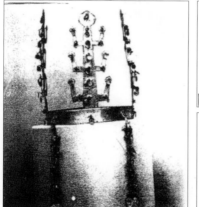

(clockwise from left)
Fig. 2.65: A Silla gold crown. National Treasure No. 87.
Fig. 2.66: Spread out diagram of the gold crown (NT No. 87).
Fig. 2.67: The *san* (山: mountain) motif usually found in a Silla gold crown. Note the same motif in the Siberian shaman's headgear (Fig. 2.47).

Were these gold crowns originally made to be worn by the Silla king (also a shaman?) for shamanistic rituals? Was Cheomseongdae originally built for the purpose of inviting the spirits to descend into it for shamanistic rituals?

The degeneration of Korean shamanism from the central morality religious belief system to a cult of the "lowly" women and the uneducated masses interestingly coincided with the rise of patriarchy and male dominance in Korean society. After the introduction and establishment of Buddhism, the "rational" world religion, and Confucianism which emphasizes the superiority of men over women, shamanism was derogated as a "primitive superstition." The successive rationalized elites of Korean society tried to eradicate it, while it was embraced by the marginalized people as a source of subversive "power" and comfort in a social system which was so unfair to them. Since the emergence of written Korean history, frequent mention has been made of Korean shamanism, albeit obliquely and in derogatory terms. So the history of Korean shamanism since the Three Kingdoms Period is largely a story of persecution, but also of persistence. While not so obvious as in ancient Korean culture, shamanistic elements can still be detected in many aspects of Korean culture. Therefore for a deep understanding of Korean culture, especially of the ancient times, it is important to have a proper knowledge of shamanism.

Part 3

RECIPROCITY, STATUS
AND THE KOREAN SHAMANISTIC RITUAL

Introduction

Despite the fascination that shamanism exerts on most people who come across it, it has been rapidly disappearing in many societies, rejected and scorned by rationalized people. Even in Siberia, where its practices were first spotted among the Tungus by western travellers in the late 17th century, thus giving it its name, shamanism is no longer widely practised. Recent studies on Siberian shamanism has been conducted through staged "performances" by elderly shamans for the benefit of scholars in abbreviated form, or through shamanistic elements in folk customs or folktales.[1]

In Korea, however, shamanistic rituals, called *gut*, have persistently been performed, despite centuries of persecution by the authorities, mainly by oppressed female and peripheral male members of the society. Today, as Prof. Seo Jeong-beom has told me, nowhere in the world can one find such highly organized, elaborate, spectacularly dramatic shamanistic rituals as *gut*. Why, then, does this essentially "primi-

---

1 For example, a Yakut participant gave a paper about a Yakut shaman based on his staged performances at the Second International Conference on the North-Asian People's Culture, held in Seoul, on 13-14 November, 1993.

tive" polytheistic religious phenomenon persist, even today, in rapidly industrializing Korea, which boasts being the ninth largest trading nation in the world?[2]

I became aware of the significance that shamanism holds to Koreans in 1987, when I returned to Korea on my husband's posting to the British Embassy in Seoul, after an absence of twenty years. Until then I had had little contact with, thus virtually no knowledge of it, *gut* having more or less died out in central Seoul, where I had been brought up. I was surprised however to witness a public revival of *gut*, even by some educated urbanites such as university students, and serious academic discourse on it. The next four years was an age of rediscovery of my native country for me. Through getting heavily involved with the Korean branch of the Royal Asiatic Society, my husband and I combed through the width and breadth of South Korea. On our travels, we encountered shamanistic rituals, or shamanistic elements in Korean culture, time and time again. On my return to England in 1991, I decided to research into shamanism in a serious academic fashion, fitting it into the framework of social anthropology, since it is after all a very social phenomenon. My MA dissertation, entitled, "Korean Shamanism and Cultural Nationalism" was based entirely on library research, aided by my sketchy memories of the *gut*. The conclusion that I arrived at then was that there was a sense in which Korean shamanism was revived as a reaction against global cultural homogenization and cultural colonialism by the West.

It seemed to me that *gut* was more and more regarded as a "performance," a piece of traditional Korean folk culture, to be enjoyed, without any religiosity or serious purpose attached to it. My PhD research proposal put an emphasis on the folklorization and entertainment aspect of the Korean shamanistic ritual. With this in mind, I set out on my fieldwork in 1993, armed with two cameras, a camcorder, a tape recorder and a clipboard. I endorsed in principle the Boasian approach of data collection, aiming at "total recovery," since I felt that premature generalizations were too frequently attempted, resulting in theories far removed from reality and forced or false analogies, etc, in anthropology. Maurice Freedman (1967) also remarks on the paucity of ethnographic descriptions, since anthropologists tend to discard ethnographic details for the sake of excellence in analysis. During my library research, I also wished

---

2 According to a commercial officer at the British Embassy in Seoul.

for some detailed information on certain aspects of Korean shamanism, particularly on a wider variety of the sponsors of the *gut*, and their interactions with the shamans. Taking heed of the wisdom contained in an old Korean proverb, "Intelligence is inferior to even bad handwriting," I was determined to record every minute detail of all that I saw, heard and felt, as it happened, so that my memory or wishful thinking would not play a trick later during my analyses.

My fieldwork was conducted between 1993 and 1994, mainly in Seoul, since it seemed quite apparent to me that Seoul is the place that has hegemony over all of South Korea, hence most shamans congregate there. Once in the field, however, I soon realized a complete change of direction was called for. The *gut*, far from being performed as a curious diversion for spectators, or just to exert national identity as I had previously thought, was still very much alive, being performed seriously as a ritual for real purposes, such as curing, praying for good luck, consoling the dead and the bereaved, etc. My fieldwork experiences, and the difficulties concerning my penetration into the shamanistic community are dealt with in my thesis. Despite the initial difficulties, mainly because of a great social stigma attached to not only the shamans, but also the sponsors of *gut*, I managed to succeed in winning the good opinions of numerous shamans and sponsors. It was achieved mainly through showing my dedication by arriving early to talk to them informally during the elaborate preparations for the *gut*, recording every detail, and staying until the very end, every time. Thus spending a whole day with them, sharing all my meals, brought us close together, creating a tremendous rapport among us.

I must express my gratitude to the late Mr. Choe Nameok, president of a shaman society called, Daehan Seunggong Gyeongsin Yeonhaphwo (the Korean Spirit Worshippers' Association for Victory over Communism), who opened the firmly-closed doors of some shamans for me. My gratitude also goes to some 200 shamans, whom I met in the field, for showing so much respect for my research and particularly to some of them, for their warm friendship. My research yielded over 800 pages of field notes, some 5,000 pictures and slides, over 40 videos, over 30 interview cassettes, as well as some rare shamans' textbooks and talismans, etc.

One of the reasons why I rejected concentrating on one shaman and his/her followers, which would be more in keeping with the classic anthropological method. is that there is a great deal of "invention of tradition" going on, in contemporary Korean shamanism. In the absence of the scriptures or any other form of systematic written texts, *gut* being all there is, minor variations or additions are constantly made to the ritual. Since Korean shamans are usually very creative artistic people, they occasionally make misleading alterations, to impress sponsors or spectators. Also there is a real danger of them even fabricating some or parts of her/his life story or various aspects of *musok* to impress the naive "scientific" researcher, who would take her/his word for face value. Therefore, in studying *musok*, it is important to get friendly with a large number of practising shamans, through whose gossips, casual unthinking remarks, etc, a true picture often emerges. It is dangerous to rely on only one, or a handful of shamans, who could actually mislead you in some ways, however good your scientific sampling method may be. Therefore, I have decided to base my thesis on 52 *gut* which I attended and recorded, my conversations with 70 shamans of both sexes, and a number of sponsors with whom I established a measure of rapport. In this way, I think I am striking a balance between Laurel Kendall's one shamaness informant and Youngsook Kim Harvey's six shamanesses, and Seo Jeong-beom's 3,000 and Gim Taegon's unspecified vast number of informants.

To sum up, this paper examines the basic principles underlying the Korean shamanistic ritual, called *gut*, through analyzing the three groups of participants in it, namely spirits, shamans, and sponsors, and the social interactions between them, to divulge its idiosyncrasies. It is based on my PhD thesis, which is scheduled to be submitted soon. I would appreciate any critiques and comments from the audience, which might help improve it. Since it is impossible to convey all the ideas contained in my 340-page thesis within the time limit, this paper has taken on a nature of synopses. Afterwards, I would be very happy to clarify any points, which may well have been lost in the process of condensation.

Definitions

First the definitions of shamanism. Shamanism is notoriously difficult to define, since there is still considerable ambiguity and controversy surrounding various aspects of shamanism, despite comprehensive studies spanning over two centuries and a large number of publications on it. Shamanism is best defined in terms of who and what the shaman is. Since "shaman" is generally thought to have come from the Tungusic *saman*. North Asia seems to be a logical place to look for a definition of it. According to Shirokogoroff (1935), shamans are capable of having direct contact with the spirit world through ecstasy, controlling spirits and using their power for helping other people who suffer from illnesses or misfortune, attributed to the influence of malignant spirits. Thus shamans have the socially recognized abilities to achieve ecstasy, summon their guardian spirits, and with their help ascend to heaven or descend to hell, to bring back the lost soul, or fight with and win over evil spirits, which cause illnesses or misfortune, and this obtain the cure. They have socially-sanctioned ritual codes and paraphernalia, and enjoy a privileged social status.

Korean shamans, collectively called *mudang*, largely fit into this paradigm in principle, although there are considerable differences. The main difference lies in the fact that Korean shamans invite the spirits, who then manifest themselves through possessing the shamans at the ritual and speaking through them. In other words, the shamans "become" the spirits. Erika Bourguignon (1971)'s division of institutionalized altered state of consciousness into "trance," and "possession trance" linking it with the type of society in which they occur largely applies to Korean society. Thus the Korean shamans, predominantly women, mostly utilize possession trance, which according to Bourguignon's model usually occurs in agricultural societies. Although in traditional Korean society, *mudang*'s social status is the lowest of the low, they enjoy a special status, at least in their community, particularly during the shamanistic ritual.

The Korean Shamanistic Ritual

The *gut* is a comprehensive shamanistic ritual in which *mudang* invite the spirits by entering into ecstasy, and through entertaining them, supplicate them and propitiate evil spirits, which are believed to be the cause of misfortune and illnesses, send off the dead to the other world, or merely seek health, happiness and prosperity of a village or an individual family.

Gluckman's (1962) dichotomy of "ritual" and "ceremony" applies strictly in Korean society, although the division is made by the criteria of sacredness and profanity, rather than religiosity and technicality. Thus a ritual, i.e. a sacred formality, is called *-je*, (as in *jesa*= ancestral sacrifice), and a ceremony, that of profane nature, is called *–sik*, as in *gyeorhonsik*=weddng, *jangnyesik*=funeral, *joropsik*=graduation ceremony) in Korean society. However, the Korean shamamstic ritual is called neither *-je* nor *-sik*, which implies its ambiguous nature. Instead of being called *muje*, a literal equivalent of "the shamamstic ritual," it is called, *gut*.

Unlike many Korean words, *gut* does not have an equivalent Chinese character. Yi (1927) interprets *gut* as based on a pure Korean word, "*gut-da*." meaning "nasty, foul or unfortunate," as in *gujeun nal* (a rainy day), or *gujeun il* (a nasty affair, i.e. a bereavement). Thus *gut* is concerned with solving the problems of misfortune, particularly illness and death. That is why *gut* is also sometimes called *puri* ("solving" or "dispelling"). Ramstedt (1949) traces the origin of *gut* to the Tungusic "*gutu*," the Mongolian "*qutug*" and the Turkish "*qut*" winch all mean "happiness" or "good fortune." Thus the purpose of a *gut* is to bring about happiness and good fortune. However, both Yi's and Ramstedt's interpretations are in essence the same in that the aim of a *gut* is to bring about happiness for everybody, which is achieved through dispelling unexpected disasters.

A *gut* basically consists of twelve *geori*; each *geori* is a small independent *gut*, dedicated to a specific god. Twelve does not always represent the exact number of parts inside a *gut*, but a number symbolizing "a whole" or "completeness," as twelve months complete a year. (Yu, 1975) As we have seen earlier, the contents and the number of *geori* can vary according to the officiating *mudang*, but the basic structure of the *gut*, i.e. 1) the evocation, 2) entertainment. and 3) finally the send-off, of the gods, remains unchanged. The same pattern applies to each *geori*, which is a part dedicated to one or a group of spirits.

The *gut* can be broadly classified into four kinds, 1) *gut*, performed for the dead, *jinogi gut* (in the Seoul area), *ssitgim gut* (in the south), etc. 2) healing *gut*, called *uhwan gut*, *byeong gut*, etc. 3) *gut* performed to pray for good fortune, called *jaesu gut*, etc, and 4) *gut* performed for *mudang*, i.e. the initiation *gut* (*naerim gut*), and the seasonal offerings to the shaman's tutelary gods (*jinjeok gut*).

My analyses of the *gut* that I attended reveal that there exist seasonal variations for types of *gut* performed. Thus over 60% of the *gut* performed at the beginning of the lunar New Year are rituals praying for good luck if you include the *jinjeok gut* in that category. On the other hand, the community *gut* occupy about 35% of the rituals performed in the autumn. The shaman's initiation rites and *jinogi gut* do not seem to have similar fluctuations, occurring more or less consistently at the mean average of around 20% and 15%, respectively. What is interesting is that unlike shamanistic séances in other parts of the world, where the main purpose is curing diseases, purely healing *gut* account for a mere 4 to 5%

of the total number of the *gut* that I attended, since for somatic diseases, people go to the hospital for cure, the shamans actually telling them to do so. Inexplicable or incurable diseases are attributed to the noxious influence of malignant spirits, often the spirits of one's own recently dead relatives. Thus a *jinogi gut*, is held to console them through gifts and entertainment and send them safely to the other world, often described as *joeunde* (a nice place).

In Korean shamanism, gods are not worshipped as metaphysical beings, but materialize via possessed shamans, and in a sense manipulated by humans as a means to obtain this-wordily goals, such as long life, wealth, health and children Thus a *gut* is not a sacred exercise, but a very profane "strategic party" in which gods participate as honoured guests, enjoying food, drink, drama, and other entertainment provided by man. By offering sumptuous feasts, liberally accompanied by gifts of money, etc, humans bind the supernatural beings in an obligation to reciprocate, forcing the latter to return their hospitality by granting them their wishes. In other words, gods and humans communicate freely with one another on equal terms at a *gut*, bound by the rules of Maussian obligation to give, receive, and reciprocate. Before analyzing the reciprocal relationships that exist among the participants of *gut*, it is necessary to divulge their characteristics, dividing them into three groups, i.e. the spirits, the shamans and the sponsors.

The Spirits

Innumerable gods and spirits occupy the Korean shamanistic pantheon, which is reflected in a polite term of address for a shamaness, "*mansin*," meaning literally "ten thousand (literally meaning a myriad) spirits." It implies that a competent shaman/ess is capable of controlling all the spirits, which number "ten thousand," a number often used in the sense of "countless" in Korean, as "a myriad" is in English. My research into the Korean shamanistic pantheon was carried out through shamanistic paintings and statues, which are their anthropomorphic reification, and the songs and recitations by the shamans during *gut*, commonly termed, *muga*, or the shaman songs.

According to Wolf (1974), the spirit world is viewed as a replica of people's social world; in traditional Chinese society, gods, ancestors and ghosts are viewed as bureaucratic officials, family and beggars, respectively, which also applies to the Korean spirit world. Gods correspond to bureaucratic officials, who should be supplicated and propitiated. This concept is manifest in the Korean shamanistic costumes, which are donned by the possessed shamans, during *gut*. The spirit costumes are based on those of the Joseon dynasty government officials of various ranks, which prompts some scholars (Jo 1983) to describe the Korean shamanistic pantheon as reflecting the Joseon dynasty (1392-1910) social structure. However, on account of the long history of Korean shamanism, it is much more complex, reflecting the Korean people's belief system over the ages. Ancestors, on the other hand, are rather like family elders, who have to be appeased, soothed and served, after death, as well as in life. Thus the shaman casually throws on a particular costume, bought and prepared for each ancestor, while performing the part for ancestors. Ghosts should never be neglected, in the sense that beggars should not, because the obligation of the rich to give to the poor exists strongly in Korean society. If this obligation is not met, the rich become the object of moral condemnation by the less fortunate. Likewise, if the ghosts do not get "given alms" at the end of *gut*, they inflict all sorts of misfortune on those who are fortunate enough to sponsor it. However, just as one does not stand on ceremony, while "feeding" the beggars, the shaman wears their everyday clothes, while performing the *twitceon*, while the other shamans get ready to leave, distributing the money and the ritual food, clearing up the table, packing the costumes, etc.

Gods are most often classified by shamans themselves into *cheon-sin*, *jisin* and *insin* (heavenly gods, earthly gods, and human gods). The first group of gods are derived from the ancient indigenous belief in Heaven, and the second based on animism, which decrees everything that exists in the universe has a spirit. hence "ten thousand spirit." What is interesting and very idiosyncratic about the Korean shamanistic pantheon is the third group of spirits, i.e. those derived from humans, often historical personages, such as kings, queens and culture heroes.

The third group of gods present us a most intriguing question: "What kinds of historical personages are apotheosized?" Gim Taegon (1981) calls human-derived gods "hero gods," indicating that they are the spirits of the culture heroes, who were larger than life personalities in their life time. *A priori*, many seem to have lived extraordinary lives, eventually dying for an altruistic cause, such as the defence of the nation or the betterment of the suffering mass. However, many great historical personages are not accorded the same prominence comparable to that given to them in mainstream Korean society. The best two examples are the two most famous Korean heroes of all time, Admiral Yi Sun-shin, often referred to as an Admiral Nelson of Korea, and King Sejong the Great, who invented the Korean alphabet, originally called *hunmin-jeongeum* (The Correct Sounds for Instructing People) and now known as *Han-geul* (The Great/Korean Script), in 1443 so that the "poor ordinary Korean masses" would not have to struggle with the alien Chinese script.

What then are the criteria for shamanistic apotheosis? I have already mentioned briefly that the common denominator of most kings, generals and culture heroes which feature prominently in *gut* is the fact that they all lived tempestuous lives and/or died tragic deaths.

The deified culture heroes themselves possess other qualities, which generate sympathy and pathos among the Korean mass, than mere tragic lives. What then are the elements in their lives which capture the people's sympathy? The answer can be found in a brief look at the lives of the most popular deities, which are derived from the Joseon dynasty kings and generals. A brief study of the three tragic kings, included most frequently in a group of shamanistic deities, called Byeolsang, Yeonsan-gun (1476-1506; r. 1494-1506), Gwanghae-gun (1575-1641; r. 1608-1623), and Crown Prince Sado (1735-1762), reveals that they all lived in a turbulent period of Korea's history, eventually becoming unjust victims of political factional wrangling. Crown Prince Sado, in particular, met a gruesome end, having been put to death in a rice chest by his father King Yeongjo. He was posthumously named Jangjo by his son King Jeongjo (r. 1776-1800), and features prominently in the Seoul area *gut* as *Dwiju daegam* (Lord Rice Chest), or the Coffin King.

The three deified generals, appearing as *Gunung*, General Choe Yeong (1326-1388), who is invariably cited in the shaman songs, with his shrine site Deokmul-san (now in North Korea), General Yim Gyeon-geop, an illustrious general in the courts of Gwanghae-gun (r. 1608-1623) and Injo (r. 1623-49), Hong Gyeong-nae (1780-1812), all had a profound, lasting influence on the ordinary people of Korea, as champions of their cause, and spokesmen of their dissatisfaction with the unfair social system, giving rise to a series of similar people's movements in the case of Hong.

As seen above, most deified historical personages were members of either royal or aristocratic lineages, whom the common Korean folk looked up to in fear and adoration. However, despite their high births, which entitled them automatically to a life of luxury and prestige, they all had eventful lives and met tragic ends. This fact alone should be enough to generate pathos, and the sympathy of the downtrodden masses, who, although dissatisfied with the social system, accepted the unfair social stratification as the basic cosmological principle. The sorrow of the ill- fated royals and nobles, persecuted by the very establishment, which put so much oppression on the women and the lower-class masses, is shared by the latter, through cathartic tears in shamanistic rituals, thus cleansing away the grievances of the former.

However, pathos alone is not sufficient to move the people enough to apotheosize someone, since there are numerous others with a similar fate, who do not get a mention, for example, Gwanghae-gun's young half-brother Yeongchang-daegun. All the above personages have another common denominator; that they were either blatantly active opposers, or wretched victims of the Confucian establishment, which severely persecuted shamanism and cast the shamans into the lowest of the low in the social hierarchy, and moreover, had shamanistic elements in their characters. This explains why Yeonsan-gun, who is recorded as the worst king in history, features prominently, while King Sejong the Great and Admiral Yi Sunshin do not. The former was an antithesis of the Confucian hero, his life philosophy, i.e. entertainment, being more or less the same as that of Korean *musok*, while the latter two were quintessential Confucian paragons. They were very much part of the Confucian establishment, who immortalized them, thus not requiring the compassion and consolation of the common mass.

The same principle applies to the second group, the ancestral spirits, who, in sharp contrast to the "ancestors proper" worshipped in Confucian style ritual, called *jesa*, include the spirits of those ascendants who cannot achieve ancestorhood for reasons of their "bad deaths" and/ or failure to leave legitimate descendants. They are embraced into shamanism by women, who dispel their grief of not being offered proper and regular food offerings. What is interesting is the fact, unlike *jesa*, which is offered by male descendants to their agnatic ascendants, *gut* are offered to all cognatic kin, not only ascendants but also descendants. The importance of ancestors in the *gut* is such that it is often identified with "treating ancestors" by many sponsors whom I talked to.

The third group, the ghosts, consist of all kinds of malevolent spirits, including those which wield noxious influence through wood, earth, stone, and arrow which hits people at a feast, and the ghosts of victims of all manners of bad deaths. Also included in this category are as Wolf's definition of the Chinese ghosts, "the souls of all the people who die as members of some other group," who are potentially dangerous. By treating them all to feast, albeit without due ceremony, they are prevented from wielding noxious influence on the sponsors and their families.

The fact that so many shamanistic spirits had tragic lives and died untimely deaths has been used to support the theory that the essence of Korean shamanism is *han*. *Han* is a frequently-used Korean word, which, although it has no exact equivalent in English, translates roughly as "grudge," "unfulfilled desire" or "deep- rooted grievances." Thus *mudang*'s function is to appease the vengeful spirits, full of *han*. Gim Yeolgyu (1977) claims that it is manifest in the representative ambience of the shamanistic rituals, which is mournful, underneath its often boisterous appearance. Choe (1990) attacks it, claiming that most of what he calls "proper deities" actually bear no grudges of any kind, and even the ghosts who are generally believed to have some sort of *han*, in fact do not always bear it.

The ambience of pathos is indeed immediately apparent to any spectators of *gut*, particularly mortuary *gut*, during which the shaman, as well as the sponsors and the audience, invariably shed copious tears at one time or another. However, tears are viewed as cathartic and purifying, therefore therapeutic, rather than signifying hopeless grief and unfulfilled *han*. Many parts of *gut* are cheerful and entertaining, giving an impression of a party which include theatrical performances enjoyed by all. As Choe says, many spirits, particularly those belonging to the "god" category do not bear *han*. Therefore, *han*, per *se*, cannot be said to be the essence of Korean shamanism, being just one of the obstacles to the ideal condition of total happiness. What is of paramount importance is getting involved with others' *han*, or grief. By helping dispel others' grief, and exposing all the skeletons in the family as well as societal cupboards, at a very public social gathering, reciprocal solutions are attempted and often found through catharsis, by all the participants, the spirits, the shamans and the sponsors, alike. Thus it would be wrong to say that *han* itself is the essence of shamanism, dispelling it being a means to the ultimate objective of the *gut*, which is as Ramstedt's etymology suggests, "happiness."

The shamans and the sponsors

Gut are parable from the shamans, collectively called *mudang*, since depending on the officiating *mudang* the form of *gut* also changes. Although there exist a great number of words referring to them because of its long history, and the stigma attached to them, there are basically two types of *mudang*; inspirational or god-descended type called *gangsinmu*, and the hereditary type, called *seseummu*. The former are the norm to the north of the Han River, and the latter to the south, and along the East Coast. The shamans among whom I conducted my fieldwork are all *gangsinmu*, since I consider them 'shamans proper,' *seseummu* in my opinion being degenerated or socially patterned variations. Max Weber's routinization of charisma might well account for their proliferation at one time, although since the abolition of the hereditary cast system, *seseummu* have been rapidly disappearing, even in the South.

According to Mr. Choe, President of the Korean Spirit Worshippers' Association for Victory over Communism, there are about 55,000 registered members- of whom 35-000 are female. His reckons that they account for about 55% of the total number; thus it can be said that there are about 82,200 practising *mudang* in South Korea.

My research method is random sampling, and my analyses were eventually based on 70 shamans with whom I interviewed in some depths. Towards the end of my fieldwork I tested some of my hypotheses, which seemed to work fairly well, to my satisfaction.

First of all, my research revealed that the male:female ratio is roughly 20:80. Despite sometimes conflicting information provided by my shaman informants concerning their private lives, they were unanimous on the fact that *mudang* were all unfortunate wretched people, who have suffered all sorts of disasters and misfortunes in their lives. They are invariably from derived backgrounds, often from broken home, and suffered severe lack of love, often having lost one or both parents early in their lives. Largely because of their circumstances, most of them received little formal education. Another important aspect of their background is the fact that most shamans have what is commonly called *buri*, literally meaning root. In other words, there exists a shamanic ancestry in the lineage, even in the case of *gangsimu*, which is consistent with Akiba's observation (1950) that shamanic ancestry seems to be hereditary. However, since the *buri* also exists among a woman's affines, which is moreover supposed to be stronger, the hereditary theory becomes weak in the Korean case. Thus *buri* is more culturally constructed than biologically inherited through genes, conforming more Bourguignon's "prelearning" theory (1971).

Nevertheless,there are certain personal traits that all the shamans share, such as unusually high level of intelligence despite their lack of formal education,hyper-sensitivity, their subversive ambition, and super-fluity of what Prof. Seo Jeongbeom calls *gi*, or equivalent to what Freed-man calls "cosmic breath."In English a parallel for *gi*, would be "spirit" in the sense of "high-spirited"or "in high spirits."

The sponsors of *gut* are much more diverse than the shamans, since they include a cross section of people with a wide variety of socio-economic background. Since as the proverbs go, "Misfortune comes to all men and women" and "Nomortal escapes death," everybody is a potential sponsor of *gut*. I have classified them into 1) Sponsors of pri-vate *gut*, divided further into believers/regular clients, called *danggol sindo* and non-believers, i.e. occasional sponsors, who can be Buddhists, Christians, or atheist, and 2) Sponsors of community *gut*. What most of them have in common is illness, grief, insoluble life problems, or worry over uncertain future. When faced with a dilemma in their lives, which cannot be solved with modem science and technology, they try to find an answer, through turning to what their ancestors did, by first offering them gifts, much like the ones they themselves would like to receive in return.

What is interesting is the existence of fictive kinship in the sha-manistic community. The teacher shaman is called spirit father/mother, the neophyte shaman, spirit son/daughter. Regular clients or believers sell their children, by hanging a long piece of cloth, called *myeongdari* (long life bridge) at the *mudang*'s shrine to pray for their long life, who are then called the shaman's *suyang adeul/ddal* (adopted son/daughter). The regular client often addresses their *mudang* "*eomma*" (Mum). Thus their social relationships are modeled on natural kinship relations, Sah-lin's generalized reciprocity being often practised.

Reciprocity and Korean society

The ideology and ethos of mainstream Korean society is directly reflect-ed in *gut*. Therefore, it is necessary to discuss the principles underpin-ning all social relationships in Korean society in general.

Polanyi (1968) divides the types of economy into three, namely primitive, archaic and modem economies, based on reciprocity, redistribution and market exchange, respectively. In Korean economy, which undoubtedly belongs to the third group, reciprocity plays an important role, since all social relationships are based on it. Extensive gift exchange is immediately apparent even to a least observant casual visitor to Korea. Gifts are taken even on a causal unannounced visit, extensive gift exchange takes place on special occasion, particularly at rites of passage. Extravagant feasts are given by hosts, and guests bring hosts money, usually put in envelopes which act as a symbolic barrier, to distinguish the gift from trade. Since overall in a person's lifetime, the actual economic gain/loss is insignificant, gift exchange is more symbolic, rather like the Melanesian *kula*, which goes around in a circle. What is of paramount importance is the act of giving, which carries Maussian obligation to receive and reciprocate.

Marshall Sahlins (1972) analyzes reciprocity into "generalized reciprocity," "balanced reciprocity" and "negative reciprocity," linking the type of reciprocity to the kinship and residential distance. Thus generalized reciprocity, or sharing of resources without any strict expectation of return, applies to the relationships between closest kinsmen. However, in Korean society, I would argue that relationships between the closest relatives, even those of parents and children are essentially based on balanced reciprocity. The children are never allowed to forget the debt they owe their parents for the gift of life and their upbringing: thus *hyodo* or filial piety, is considered a supreme human virtue. The former are expected to show them deference when young, render them financial, emotional assistance when grown up, and offer ancestral sacrifices to their spirits after the latter's death. Life can only be repaid with the like: thus the children can repay their parents by keeping them "alive" as it were, after death, by offering them food and drink on a regular basis. One of Griffin Dix's informants told him, "the ancestor worship is not useless. Wearing mourning clothes is labour exchange, *pumasi*." I would argue that Korean parent-child relationships, the most vital in Korean social life, which are imbued with implicit *hyodo* in the parents' lifetime, and ancestor worship after their death, are based on balanced reciprocity in principle. So are most regular/long-term social relationships, generalized and negative types occurring only sporadically or aberrantly in Korean society.

Gut is often identified with ancestor worship by many *mudang* and sponsors, as one sponsor said: "We treat our ancestors to food and money, with all out hearts, and cleanse away any *han* they might harbour.

That's what *gut* is all about in a nutshell. It is not really much different from *jesa*." Mr. Choe, President of the Korean Spirit Worshippers' Association for Victory over Communism, also said, "Sponsoring a *gut* is no different from seeking advice and assistance from your parents."

However, although *gut* and *jesa* share a commonality of ancestor worship. in essence they represent polarization of ideology of Korean society. Put it simply. *gut* is to *jesa* as nature is to culture. *gut* is performed mainly for and by women while *jesa* is officiated by men: the former is born of heart, while the latter of duty; the former temporarily abolishes social codes and restrictions, while the latter imposes and strengthen them. All these concepts are well represented in ritual procedures, music, costumes and paraphernalia, which I examine in some depths in my thesis. Even ritual food offered manifests this ideology, in that food offered at *gut* is mostly raw, while *jesa* food is mostly cooked. The most important difference, however, is the shamanistic worshippers' implicit faith in obligation to reciprocate, which is universally found in human societies, as Marcel Mauss (1925) so convincingly argues in his famous essay, *The Gift*.

Let us briefly examine the "emic" and "etic" interpretations of what the sponsors receive for their sacrificial (in some cases literally because of the high costs of the *gut* offerings. I will present a few case histories.

1. A healing *gut* was sponsored by a 54 year-old market woman, to cure her 26–year–old daughter-in-law's Bell's Palsy. Cost about £1,800. The patient was said to be cured soon afterwards.

2. A *jinogi gut* sponsored by a 36-year-old woman for her recently dead mother-in-law, and also to cure her mild illness, attributed to the latter's restless soul. Cost £3,000 plus. During the *gut*, her mother leapt at the spirit of the mother-in-law, i.e. the possessed shaman, accusing the latter of having given her daughter such a hard time. The spirit apologized, and they all fell on one another's shoulders, weeping for some considerable time. She told me afterwards that her heart was much lighter ("*gaseum-i shiweon hada*") for having had a "go" at the previous source of her daughter's misery. The patient's health improved soon afterwards.

3. A *jinogi gut* was held for a three-year-old boy, killed by a lorry nine days previously. A few days after the accident, his then

pregnant 26-year-old mother had a miscarriage, the foetus was a boy. The cost; £3,000. The whole family, parents, grandparents, father's two sisters, cousin, present. The little boy's spirit possessed the shaman, and they all wept their eyes out. All of them told me that they felt now that the little boy had gone safely to the other world, the misfortunes would no longer come to them.

4. A *jinogi gut* held for a 58-year-old mother of three grownup children, who had died of liver cancer. Cost £5,000. The extreme grief of the three children, all highly educated, the eldest a doctor, was exacerbated because they would have no opportunity to repay their debt to their mother, who had gone through all sorts of hardship for their upbringing and education. All three told me that they arranged the *gut* to show their true heart to their mother, which made them feel better.

5. A small-scale *jaesu gut* was sponsored covertly by a battered wife, aged 43, of a moderately affluent timber merchant. Only herself and her young son were present. Cost about £1,500. She wept, confided in the shamans, who all sympathized with her, condemning her brutal womanizing husband. She told me that Ms. Jeong, the chief shaman, was like her mother, who had died long ago.

6. A medium-scale *jaesu gut*, sponsored by a couple who jointly ran a small beer hall. The couple, originally from the countryside, regularly held a *jaesu gut*, to which they attribute their success of their business. Total cost: about £3,000, They told me that of course they got value for money and asked me where they would be without the blessings of the spirits and their ancestors.

7. A top rate combined *jaesu/jinogi gut* was sponsored by an affluent business couple, who each owned a business. The cost of the *gut* about £8,000. The wife told me that they had no problems, but were thanking their ancestors for their success and asking for their continued support by treating them to a feast and offering them money.

Thus the "emic" view of what the sponsors got from *gut* is 1) cure

2) solace for themselves and the soul of the recently dead so that it can safely go to the other world, leaving the living in peace 3) psychological relief and catharsis and 4) hope and confidence vis-à-vis the future.

The etic interpretation of the above has been presented by various psychoanalysts such as Dr. Yi Buyeong, who discusses the beneficial effects of "emotional relief" through encounters with the ancestors. It is a well established fact in medicine that a patient's emotional well-being influences the course of even a somatic disease. However, as seen above, *gut* are most effective in curing psychosomatic complaints. My case histories support Kleinman's (1980) stipulation that indigenous practitioners must successfully heal, since they primarily treat three types of disorders: (1) acute, self-limited (naturally remitting) diseases, (2) non-life threatening, chronic diseases in which management of illness (psychosocial and cultural) problems is a larger component of clinical management than biomedical treatment of the disease; and (3) secondary somatic manifestations ("somatization") of minor psychological disorders and interpersonal problems.

The woman's illness in Case History 2, for example, might well have been caused by her guilt about feeling a great relief at the death of her cantankerous mother-in-law. According to her mother, who made an outburst during the *gut*, the old woman, who had been ill for a long time before her death, had continuously bullied and pestered her. The understandable feeling of elation at having been released from her bondage must have been accompanied by a severed sense of guilt, for the woman, who had been brought up by the rigid Confucian principles. Applying the Freudian projection theory (1950), her sense of guilt was projected onto the mother-in-law's spirits, who got blamed for being guilty of inflicting an illness on her. By treating her mother-in-law's spirit well with gifts of food, clothes and money, and sending her happy to the other world, her guilt feeling may well have been assuaged, thus effecting a cure for her mild illness.

Despite the great advancement in medicine, there are so many diseases, and many aspects of them, particularly the causes, which are still beyond human comprehension. As many doctors admit, many modern medical practices merely cure the symptoms, while the disease runs its course, and many causes of diseases are unknown. Shamanism, which blames the various malignant spirits, can be said to be an attempt to explain the incomprehensible. In many cases, the care shown the patient by the shamans and the resulting relief of psychological tension which could well be the cause of a particular disease, often have a great therapeutic effect. When all fails, *mudang* are clever enough to emphasize the inevitability of one's *palja*, i.e. fate, claiming that they can only prevent minor misfortunes, not change the course of one's fate.

More importantly, the sponsors derive from *gut* new hope, confidence, and optimism about the future. One of Ms. Jeong's clients told me that the *jaesu gut* was effective, because of the confidence it gave the sponsor. They strove harder, safe in the knowledge that all the spirits were helping them, and by trying harder they achieved good results. The successful couple in Case History 7 told me that they felt more confident vis-à-vis many important financial decisions, after sponsoring a *gut*. That very confidence might well help them become more decisive in their business ventures, making them more successful.

The sponsors whom I interviewed invariably told me that they felt the cost of *gut* was money well spent. *mudang*'s whole-hearted preparations and the execution of the elaborate ritual gave them a great sense of self-importance. It was as though they and their problems were at the centre of the universe, during the *gut*, all the participants sharing their grief and thus giving them a catharsis, as well as a boost to their morale. Catharsis achieved through shared tears is a well-known theme in Greek and other tragedies. In Korean *gut*, the effect is much greater, since the audience also participate in the drama as actors/actresses. Viewed from this perspective, what prima facie is an outrageously extravagant fee does not seem so unreasonable. The sponsors get a psychoanalytic session, lasting eight or more hours, plus a banquet complete with an orchestra and live theatre, not just for the sponsors themselves, but for all the ancestors who join them. It was no surprise, therefore, to hear the sponsors say that they had value for their money.

Because of the limited time, I cannot discuss in detail an important aspect in the reciprocal relationships, namely status of the donors and recipients. However, I would like to emphasize that the spirits, as supernatural beings, enjoy the highest status, while the shamans' traditional status is the lowest of the low. It is manifested in the mode of speech, used by the participants. Even child spirits are addressed in the honorific mode, while the former use the blunt speech even to their grandparents, who carry seniority, on account of their age. The paradox that arises from the fact the "lowly" shaman assume the lofty status of the spirits may well account for the fact that the shamans become ill, if they break away from their profession.

The status of the recipients is well reflected in the gift, as much as, and in some cases more than that of the donor. In Korean society, traditionally the social subordinate must first make a gift to their super-ordinate, in acknowledgement of their inferior or junior status. Also the quality of the gift is important, in that the recipient get offended if they deem the quality and value of the gift to be beneath their status, which accounts for the exchange of extravagant and sometimes financially ruin-ous gift exchange. Thus in *gut*, the first thing a spirit invariably do, when they materialize through the possessed shamans, is to complain about the paucity of the offerings, however, sumptuous they are. The sponsors must apologize abjectly for the inadequacy, showing their full hearted devotion, which then appease the spirits, who then proceed to give them blessings. Maintaining harmony through keeping to the Confucian-based cosmological statuses of all entities, both living and spiritual, is one of the essential elements in Korean shamanism.

Conclusion

Homer Hulbert, writes in *The Passing of Korea*, "As a general thing, we may say that the all-round Korean will be a Confucianist when in soci-ety, a Buddhist when he philosophizes and a spirit-worshipper when he is in trouble." He argues that to know a man's true religion you should see what he does when in trouble. Despite the centuries of the attempts by the authorities to obliterate the above notion, more and more Koreans, including the social eletes, are acknowledging an element of truth in it.

To learn Korean society and culture, it is important to understand Korean shamanism, which reflect the centuries of Korean culture, society and its ethos. The Korean shamanistic ritual, *gut*, is based on the princi-ple underpinning all social interactions in Korean society, i.e. reciprocity, particularly the Maussian obligation to reciprocate. The *gut* is a festive gathering of the supernatural and human beings, most of them troubled beings, to help another, exchanging gifts of cure, consolation, new hope for the future through catharsis. They are, as Eliade postulates, back in the primordial paradisiac age, when gods and humans freely communi-cated with one another, on equal terms. In Korean society, because of a long history of social stratification, the superior status of the spirits as immortals is firmly recognized by mortal, which is reflected in the sumptuous and costly ritual offerings. However, the status in the *gut* is highly ambiguous, the shamans, mere mortals, changing from traditionally low-ly *mudang* to lofty gods. The ambiguous status are highly suited to modern Korean society with highly mobile class system, which is why some university students recently performed parts of *gut* in anti-government demonstrations. (For details, see Gim Gwang-eok)

The basic ideology of the *gut*, i.e. an implicit faith in the Maussian obligation to reciprocate, however, is the essence of Korean shamanism. The ever present *hyodo*, which is the essence of ancestor worship, can also be explained through "reciprocity." It is not surprising, then that the two are frequently linked, if not identified with each other by today's Korean shamanists. When one is drowning. one would even try to clutch at a straw. When faced with a terminal disease, or other inexplicable disaster, well beyond modern science and technology, sponsoring a *gut* is a positive move in a attempt to alleviate the pain and despair.

According to the contemporary Korean shamanists, in the days gone by, before the advent of advanced science and technology, that was all their ancestors had and did. Therefore, in a situation which cannot be helped by modem science, they turn to the methods used by their ancestors. Their faith in their ancestors reciprocating their whole-hearted gifts gives them confidence and hope for the future, which helps them get over difficult times.

What will happen to the *gut* in the future? Despite its persistence, there still exists a considerable stigma attached to the practitioners of *gut*, the shamans and the sponsors alike. *Gut* is performed covertly, one would never dream of saying, "I am going to the *gut*," in the way one says, "I'm going to church not to a Buddhist temple." *Mudang* themselves still feel offended to be called *mudang*, preferring various other euphemisms, such as *musok-in*, *gyeja*, *mansin*, *bosal*, etc. Ms. Pang said (7 March 1994), "Maybe in ten years' time, our time will come." They may be recognized and will take pride in their profession. Already some successful *mudang*, who have achieved financial independence have gained a measure of self-confidence. When their true identity is divulged, they will no longer be shunned or feared. It is possible that they will rightly be regarded as novel ritual specialists who might do a lot of good under certain circumstances, which are beyond modern science and technology. Once recognized and earning a decent living, their much-deprecated obsession with money may even recede, making them respected, if not bizarre, practitioners of by-gone religious beliefs and carriers of traditional Korean folk culture.

As has been already happening, the folklorisation of *gut* will take place However, *gut* in its original form, i.e. for specific purposes of praying for good luck, sending the dead off to the other world, curing, etc., will not disappear in the near future. Private *gut* will possibly be performed mostly in abbreviated form as the one that I attended on 1 March, 1994. Being less costly and time consuming, it will appeal to busy people, since although much shorter, it nevertheless contained all twelve *geori*.[3] Community *gut*, which, according to Dr. Yi Buyeong are to be encouraged for maintaining solidarity, may well be performed more frequently in the future. They have an advantage of incurring minimum costs to individuals, whilst achieving maximum effects, creating community spirit and maintaining solidarity, while providing them with entertainment and catharsis through group therapy.

---

3 **Geori** has a variety of meanings, such as "subject," "stuff," "task" or "cause," etc.

Part 4

THE POWER STRUCTURE BETWEEN BUDDHISM AND SHAMANISM IN CONTEMPORARY KOREAN SOCIETY

Introduction

This paper discusses the power structure between Buddhism and shamanism in contemporary Korean society within the context of the religious practice pattern of modern Korean people. "Shamanism and Buddhism are like two grafted trees. You can't tell them apart," said one of
my informants to me during my fieldwork. This view was echoed repeatedly by many other shamans and their followers. Her remarks succinctly
sum up the extent of the syncretism between shamanism and Buddhism
in Korean society over the ages. However, during my fieldwork, I came
across many Buddhists, monks and laymen alike, who would not admit
to the influence of shamanism on their religion. Nevertheless, there is
much evidence to suggest that Korean Buddhism has undergone considerable metamorphosis as a result of the influence of shamanism. This
bears witness to the fact that the relationship between the two is hierarchical, with Buddhism occupying a superior position over shamanism.
This vertical relationship has always been present since the introduction
of Buddhism into Korea in the fourth century.

Shamanism, or other similar indigenous possession cults, has often wielded influence on world religions, particularly Buddhism, in other parts of the world (Obeyesekere 1963, 1968; Tambiah 1970, 1984; Spiro 1971; Gombrich 1971; Jordan 1972; Ortner 1978, 1989; Southwold 1983; Carrithers 1983; Terwiel 1975, 1984). When the central morality religion of a nation is Buddhism, these cults have co-existed alongside Buddhism to satisfy the needs of ordinary people, for whom the ultimate goal of attaining nirvana is out of reach. In such cases, "orthodox" Buddhism has been compared to "the great tradition," while popular Buddhism as practised by the mass, often containing shamanistic elements, to "the little tradition," in Redfield's sense (Obeyesekere 1963). The relationship between Buddhism and shamanism is usually hierarchical, with the former having supremacy over the latter, as Spiro has shown in the case of Burmese Buddhism and supernaturalism (1967).

In contemporary Korea, the situation is more complex, since there is a multiplicity of religious practices. Buddhism, which ceased to be the central morality religion six centuries ago, has since undergone a series of crises, and its survival has often been threatened.

The existing statistics reveal that modern Korean people most frequently cite Christianity and Buddhism as their religion. Confucianism is only infrequently cited as a religion they practise, and shamanism does not get a mention at all. The general pattern has been undergoing a change in favour of Christianity in recent years (*Jonggyo yeon-gam* 1993), which suggests the existence of a power struggle between the two great world religions. I will argue that this very power struggle has enforced the hierarchy that has existed between Buddhism and shamanism for a long period of time.

The data that I use to support my argument was collected during my fieldwork conducted among the Korean shamans during 1993 - 1994.

Theodicy, Buddhism and Lay Soteriology

As Weber maintains (1948), Buddhism successfully resolves the problem of theodicy, or God's justification for the suffering of the innocent, which arises in monotheistic world religions. In monotheistic religions, the resolution of a theodicy could never be logical, for at the heart of it there exists a fundamental logical contradiction; an omniscient, omnipotent, wholly benevolent God could not in logic permit suffering (Obeyesekere 1968: 9). Buddhism provides a perfect solution to this problem through the Indian concept of karma (*eop* in Korean), the belief in the transmigration of souls. So guilt and merit in this world is compensated unfailingly in the successive reincarnations of the souls. Man is doomed to the Eternal Cycle of Births and Rebirths, or samsara (*yunhoe* in Korean), which is deemed as "suffering." Suffering in the Buddhist sense has a wider philosophical implication of impermanence than just the simple pain; all karma-produced actions are aspects of suffering in a philosophical sense. Hence salvation, the elimination of suffering, must entail the elimination of karma so that the flow of continuity can be arrested. This is nirvana, i.e. salvation, the final release from samsara and suffering.

In most world religions, salvation is the reward for the meritorious life; if you do good in this world you go to heaven in the other world after death. In Buddhism, however, even Heaven, Paradise in an earthly sense (called *geungnak* in Korean) is a form of suffering because of its transience. Thus not only the person who commits bad karma, but also the person who does good, has little chance of achieving salvation, i.e. nirvana, since everybody continues to be reincarnated. Salvation is only possible for the individual who rises above samsara altogether by renouncing society and the world, i.e. by becoming a monk and observing 227 precepts prescribed for monks. In theory even a layman could attain nirvana, but in practice it is impossible for most people, since the conditions of any human social order are such that attachments and desire are inevitable. Hence strictly speaking, Buddhism in its orthodox principle can be said to be a religion of ascetic monks in their monastic seclusion.

As Weber (1922) maintains, however, ordinary men turn to religion "so that they may prosper and have a long life on earth." Religion therefore develops in mankind what Radcliffe-Brown (1952: 175) calls "a sense of dependence." In original Buddhism, there was little provision for supernatural powers for the lay masses to depend on. Those who have achieved salvation, i.e. Buddhas, have done so through personal enlightenment, and having achieved their goal, nirvana, can no longer play an active role in relieving the suffering of the lay masses, except possibly providing a role model. Although nirvana is in theory possible to attain for anybody, in practice it is virtually impossible to attain it while living in society. The inadequate provisions for the laymen to achieve salvation in orthodox Buddhist doctrines account for the development of a peasant (or little) tradition of Buddhism under pressure of mass needs. In South East Asian countries, where Theravada Buddhism dominates, the laymen have turned to shamanism or other forms of indigenous archaic religions to solve their worldly problems (Htin Aung 1962; Obeyesekere 1963; Spiro 1967/1974, 1971; Tambiah 1970, 1984; Gombrich 1971; Terwiel 1975/1984; Southwold 1983), partly because the "orthodox" (or "great") tradition was not interested in lay soteriology. Therefore the "heretical" activities carried out by the lay masses throughout Southeast Asia are based on perfect rationality. Since the lay masses, because of their involvement in the social system, are incapable of achieving salvation anyway, doctrinally heretical practices such as indigenous deity propitiation or astrology make little difference to their ultimate future prospects. Therefore, they might as well improve their lot in this life and next lives by whatever means available to them. From the sociological, particularly functionalist, point of view, then the forms of secular Buddhism practised in Southeast Asia, though they involve theological "heresy," can be regarded as the successful transformation of essentially unsociable Buddhism into a social religion.

Buddhism and shamanism in Korea

Buddhism was first introduced to Korea in 372 A.D. from China (Clark 1932/1961: 27; et al.), and after some initial resistance, quickly established itself as the national religion. The type of Buddhism that reached Korea was Mahayana ("Great Vehicle" or "Great Way") Buddhism, prevalent in North Asia, which moreover had gone considerable metamorphosis in China under the influence of Taoism and Confucianism (Grayson 1985: 3-19).

The doctrine of Mahayana Buddhism was radically modified so as to allow for the development of the Bodhisattva cult. Bodhisattvas are saviours who have postponed their own salvation in order to save others, although they have achieved enlightenment. In Mahayana countries, this doctrinal change has now become fully "orthodox" (Obeysekere 1968). Thus although the fundamental Buddhist doctrine that salvation can only be achieved by one's own effort and ascetic renunciation of the world remains the same, over time "orthodoxy" itself has undergone changes and has diversified into different sects. Therefore "orthodoxy" in Buddhism is not an absolute, inflexible concept, and "heterodoxy" can become "orthodox," if it is generally accepted, approved and established.

Mahayana Buddhism, with Bodhisattvas and other numerous saints for the laity to supplicate, confronted little conflict with shamanism, the ancient indigenous belief system of the Korean people. Its modified doctrines made it possible for Buddhism to absorb shamanistic elements. Over time therefore, in certain cases, extensive syncretism between Buddhism and shamanism has taken place. For example, among the Korean scholars there is a consensus of the view that many State-sponsored Buddhist rituals, such as Palgwanhoe and Yeondeunghoe, of the Goryeo period were in essence shamanistic rituals hiding behind a thin Buddhist veneer (Yu 1975: 260; et al.).

The relationship between Buddhism and shamanism, however, has always been a vertical alliance. Buddhism was the officially recognized central morality religion until the fourteenth century, while shamanistic elements have always been held in contempt, castigated, disregarded, or at best hidden since the introduction of Buddhism. There remain numerous historical documents recording the official condemnation of shamans and their practices[1]. On the other hand, there is much evidence to suggest that the pride of place was given to Buddhist gods in shamanistic rituals. What illustrates this point very well is a poem entitled *Nomu pyeon* (The Old Shamaness), written in around 1241 by Yi Gyubo, a high-ranking Confucian literati government minister. The poem was written to commemorate the expulsion of his neighbour, an old shamaness, out of the capital. It vividly describes the shamanistic practices in thirteenth century Korea, which reflect many Buddhist elements. Let us briefly examine lines 26-28:

> Her rafted shrine measures barely five feet high.
> Yet she claims Heavenly Buddha Emperor is there.
> Buddha Emperor properly resides in the Six Heavens.
> How could He stay in your humble abode?

The concept of the Six Heavens and the Buddha residing there itself is a deviation from the fundamental Buddhist doctrine. Despite the minister's derision of the absurdity of the shamaness's practice, his own idea can be said to have been influenced by the indigenous Korean belief in Heaven, which was deeply rooted in shamanism[2].

Today, even a casual observer of the Korean shamanistic ritual called *gut*, would immediately notice the extent of the Buddhist influence

---

1 For details, see Yi Neunghwa 1927/1991.

2 See our previous works.

on Korean shamanism. The shamanistic shrines, both private and commercial, are, with few exceptions, filled with Buddhist artefacts, such as Buddha statues, wooden gongs and beads, Buddhist-style paintings and other paraphernalia. The costumes and some ritual procedures also reflect its influence. The shamanistic costumes for many higher-status spirits are derived from the Buddhist concept, and when the Buddhist-derived spirits descend on the scene, the animal carcass offerings are covered with a piece of white paper, in observance of the Buddhist prohibition of killing. Moreover shamans often recite the Buddhist scriptures, believing that they possess powers to chase away evil spirits[3]. Some of the most important shamanistic spirits, such as Jeseok (the Buddha Emperor), Bulsa (the Buddhist Guru Grandmother), Sambul (the Three Buddhas), Siwang (the Ten Kings of the Netherworld) are derived from Buddhism. What is interesting is the fact that these spirits are accorded the highest ranks in the pantheon, and therefore "entertained" before the "purely" shamanistic spirits, such as Changbu (the Performer Spirit).

While the Buddhist influence is proudly displayed in most shamanistic practices, the shamanistic elements in Korean Buddhism are much more played down. A shrine dedicated to the shamanistic Holy Trinity (Samseong), comprising of the Seven Stars Spirit (Chilseong), the Mountain Spirit and the Solitary Star Spirit, is usually found in all Buddhist temple grounds. However, what is interesting is the fact that these shrines are very small and insignificant in size and shape in comparison with the main temple buildings. Moreover, they are usually situated discreetly in an inconspicuous position.

Despite these outwardly low-key shamanistic elements, some areas of Korean Buddhism have undergone extensive syncretism with shamanism, particularly in terms of its ideology (Yi Neunghwa 1927/1991; Akamatsu & Akiba 1938; Yu 1975; Choe 1978; Gim Inhoe 1987). Let us briefly examine the reasons that the ordinary Koreans give for visiting Buddhist temples. They are:

1. To attend festivals, such as the Buddha's Birthday

2. To perform mortuary rites, such as the 49th Day Ritual and

---

3 For details of the shamanistic incantations based on the Buddhist Scriptures, see Akamatsu & Akiba 1938: II, 239-246. An interesting parallel can be founded in northern Thailand, where the people also believe in the powers of the Buddhist Scriptures (Tambiah 1970).

100th day Ritual to pray for the wellbeing of the dead

3   To pray for long life, prosperity and healing and preventing other disease and misfortune.

The above suggests in ideology Korean Buddhism is closer to shamanism, which is this-wordly, corporeal and existential. It also supports Yu's view (1975: 263) that Korean Buddhism can be said to be "Buddhism of prayer."

Although outwardly the influence of Buddhism on Korean shamanism has been greater than the latter on the former, in essence the opposite can be said to be true. As Gim Inhoe shrewdly observes (1987: 217), Buddhist paraphernalia merely serve as external decorations in Korean shamanism, while Korean Buddhism has undergone a metamorphosis to such an extent that Buddhism as practised by the Korean laymen can arguably be said to be closer to shamanism than the "orthodox" Buddhism.

Among the regular sponsors of *gut*, the Buddhists account for the largest proportion. Many of them switch from one to another in the course of their lives, or alternatively they tend to practise both alongside each other, adapting to the situation.

Buddhist festivals bring the Buddhists and shamanists together. *Prima facie*, they are indistinguishable. However, after a few months in the field, I learned to distinguish between them by the way they pray. It seems to me that when they bow in prayer, Buddhists seem to Stand on one spot and bow several times, while the shamans and their followers bow to all directions, turning 360 degrees around in the process. The Buddhist monks and officials, who must also know that some of their congregation members actually engage in shamanistic practices as well, treat them as though they were simple Buddhists.

It seems to me that the Buddhist officials regard the shamanistic elements in their religion highly undesirable and shameful. 1 will give an example from my field experience, *Bansaengje,* meaning "Liberating Life Ritual," is a Buddhist festival performed on the 3 March in the lunar calendar. A large crowd of mainly women gather by the riverside and perform the act of releasing fish or sometimes turtles into the river for merit-making on the third day of the third month in the lunar calendar. This same ritual is called *yonggung gut* (Dragon Palace shamanistic ritual) by the shamans and their clients, according to my veteran shaman informants. My shaman friends, Yi Jongnam, Jeong Wonhae and Bang Chunja told me about this *gut* to be performed on the 13 April, 1994 (3 March in the lunar calendar that year), at the Dragon Palace Shrine on the bank of the River Han, which flows through Seoul. When I got there, however, there were no signs of shamanistic activities, everybody 1 talked to denying vehemently that they had anything to do whatsoever with shamanism, which they said a mere superstition. However, I could recognize some participants as shamanists by the way they prayed. I also saw prolific displays of shamanistic talismans in the buildings. It was later confirmed again by my shaman informants that *bansaengje* and *yonggung gut* are indeed one and the same, only different terms applied by the Buddhists and shamanists. The implications were that the Buddhists were ashamed of having any connections with shamanism, which they consider a "primitive superstition."

Another visual evidence of the syncretism between shamanism and Buddhism is a place of worship for the Buddhists and shamanists alike, called *seonbawi* (Zen Rocks)[4], a group of rocks shaped like monks wearing peaked hats. Situated on top of Mount Inwang in Seoul, they attract large numbers of worshippers and other visitors. Oral tradition has it (Gim Yeongsang 1989: 64) that the eminent Buddhist monk Muhak Daesa[5], an advisor to the founder of Joseon dynasty, King Taejo, suggested that the Zen Rocks be included inside the city walls. On the other hand, a Confucian literati minister called, Jeong Dojeon, insisted that they be placed outside the walls. Eventually Jeong won, which signified the symbolic triumph of Confucianism, and defeat and further decline of Buddhism and shamanism.

These days, worshippers pray at the Zen Rocks for sons, prosperity and healing of bodies and minds. One can detect both Buddhists and shamanists judging from the way they bow and kowtow in prayer, as described earlier. I was fascinated to learn from Ms. Pang, one of vet-

---

4 *Seon bawi* could also mean 'Standing upright rocks.' Elsewhere in Korea there are various *seon bawi*, which are said be a phallic symbol, in front of which women pray for a son. However this particular group of rocks resemble monks wearing the monkish habit and peaked hoods, and are better translated as "Zen rocks" (Gim Yeongsang 1989; 219).

5 Even today Muhak Daesa appears in the shamanistic ritual as a revered deity in the Seoul area.

eran shamans that shamans climb up the sleep hill to the Zen Rocks on the eve of any *gut* to "inform the spirits of the planned rituals," however late it may be. The extreme reverence that shamans and their followers hold for this very Buddhist symbol may be interpreted in several ways. It illustrates an area in which extensive syncretism between Buddhism and shamanism has taken place, and how the shamanists recognize the supremacy of Buddhism over shamanism. It also suggests that after the fall from official grace, Buddhism may have absorbed the shamanistic elements even further from the fourteenth century, coexisting alongside shamanism at the level of the downtrodden masses during the Joseon dynasty. The extent of shamanistic elements in Korean Buddhism deserves further anthropological research at the grassroots.

Buddhism and shamanism in the context of the religious lives of the Korean people

At the beginning of this century, Homer Hulbert (1906: 403-404), an early Christian missionary to Korea, wrote, "As a general thing, we may say that the all-round Korean will be a Confucianist when in society, a Buddhist when he philosophises and a spirit-worshipper when he is in trouble." He argues that to know a man's true religion you should see what he does when in trouble.

I have argued in my PhD thesis (1995) that Hulbert's remarks are still valid in Contemporary Korean society. What is interesting, however, is the fact that the existing statistics for modern Koreans' religions reveal a completely different picture. The two most dominant religions by far are Buddhism and Christianity. According to the Ministry of Information Statistics, in 1982, there were 11 million Buddhists, and the Christians, combining Catholics and Protestants, numbered 9 million. The figures change in the Gallop Research Statistics in 1984 to 7.4 million Buddhists and 9 million Christians. The 1985 census reveals a similar trend, with just over 8 million Buddhists to 8.34 million Christians.

The problem with these figures, however, lies in the method used, which was by self-identification. According to Yun (1988), in actual terms of religious practice, the figures should more realistically show 91% Confucianists, 49.3% Buddhists, and only 36.5% Christians.

The Statistics, indicating the emergence of Christianity as a more dominant religion, is shown not only in quantitative terms, but also in qualitative terms. According to *Jonggyo yeon-gam* (1993), the Korean

Buddhists suffer graver doubts about their faith than their Christian counterparts.

Why then so many modem Koreans wish to project themselves as Christians? I would argue that it is because Christianity is associated with modernity, advanced civilization imported from the West, while Buddhism with anachronism and Korea's past (Gusan 1985: 32-55). The gradual increase in the number of Christians, sporadic incidents of fanatic Christians' arson of Buddhist temples[6], and the assertion of some Christians that Korea is now a Christian country, etc. all indicate that for many Koreans Christianity symbolizes Korea's progress in the modern world.

Buddhism, which has always been a driving force in the Korean people's philosophical consciousness despite the decline and suppression during the Confucian Joseon dynasty regime (Cozin 1987: 176), faces a strong competition from the powerful, albeit relatively newly-established, Christianity. In recent years, it seems to me that there have been efforts on the Buddhist organizations to revitalize the structure of Buddhism through mass appeal. Modernization processes include mass production and distribution of tape recordings of famous monks, mass media publicity on the occasion of the death of a renowned monk, and a popular appeal for donations for constructions of new Buddhist temples.

Against this background, for the Buddhists, any connection with shamanism, which is generally associated with "primitiveness," can only be extremely embarrassing. I suspect that this is the reason why the Buddhists that I met denied any connection with shamanism, and even showed anger at such a suggestion. I would argue that the power struggle between the two great world religions, Buddhism and Christianity, has contributed to the reinforcement of the vertical nature of the relationship between Buddhism and shamanism.

Conclusion

Akiba, a Japanese social anthropologist, conducted fieldwork among the Korean shamans in the 1950s. One of Akiba's shaman informants (1938: 512) explained to him that Buddhism was like the "great house," and shamanism like the "little house." It is intriguing to hear that an uneducated Korean shaman actually preempted Redfield in his theory of the

---

6   There were some serious incidents of arson of Buddhist temples in Seoul in April 1996, causing millions of pounds of damage. Fanatic Christians were suspected of the crimes, although there was insubstantial evidence.

great and little traditions by more than 20 years.

The existence of Bodhisattva and other saints in Mahayana Buddhism, the type practised in Korea, has made it easy to incorporate many elements of shamanism, the ancient indigenous religion of the Korean people. Their relationship, however, has been always vertical, with Buddhism having supremacy over shamanism. I have discussed how the Buddhist influence on shamanism is blatantly displayed, while the shamanistic elements in Korean Buddhism are underplayed as much as possible. That suggests that shamanism is proud to be associated with Buddhism, whereas the latter is ashamed of its connection with the latter.

The religious scene in contemporary Korean society has undergone great changes. Christianity, after suffering an initial period of gory persecution, has been firmly established as the religion of 20% of the total population, and accounts for 48.6% of the religions Korean people practise these days. Moreover, there has been a steady increase in the Christian population. There is a sense in which Christianity is associated with modernity in contemporary Korean society, and is seen as the symbol of the newly-industrialized nation-state.

Buddhism, in the face of the increased competition from Christianity, has also made efforts to modernize its practices with media publicity, utilization of modern equipment in Buddhist temples and the encouragement of the mass participation in the construction of new Buddhist temples, etc.

Against this background, any association with shamanism has become an even bigger embarrassment to the Buddhist authorities. The power struggle between these two great world religions has further enforced the vertical power relationship that has existed between Buddhism and shamanism for centuries.

Part 5

RATIONALITY, PRACTICALITY AND MODERNITY: BUDDHISM, SHAMANISM AND CHRISTIANITY IN KOREAN SOCIETY

Introduction

This paper discusses the relationship between Buddhism, shamanism and Christianity in contemporary Korea society within the context of the religious practice pattern of modern Korean people. These religions and religious belief system play important roles in the religious lives of the Korean people today. Buddhism owes its survival and growth in popularity to its inherent rationality. On the other hand, Korean shamanism, generally referred to as *musok*, addresses the basic human desire for health, good fortune and long life, which is fundamentally irrelevant in Buddhism. The increasing power and popularity of Christianity is in a sense based on its association with modernity. Although the co-existence of Buddhism, shamanism and Christianity in contemporary Korean society is not without conflict, there exists an intricate interplay between the three.

As Weber (1922) posits, Buddhism is the most rational of all world religions, since it logically explains unjustified human suffering. However, its lofty goal of achieving impossible *nirvana* is beyond reach for most mortals. Therefore, shamanism, or other similar indigenous possession cults, has often wielded influence on Buddhism, in other parts of the world (Obeysekere 1963, 1968; Tambiah 1970; Spiro 1967/1974). When the central morality religion is Buddhism, these cults have co-existed to satisfy the needs of ordinary people, who cannot realistically attain *nirvana*. In such cases, "orthodox" Buddhism has been compared to the great tradition while popular Buddhism as practised by the masses, and often containing shamanistic elements has been compared to the little tradition in Redfield's sense (Obeyesekere 1963). Thus the relationship between Buddhism and shamanism is usually hierarchical, with the former having supremacy over the latter, as Spiro (1967) has shown in the case of Burmese Buddhism and supernaturalism.

"Shamanism and Buddhism are like two grafted trees. You can't tell them apart," said one of my informants to me during my fieldwork. This view was echoed repeated by many other shamans and their followers. Her remark succinctly sums up the extent of the syncretism, between shamanism and Buddhism in Korean society over the ages. However, during my fieldwork, I came across many Buddhists, monks and laymen alike, who would not admit to the influence of shamanism on their religion. Nevertheless, there is much evidence to suggest that Korean Buddhism has undergone a considerable metamorphosis as a result of the influence of shamanism. This bears witness to the fact that the relationship between the two is hierarchical, with Buddhism occupying a superior position over shamanism. This vertical relationship has always been present since the introduction of Buddhism into Korea in the fourth century.

In contemporary Korea, the situation is more complex, since there is a multiplicity of religious practices. Buddhism, which ceased to the central morality religion six centuries ago, has since undergone a series of crises, and its survival has often been threatened. The existing statistics reveal that modern Korean people most frequently cite Christianity as a religion they practise, and shamanism does not get a mention at all. The general pattern has been undergoing a change in favour of Christianity in recent years (*Jonggyo yeon-gam* 1993), which suggests the existence of a competition between the two great world religions. I will venture to argue that this phenomenon has increased hostility that Buddhism has displayed towards shamanism for a long period of time.

The data that I use to support my argument was collected during my fieldwork conducted among the Korean shamans during 1993-1994.

Theodicy Buddhism and Lay Soteriology

Ass Weber (1948), Buddhism successfully resolves the problem of theodicy, or God's justification for the suffering of the innocent, which arises in monotheistic world religions. In monotheistic religions, the resolution of theodicy could never be logical, for at the heart of it there exists a fundamental logical contradiction; an omniscient, omnipotent, wholly benevolent God could not in logic permit suffering of the innocent and good (Obeysekere 1968: 9). Buddhism provides a perfect solution to this problem through the Indian concept of karma (*eop* in Korean), the belief in the transgression of souls. So guilt and merit in this world is compensated unfailingly in the successive reincarnations of the souls. Man is doomed to the eternal cycle of births and rebirths, or *samsara* (*yunhoe* in Korean), which is defined as suffering. Suffering in the Buddhist sense has a wider philosophical implication of impermanence than just the simple pain; all karma-produced conditions are aspects of suffering in a philosophical sense. Hence the salvation, the elimination of suffering, must entail the elimination of karma so that the flow for continuity can be arrested. This is *nirvana*, the ultimate salvation, the final release from *samsara* and suffering.

In most world religions, salvation is the reward for a meritorious life; if you do good in this world you go to heaven in the other world after death. In Buddhism, however, even Heaven, a paradise in an earthly sense, called *geungnak*, is a form of suffering because of its transience. Thus not only the person who commits bad karma, but also the person who does good, has little chance of achieving the ultimate salvation, i.e. nirvana, since everybody continues to be reincarnated. Salvation is only possible for the individual who rises above samsara altogether by renouncing society and the world, i.e. becoming a monk and observing 227 precepts prescribed for monks. In theory even a layman couyld attain nirvana, but in practice it is impossible for most people, since the conditions of any human social order are such that attachments and desire are inevitable. Hence strictly speaking, Buddhism in its orthodox principle can be said to be a religion of acetic monks in their monastic seclusion.

As Weber (1922) maintains, however, ordinary men turn to religion "so that they may prosper and have a long life on earth." The inadequate provisions for the laymen to achieve salvation in orthodox Buddhist doctrines account for the development of a peasant or little tradition of Buddhism under pressure of the needs of the masses. In South

East Asian countries, where Theravada Buddhism dominates, syncretism with shamanism or other forms of indigenous archaic religions has occurred, partly because the orthodox or great tradition was not interest in lay soteriology. Therefore the "heretical" activities carried out by the masse throughout Southeast Asia are based on practicality. Since the lay masses, because of their involvement in the social system, are incapable of achieving salvation anyway, doctrinally heretical practices such as indigenous deity propitiation or astrology make little difference to their future prospects of attaining the ultimate goal. Therefore, they might as well improve their lot in this life and next lives by whatever means available to them. From the sociological, particularly functionalist point of view, then the forms of secular Buddhism practiced in Southeast Asia, though they involve theological "heresy," can be regarded as the successful transformation of essentially unsociable Buddhism into a social religion.

Syncretism of Buddhism and shamanism in Korea

Buddhism was first introduced to Korea from China, in the fourth century and after some initial resistance, quickly established itself as the national religion. The type of Buddhism that reached Korea was Mahayana ("Great Vehicle") Buddhism, Prevalent in North Asia. Mahayana in Korea is *daeseung* which is a literal translation of "Great Vehicle." The objective of Mahayana Buddhism is thus helping a great number of people to achieve salvation. In contrast, Theravada Buddhism is referred to as *"soseung bulgyo,"* a literal translation of "Hinayana" or "small vehicle," another name for Theravada. Hinayana was so named in the sense that only a chosen few, i.e. acetic monks, can attain nirvana.

For the salvation of the masses, the doctrine of Mahayana Buddhism was radically modified so as to allow for the development of the Bodhisattva cult. Bodhisattvas are saviours who have postponed their own salvation in order to save others, although they have achieved enlightenment. In Mahayana countries, this doctrinal change has now become fully "orthodox" (Obeysekere 1968). Thus although the fundamental Buddhist doctrine that salvation can only be achieved by one's own effort and ascetic renunciation of the world remains the same, over time "orthodoxy" itself has undergone changes and has diversified into different sects. Therefore "orthodoxy" in Buddhism is not an absolute, inflexible concept, and "heterodoxy" can become "orthodox," if it is generally accepted, approved and established.

Mahayana Buddhism, with Bodhisattvas and other numerous saints for the laity to supplicate, confronted little conflict with shamanism, the ancient indigenous belief system of the Korean people. Its modified doctrine made it possible for Buddhism to absorb shamanistic elements. Over time, therefore, extensive syncretism of Buddhism and shamanism has taken place. Among Korean scholars there is a consensus of the view that many state-sponsored Buddhist rituals, such as *palgwanhoe* of the Goryeo period were in essence shamanistic rituals hiding behind a thin Buddhist veneer. (Yu 1975:260)

The syncretism of Buddhism and shamanism, however, has always been a vertical alliance. Buddhism was the officially recognized central morality religion until the 14th century, while shamanistic elements were always held in contempt, castigated, disregarded, or at best hidden There remain numerous historical documents recording the official condemnation of shamans and their practices[1]. On the other hand, there is much evidence to suggest that the pride of place was given to Buddhist gods in shamanistic rituals. What illustrates this point very well is a poem entitled, *Nomu pyeon* (the Old Shamaness), which appears in *Dongguk Isangguk jip* written in around 1241 by Yi Gyubo, a high-ranking government minister. The [poem was written to commemorate the expulsion of his neighbour, an old shamaness, from the capital. It vividly describes the shamanistic practices in 13th century Korea, which reflect many Buddhist elements. Let us briefly examine lines 26-28:

> Her rafted shrine measures barely five feet high.
> Yet she claims the Heavenly Buddha Emperor is there.
> The Buddha Emperor properly resides in the Six Heavens.
> How could He stay in your humble abode?

The concept of the Six Heavens and the Buddha residing there itself is a deviation from the fundamental Buddhist doctrines. Despite the minister's derision of the absurdity of the shamaness's practice, his own idea can be said to have been influenced by the indigenous Korea belief in Heaven, which was deeply rooted in shamanism[2].

Today, even a casual observer of the Korean shamanistic ritual

---

1   For details, see Yi Neunghwa 1927.

2   See Hogarth 1995.

called, *gut*, would immediately notice the extent of the Buddhist influence on Korean shamanism. The shamanistic shrines, both private and commercial, are with few exceptions filled with Buddhist artefacts, such as Buddha statues, wooden gongs and beads, Buddhist-style paintings and other paraphernalia. The costumes and some ritual procedures also reflect its influence. The shamanistic consumes for many higher-status spirits are derived from the Buddhist concept, and when the Buddhist-derived spirits descend on the scene, the animal carcass offerings are covered with a piece of white paper, in observance of the Buddhist prohibition of killing. Moreover shamans often recite the Buddhist scriptures, believing that they possess powers to chase away evil spirits[3].

Some of the most important shamanistic spirits, such as Jeseok (The Buddha Emperoro), Bulsa (the Buddhist Guru Grandmother), Sambul (the Three Buddhas), Siwang (the Ten Kings of the Netherworld) are derived from Buddhism. What is interesting is the fact that these spirits are accorded the highest ranks in the pantheon, and therefore "entertained" before the "purely" shamanistic spirits, such as Changbu (the Performer Spirit).

While the Buddhist influence is proudly displayed in most shamanistic practices, the shamanistic elements in Korean Buddhism are much more played down. A shrine dedicated to the shamanistic Holy Trinity, comprising of the Seven Stars Spirit, the Mountain Spirits, and the Solitary Star Spirit, is usually found in all Buddhist temple grounds. However, what is interesting is the fact that these shrines are very small and insignificant in size and shape in comparison with the main temple buildings. Moreover, they are usually situated discreetly in an inconspicuous position.

Despite these outwardly low-key shamanistic elements, Korean Buddhism has undergone extensive syncretism with shamanism, particularly in terms o its ideology (Yi Neunghwa 1927; Akamatsu & Akiba 1938; Yu 1975; Choe 1978; Gim Inhoe 1987). Let us briefly examine the reasons that the ordinary Koreans give for visiting Buddhist temples. They are:

1. To attend festivals, such as the Buddha's Birthday

2. To perform mortuary rituals, such as the 49th Day Ritual and 100th Day Ritual to pray for the wellbeing of the dead

---

3 For details of the shamanistic incantations based on the Buddhist Scriptures, see Akamatsu & Akiba 1938; Book II, pp 239-246. An interesting parallel can be found in northern Thailand, where the people also believe in the powers of the Buddhist Scriptures (Tambiah 1970).

3. To pray for long life, prosperity and healing, and preventing other disease and misfortune.

The above suggest Korean Buddhism is closer in ideology to shamanism, which is this-worldly, corporeal and existential. It also supports Yu's view (1975:263) that Korean Buddhism can be said to be "Buddhism of prayer for good fortune."

Although outwardly the influence of Buddhism on Korean shamanism has been greater than the latter on the former, in essence the opposite can be said to be true. As Gim Inhoe (1987:217) shrewdly observed, Buddhist paraphernalia merely serve as external decorations in Korean shamanism, while Korean Buddhism has undergone a metamorphosis to such an extent that Buddhism as practised by the Korean laymen can be said to be closer to shamanism than "orthodox" Buddhism.

Among the regular sponsors of *gut* who practise a world religion, the Buddhists account for the largest proportion. Many of them switch from one to another in the course of their lives, or alternatively, adapting to the situation, they tend to practise the two alongside each other.

Buddhist festivals bring the Buddhists and shamanists together. Prima facia, they are indistinguishable. However, after a few months in the field, I learned to distinguish between hem by the way they pray. I noticed the Buddhist seem to stand on one spot and bow several times with their hands held together, while the shamanists rub their hands together repeatedly and bow to all directions, turning 360 degrees in the process. The Buddhist monks and official, who must also perceive their identity, treat all shamanist as though they were Buddhists.

It seems to me that the Buddhist officials regard the shamanistic elements in their religion as highly undesirable and shameful. I will give an example from my field experience. Bangsaenje, meaning "liberating life ritual," is a Buddhist festival performed on the 3 of March by the lunar calendar. A large crowd of mainly women father by the riverside for merit-making on the third day of the third month by the lunar calendar. This same ritual is called *yonggung gut* (the Dragon Palace Ritual) by the shamans and their clients, 1 according to my veteran shaman informants. My shaman friends, Yi Jongnam, Jeong Wonhae and Bang Chunja told me about this *gut* to be performed on the 13 April, 1994 (3 March in the lunar calendar that year), at the Dragon Palace Shrine on a bank of the Han iver, which flows through Seoul. When I got there, however, there were no signs of shamanistic activities; everybody I talked to denying vehemently that they had anything to do with shamanism, which they said was merely a superstition. However, I could recognize some participants as shamanists by the way they prayed. I also saw prolific displays of shamanistic talismans in the buildings. It was later confirmed again by my shaman informants that that *bangsangje* and *yonggung gut* are indeed one and the same; different terms are applied by the Buddhists and shamanists. The implications were that the Buddhists were ashamed of having any connection with shamanism, which they consider a "primitive superstition."

Another visual evidence of the syncretism of shamanism and Buddhism is a place of worship for the Buddhists and shamanists alike, called Seonbawi (the Zen Rocks), a group of rocks shaped like monks wearing peaked hats. Situated on top of Mount Inwang in Seoul, they attract a large number of worshippers and other visitors. Oral tradition has it (Gim Yeongsam 1989: 64) that the eminent Buddhist monk Muhak Daesa[4], an advisor to the founder of Joseon dynasty, King Taejo, suggested that the Zen Rocks be included inside the city walls. On the other hand, a Confucian literati minister called Jeong Dojeon, insisted that they be placed outside the walls. Eventually Jeong won, which signified the symbolic triumph of Confucianism, and defeat and further decline of Buddhism and shamanism. These days, worshippers pray at the Zen Rocks for sons, prosperity and healing of bodies and minds. One can detect both Buddhists and shamanists judging from the way they bow in prayer, as described earlier.

I was fascinated, when Ms Bang, one of the veteran shamans, told me that shams climb up the steep hill to the Zen Rocks on the eve of any *gut* to "inform the spirits of the planned rituals," however late it may be. The extreme reverence that shamans and their followers hold for this very Buddhist symbol may be interpreted in several ways. It illustrates the extensive syncretism between Buddhism and shamanism, and the supremacy of the former over the latter. It also suggests that after the fall from official grace, Buddhism, may have absorbed shamanistic elements even further from the 14th century, thus co-existing alongside shamanism at the level of the downtrodden masses during the Joseon dynasty. The shamanistic elements in Korean Buddhism deserve further anthropologi-

---

4 Even today Muhak Daesa appears in the shamanistic ritual in the Seoul area as a revered deity.

cal research at the grassroots.

Buddhism and shamanism in the context of the religious lives of modern Korean people

At the beginning of the 19th century, Homer Hulbert (1906:403-404), an early Christian missionary to Korea, wrote, "As a general thing, we may say that the all-round Korean will be a Confucianist when in society, a Buddhist when he philosophises and a spirit-worshipper when he is in trouble." He argues that to know a man's true religion you should see what he does when in trouble.

I have argued (1995) that Hulbert's remarks are still valid in contemporary Korean society. What is interesting, however, is the fact that the existing statistics for Modern Koreans' religions reveal a completely different picture. The two most dominant religions by far are Buddhism and Christianity. According to the Ministry of Information statistics, in 1982 there were 11 million Buddhist, and the Christians numbered 9 million, combining Catholics and Protestants. The figures change in the Gallup Research statistics in 1984 to 7.4 million Buddhists and 9 million Christians. The 1985 census reveals a slightly different trend, with just over 8 million Buddhists to 8.34 million Christians.

The problem with these figures, however, lies in the method used, which was by self-identification. According to Yun (1988), in actural terms of religious practice, the figures should more realistically show 91% Confucianists, 49.3% Buddhists, and only 36.3% Christians.

The statistics indicate that the emergence of Christianity as a more dominant relgion is shown not only in quantitative terms, but also in qualitative terms. According to *Jonggyo yeon-gam* (1993), the Korean Buddhists suffer graver doubts about their faith than their Christian counterparts.

Why then do so many modern Koreans wish to project themselves as Christians? I would argue that it is because Christianity is associated with modernity, industrialization and "advanced" civilization from the west, while Buddhism is associated with anachronism and Korea's past (Kusan 1985:32-33).

The gradual increase in the number of Christians, sporadic incidents of arson of Buddhist temples by fanatical Christians, and the assertion by many Koreans that Christianity symbolizes Korea's progress in the modern world.

Buddhism, which has always been a driving force in the Korean people's philosophical consciousness despite the decline and suppression during the Confucian Joseon dynasty regime, faces strong competition from powerful albeit relatively newly-established Christianity. In recent years, it seems to me that there have been efforts on the art of Buddhist organizations to revitalize the structure of Buddhism through mass appeal. Modernization processes include mass production and distribution of tape recordings of famous monks, mass media publicity on the occasion of the deaths of renowned monks, and popular appeals for donations for constructions of new Buddhist temples. The self-image that Korea Buddhism tries to project is well represented by a ubiquitous poster, representing a sect of Korean Buddhism. The poster features a Buddhist monk with an affluent-looking middle-aged woman with gently-permed hair, wearing sophisticated smart casual western clothes and smiling contentedly. The image of this woman is a far cry from my own conception of a Buddhist, which is that of a saintly old man or a wizened long suffering woman of the countryside.

Against this background, for the Buddhists, any connection with shamanism, which is generally associated with "primitiveness," can only be extremely embarrassing. This may well be the reason why the Buddhists met denied any connection with *musok*, and even showed anger at such a suggestion. I would argue that the competition between the two great world religions, Buddhism and Christianity, has contributed to the enforced hostility of Buddhists towards shamanism. Christianity, being closely associated with modernity in contemporary Korean society, condemns *musok* as a primitive superstition. Nevertheless, the Korean Christian churches, both Catholic and Protestant, also contain many shamanistic elements despite their persecution of *musok*. The detailed discussion of this fascinating subject is beyond the scope of this paper. I will just mention that I have come across some Christians, including one or two minsters, sponsoring *gut* for various reasons. Their views of *musok* are more from the perspective of cultural nationalism, than anything else. However, they would never publicly admit that they sponsored a *gut*.

Conclusion

Akiba, a Japanese social anthropologist, conducted fieldwork among the Korean shamans in the 1930s. One of Akiba's shaman informants (1938: 312) explained to him that Buddhism was like the great house, and shamanism like the little house. It is intriguing to hear that an uneducated Korean shamans actually pre-empted Redfield in his theory of the great and little tradition by more than 20 years.

The existence of Bodhisattvas and other saints in Mahayana Buddhism, the type practised in Korea, has made it easy to incorporate many elements of shamanism, the ancient indigenous religion of the Korean people. Their relationship, however, has been always vertical, with Buddhism having supremacy over shamanism. I have discussed how the Buddhist influence on shamanism is blatantly displayed, while the shamanistic elements in Korean Buddhism are hidden as much as possible. That suggest that shamanism is proud to be associated with Buddhism, while the latter is ashamed of its connection with the former.

The religious scene in contemporary Korean society has recently undergone treat changes. Christianity, after suffering a period of gory persecution, has been firmly established as the religion of 20% of the total population, and accounts for 48.6% of the religions that Korean people practise these days and the number is rapidly increasing. Moreover, there has been a steady increase in the Christian population. Christianity is associated with modernity, and is seen as the symbol of the newly-industrialized nation state.

Buddhism, in the face of the increased competition from Christianity, has also made efforts to modernize its image with media publicity, utilization of modern equipment in Buddhist temples and encouraging the masses to participate in the construction of new Buddhist temples, etc.

Against this background, any association with shamanism has become an even bigger embarrassment to the Buddhist authorities. The competition between these two great world religions has further forced Buddhists to deny any close link with shamanism, which has existed for centuries. In time of unexplained great disasters or anxiety, many Korean People including Buddhists and some Christians, turn to *musok*. There are only a few adult female Koreans who have never consulted a fortune-teller. Many fortune-tellers are actually *gut*-performing *mudang*, although of course many practise statistics-based *yeokhak*. In the current so-called "IMF Age," when the Korean economy has suffered a severe setback, and the unemployment situation has become grave, the number of people visiting *mudang* has increased, according to my shaman informants. Fewer *gut* are being sponsored, however, on account of the lack of, and people's reluctance to part with, ready cash, which clearly reflects the practical nature of *musok*.

Even those who deprecate *musok*, cannot seem entirely to eliminate shamanistic elements in their religious lives. The manners in which Korean worshippers pray to various spiritual beings, such as Buddhist Bodhisattvas and Christian saints, to alleviate their immediate physical and mental sufferings is in essence the same as the shamanists supplicating to various spirits. I would go as far as to say that the modern Koreans praxis of Buddhism and Christianity are in principle underpinned by their indigenous belief system, i.e. *musok* (Korean shamanism).

Part 6

TRANCE AND POSSESSION TRANCE

This paper examines Bourguignon's analysis of institutionalized altered states of consciousness from the perspective of Korean shamanism. Bourguignon presents a paradigm of trance[1] and possession trance (1979) to analyze the institutionalized utilization of altered states of consciousness in various societies. However, when dealing with shamanism, an important distinction can be made between spirit possession, spirit mediumship, and shamanism, which to my knowledge was first presented by Firth (1967), and which helps clarify some of the ambiguities surrounding shamanism.

The Korean case fits quite well within Bourguignon's general theoretical frame. It helps establish an evolutionary theory in which "trance" is the prototype of an institutionalized altered state of consciousness, while "possession trance" is a more developed form. Here, I examine the

---

1. Gilbert Rouget (1980: 36) further differentiates trance from ecstasy, reserving the former to describe an active, agitated, noise-filled state that the shaman enters into, and the latter a passive, tranquil, mystical experience of possession. Michael Harner (1980), in contrast, prefers not to use the term "trance," claiming that it implies an involuntary, unconscious condition that spirit mediums enter into. Thus, a distinction between trance and ecstasy only confuses, rather than clarifies, the relationship of shamanism to possession. In this paper I shall use "trance" to mean an altered state of consciousness without possession, and "possession trance" where spirit possession is deemed to occur.

types of altered state of consciousness in the context of societal evolution and the various stages of development in Korean shamans' professional careers. I use data gathered during fieldwork among Korean shamans and historical documentary material.

Shamanism and altered states of consciousness

Shamanism is notoriously difficult to define; the theoretical debate continues today without any real consensus. Most would agree that one of the most important features of shamanism is the utilization of an altered state of consciousness for the purpose of making direct contact with supernatural entities (for example, Shirokogoroff 1935; Eliade 1951/1964; Underhill 1965: Harner 1973, 1980; Rogers 1982; Hoppál (ed) 1984; Hoppál and Pentikainen (eds) 1992; Drury 1989). Altered states of consciousness are institutionalized in many societies ancient and modern, although in differing forms. Bourguignon classifies altered states of consciousness into "trance" and "possession trance," linking them to differing levels of social complexity and, ultimately, to types of subsistence economies. To Bourguignon, trance is typically, though not always, utilized by men, and possession trance by women. Trance involves interaction with supernatural beings through hallucinations, visions, or dreams, often by sending the subject's soul on a journey, so that he sees, hears, and interacts with the spirits while retaining his identity. Possession trance, on the other hand, involves an impersonation of the spirits; the trancer, in amnesia, becomes the spirit. Trance is generally induced by hypoglycaemia, brought on by fasting, sensory deprivation, isolation, mortification, or hallucinogens,[2] whereas possession trance is usually induced by drumming, singing, dancing, crowd contagion or—but more rarely—drugs. Trance is a private experience, reported from memory to the community. Possession-trance is a public performance, to be observed by all present, and it requires an audience.

Bourguignon bases her initial discussion on a comparative study of 488 societies, later whittled down to 84. She concludes that "the greater the societal complexity and the higher the level of subsistence economy, the more likely the society is to employ possession trance rather than trance." Trance is prevalent in the Americas and amongst

---

2. Korean shamans do not use hallucinogens. For a discussion of hallucinogens, see Harner (ed) 1973.

predominantly hunting societies, while possession trance is usually found in African agricultural societies. Types of altered states of consciousness are linked to patterns of socialization and stress, to different stages of life, and to culturally defined sex roles. Thus, trance is associated with more independent and self-reliant males, with stress linked to young men pressured to achieve independence in hostile settings such as hunting, war-fare, and sex. Possession trance is utilized by obedient and compliant women, stress linked to new marriage, moving from natal homes, and domestic conflict. This picture is too neat. There is a discrepancy between Bourguignon's theory and shamanic techniques used to achieve an altered state of consciousness. In shamanism, singing, dancing, crowd contagion, drumming, and so on, are common techniques. Memory, and the degree of control exercised by the shaman during an altered state of consciousness also challenge Bourguignon's view. I note that, although a Korean shaman has no knowledge of what the spirits will say through him or her before trance possession, the oracle is clearly remembered afterwards. A shaman might say, "Let's receive an oracle, and see what the spirits say," and afterwards ask rhetorically, "Didn't they say: 'Don't do it!'?"

Firth's distinction between spirit possession, spirit mediumship, and shamanism allows me to go further. To him, spirit possession refers to abnormal personal behaviour, interpreted as evidence that a spirit is controlling personal action and is probably inhabiting the body. Spirit mediumship, in contrast, uses behaviour appropriate to communicate with the spirit world. The behaviour must be intelligible, so it must follow a regular and predictable pattern. Shamanism can apply to mediums, since it is defined as a phenomenon in which the practitioner controls spirits, exercising mastery over them in socially recognized ways (Firth 1967: 296). Control, then, is the vital clement in shamanism. Korean shamans often refer to themselves as "people who manage the spirits (*sin-eul burineun saram*)." Further, they have the socially acknowledged ability to go into an altered state of consciousness at will. This ability is a form of power, used for socially approved, largely altruistic ends, such as curing ill health, praying for good luck, and consoling the newly-dead and the bereaved. Even where their status is low, shamans occupy central positions in their community.

I must at this point extend my discussion beyond Bourguignon and Firth. Where the main mode of production is hunting and gathering, notably in Siberia, and North and South America, trance features, but in horticultural societies, including Korea, Taiwan, and Burma, possession trance is more common. Trance, if we follow I. M. Lewis (1971), is more likely where shamanism is central to society, and possession trance where it is peripheral. Both types can occur in one society, hence Potter (1974) describes how a Cantonese shamaness makes an upward journey into the Heavenly Flower Garden, possessed and helped by her "familiar" spirits, and speaks with her clients' dead relatives and neighbours. And, given the truism that human society has evolved by developing complex political and jurisdictional hierarchies and greater degrees of dependence on production, it is trance, the phenomenon of the more simple societies, which should be considered the prototype, and possession trance a later development (Eliade 1951/1964).

Altered states of consciousness and Korean shamanism in a historical perspective

Archaeological relics and documents point to the strong possibility that Korean shamans were once men with political, jurisdictional, and religious leadership functions. Many Korean scholars trace the beginnings of shamanism to the origin myth of Dan-gun (see, for example, Yu Dongsik 1975), which adds support to the theory of leadership. The Dan-gun myth, relating the birth of the founder of Korea to a deity and a bear who had been transformed into a woman, contains many elements common to Siberian shamanism (Hogarth 1999). Later, essential public festive rites such as the *Mucheon* of the Ye tribe, the *Yeonggo* of the Buyeo and the *Dongmaeng* of Goguryeo, contain shamanic elements, and it can be assumed that ritual officiates were shamans (see, for example, Yi Neunghwa 1927b; Han Woo-keun [Han Ugeun] 1970; Gim Taegon 1982a; Yu Dongsik 1975; Grayson 1985). Similar shamanic functions extended through the Three Kingdoms period (traditional dates 57 BC- 668 AD). For example, the second king of Silla (the kingdom in the southeast), who is said to have reigned from AD4-23, was Namhae *Chachaung*. *Chachaung* uses three Sino-Korean characters to transcribe a pure Korean word, *seuseung*, meaning "teacher"; in Hamgyeong Province, a male shaman was still called *seuseung* early in the 20th century (Akamatsu and Akiba 1938).

Relics and royal regalia that suggest Korean kings fulfilled a shamanic role were excavated from the Cheonmachong (Tomb of the heavenly horse; 4th or 5th century AD), a royal tomb in Kyongju, the capital of Silla (Yu Dongsik 1975; Grayson 1989). The regalia consist of gold crowns and gold belts that bear a striking resemblance to contemporary Siberian shaman costumes. The crowns have pairs of antlers and feature a three-pronged fork representing a branch of the cosmic tree, elements common to shaman headgear. Jade pieces hung from the crown and the belt, often said to be "comma-shaped," look similar to the bear or tiger claws used to decorate Siberian shaman clothing, which are considered to give the shaman the power of animals. Ornaments also have ornithological themes, and the tomb contained a mural of a flying horse painted on birch bark (the cosmic tree in the form of a white birch is a classic concept in Siberian shamanism). The recurring theme is of a flight to heaven.

A more concrete account of shamanic trance during the Three Kingdom period exists. *Samguk sagi* (History of the Three Kingdoms, *kwon*) describes General Gim Yusin, a famous *hwarang* who masterminded the unification of the Three Kingdoms in the seventh century.[3] It contains a detailed account of trance:

> In the 28th year of the reign of King Jinpyeong (AD 611), when the general was seventeen, feeling indignant at the repeated invasions by Goguryo and Baekje troops into Silla territory, he went alone, with the intention of planning to conquer these enemies, into a stone cave in Jungak mountain. After purifying himself, he prayed to Heaven: "We have no peace, because of repeated invasions by our enemies, who indiscriminately bully us like ferocious tigers. I, though weak and without any talent or power, cherish an ambition to finish these disastrous wars. May Heaven listen to my prayer, and give strength to my hands." Four days later, an old man mysteriously appeared, saying: "It is admirable that you, a mere child, should have an ambition to unite the Three Kingdoms." He taught Yusin secret skills, telling him to use them wisely and discreetly, then disap-

---

3. *Hwarangdo* was a national institution founded in the sixth century to train high-born youths as a warrior elite. It is often said to have had strong shamanistic connections. *Hwarang* means "flower youth." The youths were trained in military skills and travelled throughout the country, indulging in Dionysian activities such as drinking, singing, and dancing.

peared into thin air. Yusin ran after him for about two miles, but could find him nowhere; only resplendent light lingered, sending colourful rays in all directions.

This can be compared to the uncannily similar description given by Rasmussen of an Eskimo neophyte shaman:

> There, I soon became melancholy. I would sometimes fall to weeping and feel unhappy without knowing why. Then for no reason all would suddenly be changed, and I felt a great, inexplicable joy, a joy so powerful that I could not restrain it, but had to break into song, a mighty song, with room for only one word: joy, joy! And I had to use the full strength of my voice. And then in the midst of such a fit of mysterious and overwhelming delight I became a shaman, not knowing myself how it came about. But I was a shaman. I could see and hear in a totally different way. I had gained my enlightenment, the shaman's light of brain and body. and this in such a manner that it was not only I who could see through the darkness of life, but the same bright light also shone out from me, imperceptible to human beings but visible to all spirits of earth and sky and sea, and these now came to me to become my helping spirits (Rasmussen 1929: 119).

Vestiges of possible *hwarang* links with shamanism remain. In Korea's south and along the East coast, a male shaman is sometimes called a *hwarang* or *hwaraengi*. Gim Yusin remains a popular deity in the shamanic pantheon, and regular rituals are performed at his tomb in Gyeongju. His mother, Manmyeong, also features as a shamanic goddess, and one item kept by shamans at their spirit shrines is a round convex copper mirror called the *myeongdu*, supposedly named after Manmyeong (Yi Neunghwa 1927b). The brass mirror is also a common incarnation of a Tungus shaman's familiar spirits (Shirokogoroff 1935).

The degeneration of shamanism from centre to periphery is believed to have begun with the introduction of Buddhism from China in the 4th century (Yu Dongsik 1975; Gim Taegon 1987). However, extensive syncretism took place, and shamanism survived alongside state Buddhism. Scholars consider that women took over shamanism as men discarded it in favour of the more sophisticated and rational world religion.

Throughout the Goryeo period (918-1392), numerous documents refer to shamanism, though sometimes only obliquely (Yi Neunghwa 1927b: 22-50). *Goryeosa* (History of the Goryeo dynasty; completed 1451) mentions shamans in connection with *kiuje*, prayers for rain and divination. Shamans were already deprecated, and *Goryeosa*, like the *Dongguk tonggam* (Comprehensive mirror of the Eastern Country), includes petitions from courtiers to the king recommending that shamans be banished outside the city walls. The most celebrated writing about shamanism at this time is a long poem written by Yi Gyubo (1168-1241). He talks about his euphoria when an old shaman who had been his neighbour was expelled. This poem contains valuable information about the shamanic practices of his day. Shamanic practices appear to have been popular, and possession trance was already utilized:

> They themselves claim that the spirits have descended on them (line 11);
> Men and women gather in a room like clouds, leaving their shoes at the door.
> They leave the room rubbing shoulders, and enter it with their heads touching (lines 17-18).

Some aspects of contemporary shamanism were already well established, and the poem can also be interpreted to suggest that most shamans were women[4]:

> They mumble words in their throats, like birds, incoherent, sometimes fast and sometimes slow (lines 19-20);
> They rise, and leap up and down until their heads hit the cross-beam (line 24);
> On the walls are colourful paintings of the spirits, and framed pictures of the Seven Stars Spirit and Nine Stars Spirit (line 29-30).

Full-scale persecution of shamanism began with the adoption of Confucianism by the Joseon dynasty. Shamans were ostracized as mem-

---

4. Yi's writing translates as "female shamans are called **gyeok** and male **mu**." Yu Dongsik (1975: 155-7) changes this around in his translation. I, along with other scholars, agree with Yu, for it is axiomatic that **mu** refers to a female shaman.

bers of the lowest social class, and special taxes were levied on them to discourage their practices (Yi 1927b). However, documents still mention shamanic rituals praying for rain. More significantly, shamanism appears to have continued to thrive among the downtrodden masses and among women of all classes, providing cathartic release from oppressive patriarchy and the rigid social hierarchy through a reciprocal interaction with spirits. Women exerted their power through shamanism, even though they lived in a society with overt sex role asymmetry (Rosaldo & Lamphere 1974). Despite its universal ethos of *namjon yeobi* ("honoured men and subservient women"), Korean society allowed women power in socially vital ritual work since, as Hulbert (1906) points out,[5] all Koreans have turned to shamanism, normally through women, to solve a given crisis.

The altered state of consciousness in contemporary Korean shamanic praxis

Although Korea has recently undergone rapid industrialization, the ethos is still that of an agrarian society. Therefore, it is not surprising to find that the altered state of consciousness utilized by shamans remains possession trance. It is interesting to note that the type of state changes as a shaman's career progresses. Initially, particularly while suffering possession sickness (*sinbyeong*), the neophyte can neither sleep nor eat. He or she experiences symptoms similar to the trances of shamans in hunting societies, in which she has visions and discussions with spirits in dreams (Akamatsu and Akiba 1938/1991; Akiba 1950; Harvey 1979a; Gim Taegon 1982a; Seo 1993; Hogarth 1995). Later, during *gut*, only ritualized possession trance is utilized. To illustrate this, I will present three case histories from Seoul.

Bang Changhwan (b.1943) first suffered possession sickness when aged 19. He was committed three times to a mental hospital, and repeatedly attempted suicide. His father died, and on the third night following his death, at around 1 a.m., Pang had a vision. He saw his father's tomb burst open. His father emerged with an octagonal table in his left hand and a staff in his right. He came from his tomb down from

---

5. Hulbert writes: "As a general thing, we may say that the all-round Korean will be a Confucianist when in society, a Buddhist when he philosophises, and a spirit worshipper when he is in trouble (1906:403-4)."

the hillside and told Pang to get up and take the table. Pang took it, and became a shaman.

As a child, Jo Jaryong (b.1946) often had visions of his grandfather, who had covertly practiced as a shaman. His mother's constant nagging to study so stressed him out that at the age of 13 he decided to kill himself. He collected sleeping tablets from several chemists, and one night sneaked into a deserted alley to take them. But his grandfather suddenly appeared and rebuked him, hitting him on the head with his staff. Jo swallowed the tablets anyway, swigging them down with rice wine, but they failed to kill him. He recovered without suffering any long-term damage.

One night, when Jeong Wonhae (b.1932) was suffering from possession sickness, she heard a voice saying, "I have come." She asked who was speaking and the voice revealed itself, winding around her body, "I am the General Dragon. Since it is a wonderful world, I have come to you down the telephone line." The spirit offered her a bowl filled with water, but she hesitated, saying, "If I receive this, they say I'll become a shaman." The spirit responded, "You are different from an ordinary shaman." She still hesitated, so he continued, "If you don't trust me, go to Noryangjin market south of the Han river in Seoul and look for a Mr. Go, whose business recently folded. I caused it to close down, because I was displeased by the selfish neglect he had for his staff's safety. Two employees lost their hands in an accident involving machinery." The next day, she went to look for Go and, to everybody's astonishment, found him and discovered that his grain shop and mill had closed two months earlier.

In each of these cases, possession sickness is coupled to trance and a vision. The neophyte's first socially acknowledged possession trance takes place during the later initiation ritual (*naenm gut*). This is accompanied by the first oracle, described as *malmun-eul yeolda*, literally, "opening the word gate." From here onwards, possession trance features in the institutionalized ritual, while trance experiences are restricted to private dreams and visions at times of personal stress or crisis. [6] Trance, then, characterizes the initial calling, while possession trance is

---

6. As a further example, Ha Bubang (b.1953), a neophyte shaman, told me on 17 April 1994 that whenever she doubted the power and existence of spirits, her "grandfathers (her tutelary spirits)" would appear to her in a dream and rebuke her.

utilized after the initiation ritual. This supports my view that trance is the prototype of the shamanic altered state of consciousness, but that possession trance is a later development. The changing type of altered state of consciousness is, thus, linked not only to social evolution, but also to the evolutionary process of becoming a Korean shaman.

Part 7

THE GANGNEUNG DANOJE: THE FOLKLORIZATION OF THE KOREAN SHAMANISTIC HERITAGE

Introduction

This paper discusses the "folklorization" of the shamanistic heritage as appears in one of the most popular festivals, called Gangneung Danoje. What I mean by "folklorization" is the process by which an old tradition is revived and firmly re-established in its modified form. In contemporary Korea, folklore is closely linked with the Korean national identify and cultural nationalism. Since shamanism is an integral part of Korean folk culture, the folklorization of shamanistic heritage can often be found.

Gangneung Danoje, one of the most celebrated festivals in contemporary Korea, provides the ethnographic material.[1] The Festival, designated by the Korean government as the Important Intangible Cultural property No. 13, is held annually in spring on the east coast of Korea. A

1. My fieldwork was conducted between the 10th and 30th of May 1998, in Gangneung and its vicinity. I owe a debt of gratitude to many people, particularly to Mr. Jeong Hodon, President of the Gangneung Cultural Centre, Ms Gim Yeongsuk, a veteran hereditary shaman in that area, and the Choe family for their accurate information, kind hospitality and consideration.

special group has been formed for its preservation, headed by an old inhabitant of the area, called Gim Jindeok, who is well versed in the ritual details.

The field data will be supplemented by a comparative study of the previous ethnographies of Gangneung Danoje, by scholars such as Hong (1849/1989), Akiba (1954/1993), Im (1971) and Gim Seongwon (1987). Analyses of such data spanning a long period of time will help us understand what I term "folklorization," i.e. the establishment and confirmation of the myths and ritual process, and sometimes a reinvention of tradition.

I will define the terms "folklore" and "folklorization," and present some paradigms of "festival" in many other cultures of the world. What is interesting is Gangneung Danoje contains all the classic elements of the "festival," but at the heart of it is the shamanistic ritual, which is its essence. We will examine how the shamanistic heritage lives on in popular folk festivals such as Gangneung Danoje in contemporary Korean society, by analyzing its ethnographic details.

Definitions of folklore and folklorization

The scholarly study of folklore began in the mid-19th century, although there were precursors such as Johann Gottfried von Herder (1744 - 1803), a German critic and poet. His love of popular songs and for "unsophisticated" human nature led to the publication of his famous anthology of folksongs, *Stimmen der Völker in Liedern* in 1778-79. He used such terms as *Volkslied* (folksong), *Volksseele* (folk soul) and *Volksglaube* (folk belief). But the English term "folklore" was coined much later by William John Thomas, a British antiquarian, much later in 1846. He defined it as "the manners, customs, observances, superstitions, ballads, proverbs, etc., of the olden times" (cited in Bauman 1992). Stemming from the 19th century notions of romanticism and nationalism, folklore became a subject of serious study among "individuals who felt nostalgia for the past and/or the necessity of documenting the existence of national consciousness or identity." (Dundes 1980: 1)

In recent years, however, modern folklorists, such as Dundes (1980), deconstructed the concept of folklore as the study of past relics mainly for the purpose of their preservation, and considerably changed its definition. According to these scholars, although tradition remains central to folklore, the definitions of "tradition" itself and the term "folk" have taken on different meanings. The term "tradition" no longer denotes merely "relics" of the past, but has now come to indicate "temporal continuity, rooted in the past but persisting into the present in the manner of a natural object" (Bauman 1992). Thus folklore is not simply a product of the past that survives in the present, but is newly formed as the result of a complex interaction of communication, social goals, individual creativity, and performance (Bauman 1992). Dundes (1980) has maintained that the forces that produced folklore in the past are present today, and folklore is constantly shaped and created. He has also presented a new meaning for the term "folk." Modern western folklorists like him reject the 19th century definition of "folk" as illiterate, rural, technically backward peasants in literate societies, and define it as "any group of people whatsoever (Dundes 1980: 6)" who share a common feature. A folk group can consist of any number of people; in other words, "folk" can refer to a group as large as a nation or as small as a family. A folk group may be highly literate and technically advanced, since it can range from members of particular religious congregations, corporations, neighbourhoods, etc., to users of similar computers.

Folklore studies (*minsokhak*) in Korea, however, are still conceived as the study of culture rooted in the past which has survived into the present, mainly in a rural setting. Korean folklorists therefore have tended to concentrate on the collection and recording of the manners, customs, observances, superstitions, ballads, proverbs, and stories of bygone days, which have only survived in remote areas. Their stance is unabatedly nationalistic, in the sense that preserving and maintaining the Korean cultural heritage is of the utmost importance (Minsok Hakhoe 1994).[2]

It is interesting to detect the elements of cultural nationalism and the maintenance of the national identity through the folklorization of various traditions, most notably the shamanistic heritage. "Folklorization" is the process by which "folklore" is reinvented or created by a particular folk group. One of the best examples of the folklorization of the shamanistic heritage is Gangneung Danoje. Before further discussion, I will present paradigms for understanding "festivals," and some general information about the Dano Festival.

---

2. See especially the preface by Gim Seonpung.

Festivals

Festivals have been an important part of human societies from time immemorial. According to the *Encyclopaedia of Cutlural Anthropology* (1996: 484), the English word "festival" is derived from the Latin *festus* (of a holiday) and from the Indo-European *dhes* or *dhesto*, the root of several words linked with religion. Through *festus* it is related to the Latin *feralis* (concerning the dead) and *feriae* (holidays, fairs). Dhes is possibly related via *dheso* to the Greek theos (god). Thus the concept of festival contains two elements, namely ritual and play. Ritual deals with the serious (often "religious") aspect of life, while play (which often includes role reversal) temporarily eliminates tension caused by social injustice, and helps ease the stress of daily life. It is the tension between ritual and play that gives festival much of its piquancy and power. A festival is not complete without the ritual element, while it is the play aspect that attracts the participants to it.

Despite their outward differences, there are common elements in all festivals throughout the world. All festivals are "liminal" in that they constitute a break in everyday life. They are ephemeral in that they only last a short period of time, which is well represented in gaudy disposable decorations and fireworks which are instantaneous and ephemeral. There also exists a great sense of community spirit among the participants, which is also short-lived. Inversion of social roles is also commonly found (Babcock 1978), together with lampooning which is the subordinates poking fun at their social superiors.

Play and games also feature prominently in festivals. Roger Caillois (1979) categorizes play into "competition, mimesis, chance and giddiness," which can all be represented in festivals as sport, the re-enactment of founding events, gambling, dance and fairground rides. Extravagant costumes, masks, loud music, dancing, drumming, overeating, and so on, create a world different from everyday life for the participants, who spend money freely. All these elements of festival can be found in Gangneung Danoje. Let me first present some background information about the Dano festival in general.

The Dano Festival

The Dano festival, which is held on the fifth day of the fifth lunar month, has long been one of the most important festivals in the Korean folk calendar. There are documents dating from the Joseon dynasty describing the Dano Festival. Three of the best known are 1) *Gyeongdo japgi*, written by Yu Deukgong (1749-?) during the reign of King Jeongjo (1776-1800), 2) *Yeolyang sesi gi*, written by Gim Maesun (1776-1840) in 1819 during the reign of King Sunjo (1800-1834), and 3) *Dongguk sesi gi*, written by Hong Seokmo (dates of birth and death unknown) in 1849, during the reign of King Heonjong (1834-1849).

Dano Day is also popularly referred to as *surit nal* ("*suri*"-Eagle Day). *Gyeongdo japgi* (Yu 18th century/1989: 239) and *Dongguk sesi gi* (Hong 1849/1989: 93-94) state that "*suri*" is a derivation of a pure Korean word "*sure* (wheel)," and Dano Day is also called *surit nal*, because the shape of the rice cake eaten on that occasion is round like a wheel. According to *Yeolyang sesi gi* (Gim Maesun 1819/1989: 163), "*suri*" is derived from "*suroe* (swift current)." Dano is called *surit nal*, because it originated from the Chinese rituals held to appease the spirit of a loyal courtier called Quyuan during the Cho dynasty. Victimized as a result of a slanderous plot by his enemies, he committed suicide by jumping into the rapid waters of Miluo, to prove his innocence to the king. Another interpretation for "*suri*" is "high," "above" or "god," hence it is "high day or the day to serve the gods" (Im Donggwon 1971: 111). That is why Dano is also called *cheonjungjeol* (the heavenly season).

The interpretations of "*suri*" as meaning "*sure* (wheel)" or "*suroe* (swift current)" seem too contrived in my opinion. The similar sounds of these words could be completely fortuitous. The theory that Dano Day is called *surit nal*, because people make mugwort rice cake (*surichwi ddeok*) in the shape of a wheel lacks cogency. For one thing, *surichwi ddeok* that I tasted in the ground of Gangneung Danoje was not shaped like a wheel, but a square piece cut from a large cake. More importantly, that theory does not adequately explain why mugwort used for the rice cake is called "*surichwi*," since *surichwi*, as a raw ingredient, must precede the rice cake, the final product. The swift current theory is even more difficult to accept.

I would suggest that Dano is called *surit nal*, because of its shamanistic connections. *Suri* is a Korean word for "eagle," which is a classic symbol connecting humans and the spirits who are believed to live high above. (Hogarth 1999: 231) In many parts of the world, such as North-east Asia, the eagle which soars high into the skies was believed by ancient people to have the power to reach and communicate with the spirits who dwell in Heaven. That could explain why *suri* also means "high" or "above," and mugwort, which has whitish fuzz on the under-side of its leaves, is called *surichwi*. In Korea, as in many other North-east Asian cultures, white symbolizes Heaven (Hogarth 1998: 29-30). That *surichwi* is related to Heaven has a parallel in the silver birch tree, which is considered the *axis mundi*, or the sacred world tree, connecting the worlds of humans and spirits.

The folk customs of the day are described in some detail in the above-mentioned writings, but the most detailed descriptions can be found in *Dongguk sesi gi* (Hong 1849/1989), which is based on *Gyeong-do japgi* (Yu 18th century/1989). The entries for the fifth lunar month record that men, women, and children washed themselves in water boiled with sweet flags (*Acorus calamus*), and women made hair-pins out of the aromatic roots of those plants. Special festive foods, such as rice cakes made with mugwort with silver-grey aromatic foliage (*surichwi*), were prepared in abundance and consumed copiously. Play, games and competitions, were an integral part of the Dano festival, favourite games being wrestling and tug-of-war for men, and swing for women. The king distributed gifts of fans, medicinal concoctions (*jehotang*) and health-giving tablets (*okchudan*), tiger images (*aeho* or *aehwa*) made of wood or silk to be put in the hair to ward off evil spirits, to his courtiers and palace staff. Talismans (called *cheonjung jeokbu* or *Danobu*) and other forms of an apotropaic nature were widely used among people regardless of class.

Although the religious significance of Dano has somewhat receded into the background in contemporary Korea, amid the atmosphere of recreation and entertainment, Dano is still celebrated with unabated enthusiasm and enjoyment by the rural communities throughout Korea. The Dano festival par excellence is that held in Gangneung, a historical city on the East Coast, where many Korean traditional customs are well preserved. It is called Gangneung Danoje ("Dano Ritual"), because of its strong religious (basically shamanistic) significance.

A Brief History of Gangneung Danoje

Gangneung Danoje has a long history, but most extant records date back to the Joseon dynasty. In *Chugang naenghwa* (1477) a Confucian scholar, Nam Hyo-on (1454-1493), describes a ritual, dedicated to the Mountain Spirit at Daegwallyeong mountain pass on specially selected days in March, April or May, in., as follows:

> According to the Yeongdong province folklore, every year,

on selected days in March, April or May, **mudang** were welcomed and sacrifices were offered to the Mountain Spirit. The rich carrying the load on the backs of beasts, and the poor on their backs, people took the ritual offerings to the spirits' seat. For three consecutive days, they played trumpets, drums and zithers. They only came down to their homes when they were drunk. At first they did not trade with people. If they did not make sacrificial offerings, they were not allowed to sit with other people[3].

Although the above ritual cannot definitively be identified with the contemporary Gangneung Danoje, the timing and the manner of it bears a striking resemblance, and thus can be said to be at least its precursor.

Another Confucian scholar, Heo Gyun (1569-1618), who was interested in many aspects of folk culture, describes the ritual dedicated to the Daegwallyeong Mountain Spirit that he witnessed in 1603 in his *Seongso bubu go* (1611).

However, the earliest reference to it appears in *Gangneung ji* (also known as *Imyeong ji*), vol. 2, which was written by an unknown author during the reign of King Gyeongjong (1720-1724). It states that during the reign of King Taejo (r. 918-943) of the Goryeo dynasty, a sacrificial offering was made at Daegwallyeong mountain pass.[4] It can therefore be deduced that a similar festival existed as early as the tenth century, and most probably much earlier.[5]

The Three Main Deities of Gangneung Danoje

Today at the core of this festival is a series of shamanistic rituals, dedicated to (1) the Mountain Spirit of Daegwallyeong (Daegwallyeong Sansin), (2) The "National Preceptor" Guardian Spirit of Daegwallyeong (Daegwallyeong Guksa[6] Seonangsin; hereafter Guksa Seonangsin), and (3)

---

3. My English translation of the passage cited by Akiba (1954/1993:193) and Im (1971: 214).

4. Cited in Im (1971: 214) and Akiba (1954/1993: 193).

5. According to Jeong Hodon, director of the Gangneung Cultural Centre it dates back 2000 years (See below, p11)

6. The titles of **guksa** (the National Preceptor) and **wangsa** (the Royal Preceptor) were set up by the Goryeo Kings to safeguard the state-protecting role of Buddhism. Originating from the **guktong** of the United Silla Period, they were highly respected teachers and advisors to the king and royal family.

The Female "National Preceptor" Guardian Spirit of Daegwallyeong (Dae-gwallyeong Guksa Yeoseonangsin; hereafter Guksa Yeoseonangsin), the former's wife. Of these three deities, the central figure is Guksa Seonang-sin, although a short sacrifice is offered to the Mountain Spirit first.

There are various theories concerning the identities of these spir-its. Earlier documents, such as Nam Hyo-on's *chugang naenghwa* (1477) and Heo Gyun's *Seongso bubu go* (1611), only mention the Mountain Spirit, and not the male and female guardian spirits. Heo Gyun states that the Mountain Spirit of Daegwallyeong is none other than General Gim Yusin, who played a vital role in the unification of the three kingdoms by Silla. According to *Samguk sagi*[7], General Gim went to Myeongju (the old name for Gangneung) and was taught mysterious military skills by the Mountain Spirit of Daegwallyeong. General Gim Yusin is also said to have become the Mountain Spirit of Daegwallyeong after his death. This story well illustrates the multifarious nature of Korean folk gods, par-ticularly the Mountain Spirit, which is by no means one entity, but can occur in multiple numbers in one location, or in many different locations (Hogarth 1998: 76; Mason 1999).

Akiba (1954/1993: 200) does not distinguish between them, ei-ther, stating that the Mountain Spirit became the Guardian Spirit over time. He states that the "National Preceptor" Beomil (hereafter "Beomil Guksa"), a patriotic Buddhist monk who "fought against the invading Hideyoshi army in the late 16th century," was deified as the Mountain Spirit. He posits that the worship of the Mountain Spirit was metamor-phosed into that of a hero spirit. Akiba (ibid.: 199) mentions how he felt as though he was witnessing the transformation of people's beliefs in various spirits. According to him, Beomil Guksa was only one of the 12 deities enshrined at the Great Village Guardian Spirit Shrine in Gang-neung, General Gim Yusin being another.

Some 20 years after Akiba's research, Im (1971: 215) states that although there is no clear consensus among the village elders, it is gener-ally believed that Guksa Seonangsin is Beomil Guksa, while the Moun-tain Spirit is General Gim Yusin.

If there existed a confusion over the identities of these three dei-ties in Akiba's (and Im's to a certain degree) times, nowadays there does

---

7. *Samguk sagi*, Book 41, Chap. 1, Gim Yusin. For my English translation of the passage concerned, see Hogarth, 1999: 295.

not appear to be any doubt about them. Today's introductory pamphlets, the entries in encyclopaedias,[8] etc., all clearly distinguish between the Mountain Spirit and Guksa Seonangsin, stating that the Mountain Spirit of Daegwallyeong is General Gim Yusin, while Guksa Seonangsin is Beomil Guksa, and Yeoseonangsin, his wife. I suspect that Im could have influenced the establishment of the separate identities of the three deities that are propitiated today. It is interesting to note how a distinguished folklorist, such as Im Donggweon can "set the record straight," dispersing any confusion over details, in the process of inventing a new tradition.

However, the fact that Beomil Guksa was originally one of the Mountain Spirits can be detected in his portrait that hangs inside the shrine dedicated to him. In it, he is depicted as a Joseon dynasty military officer mounted on a white horse and flanked by two tigers. Yi Gangyeol (1989: 233) also states that the status of Guksa Seonangsin is that of the Mountain Spirit.

What is significant is the fact that of the 12 deities enshrined in the Great Guardian Spirit Shrine, the two national military heroes were apotheosised as the main deities of the occasion. General Gim Yusin who greatly contributed to the formation of a unified kingdom for the Korean people, and Beomil Guksa who is erroneously believed to have protected the weak helpless people from the powerful invading Japanese army/ navy, were powerful symbols of the Korean national identity and solidarity. It is no mere coincidence that the inhabitants of Gangneung should choose two such national heroes as the central objects of their adoration in their favourite festivals.

The Legend of Beomil Guksa and the Jeong Maiden

Mr. Jeong Hodon, director of the Gangneung Cultural Centre, and one of the major participants in the ritual, briefly told me the legend about the male and female guardian spirits of Daegwallyeong. During the interval between the rituals dedicated to the Mountain Spirit and Guksa Seonangsin on the 10th of May 1998, he gave me detailed information about the day's rituals. The following is my English translation of his explanations, which I recorded on video:

---

8. *Han-guk minjok munhwa dae baekgwa sajeon* , Book 1. pp. 412- 414.

The history of Danoje goes back some 2,000 years. In those days, there existed *mucheonje*, which is a sort of thanksgiving festival held in the autumn, and Danoje to pray for good crops and fishing held in the spring after planting seeds.

Those festivals were held for hundreds of years, and finally to sanctify Danoje, General Gim Yusin, a famous general during the Silla period, was enshrined in the Mountain Spirit shrine (*sansin gak*). People prayed to him for the prevention of disasters in the Yeongdong area (that is the Gangneung area), good crops and successful fishing.

Likewise, here at the Seonghwangsa, they enshrined Beomil Guksa. He was a famous monk who lived during the Silla period; he was the chief monk at Gulsansa, the temple situated at Gujeong-myeon in the City of Gangneung. After his death, his spirit tablet was enshrined here.

By and by, Beomil Guksa ordered a tiger to bring him a maiden of the Jeong family. Obeying his order, the tiger carried the maiden on its back, and brought her to him. On that day, their marriage was consummated in this room.

The inhabitants of Gangneung connected this legend (of course that story is a legend) with Danoje to render the festival closer to their hearts, so that they would celebrate it more assiduously.

Today after here we are going to the shrine of Guksa Yeoseonangsin. There they will be united for fifteen days, and on the third day of the fifth lunar month, they will be escorted to the Danoje site.

Today's procedure involves the sacrifices offered to the Mountain Spirit, Guksa Seonangsin, and then the re-enactment of the union between Guksa Seonangsin and his wife for fifteen days. The deity enshrined here is Beomil Guksa, and Daegwallyeong Guksa Yeoseonangsin is enshrined in her own shrine in the city. In a little while we will escort the spirit of Beomil Guksa to his wife's shrine. These are today's events.

The biography of Beomil that Im (1971: 216-217) presents, however, contains some confusion over historical dates:

Once upon a time, there lived a maiden in the village called

Haksan-ri (The Crane Mountain Village). One morning she went to a rock spring to fetch water. She scooped up some water with a gourd bowl, and saw the sun floating in it. She thought it strange, but drank the water anyway. After that, she found herself pregnant, and gave birth to a baby boy. Being an unmarried girl who gave birth to a fatherless baby, she was ostracised and shunned by everybody, including her family. So she abandoned the baby under the Crane Rock. But she could not sleep a wink that night, and early next morning she went to the spot, where she had left the baby the night before, fearing the worst for it. To her surprise, she found the baby cosily asleep, the cranes, and all sorts of other mountain animals having protected and fed it during the night. Marvelling at the sight and deciding that the baby would grow up to be an extraordinary personage, she brought it home.

When the boy was seven, he was sent to Gyeongju to study. He eventually became an illustrious Buddhist monk, called Beomil (literally meaning "the Scooped Sun"). The reason why the reverend monk is named Beomil is that his mother conceived him after drinking the water with "the scooped sun." He was appointed a *guksa* by the king. His fame reached as far as China. On his return to Gangneung, he threw a staff, and built a temple, where it landed, naming it Simboksa.

During the Hideyoshi invasion, Beomil Guksa climbed up to the Daegwallyeong mountain pass, to protect his hometown from the invading Japanese army. Using magic, he transformed all the trees and bushes to soldiers. The Japanese soldiers thought they were hopelessly outnumbered, and dared not approach the town and fled. After death, he became apotheosized, and became Guksa Seonangsin.

In the shrine are placed the two spirit tablets, that of Guksa Seonangsin and Guksa Yeoseonangsin. There is a legend concerning the Female Guardian Spirit as follows. Once upon a time in Gangneung there lived a family called Jeong. They had a nubile daughter. One night Guksa Seonangsin appeared to the head of the family, and asked for his daughter's hand in marriage. Mr. Jeong refused the god, saying that he could not marry his daughter to a non-human spirit.

One day, when the daughter sat on the wooden floor, beautifully dressed in a yellow top and a blue skirt,[9] a tiger appeared and carried her away on its back. The tiger was the messenger sent by the Mountain Spirit. She was taken to the Guksa Seonangsin, who made her his bride. The panic-stricken Jeong family traced the tiger to the shrine of Guksa Seonangsin. There they found her already dead; her spirit had already departed and only her body was standing next to the Guardian Spirit like a statue. Her family called a painter and had her portrait painted. Only when they hung the portrait, her body became detached.

The day the tiger carried her away was the 15th day of the fourth lunar month. That is why to this day, every year on that day, the inhabitants of Gangneung re-enact their union through a ritual.

(My English translation)

The problem with this interesting legend, which has now become familiar to modern Gangneung's residents and visitors, is the discrepancies in historical facts. First of all, if Beomil was indeed a national preceptor during the Silla period, he should have been given the title of *guktong*, rather than "*guksa*" which was introduced by the Goryeo King Taejo (Suh 1993: 131). Secondly, he could not possibly have fought the invading Hideyoshi army, which took place between 1592 and 1598. Since the Silla period ended in 935, there is a discrepancy of no less than six and half centuries.

Then who was the historical Beomil? The biography of Beomil which appears in *Zutangji* (Collection of the Ancestor's Hall)[10] paints quite a different picture of him. According to it, he was the son of Gim Sulwon, a Silla aristocrat. Beomil's mother was from the powerful Mun clan, and was considered to be a "wifely paragon." She conceived Beomil after dreaming of a portent in which she "caressed the sun." She gave birth to Beomil after 13 months of pregnancy, on the tenth day of the first lunar month, in the year *gyeongin*, the fifth year of Yuanhe (17 February 810). He left home at age 15 with his parents' consent, to go to a mountain in search of spiritual enlightenment . When he was 20

---

9. Today Guksa Yeoseonangsin is portrayed as a girl wearing a red skirt and a yellow top.

10. *Zutangji* 17:107a-c, cited in Peter Lee 1993: 241-244.

years of age, he went to the capital Gyeongju and received the complete precepts of a monk. Around the middle of Taihe (c. 830-833), he went to Tang China, where he studied under learned masters, including Great Master Yanguan Qian and Yaoshan (Weiyan) (745 - 828). In the fourth year of Huichang (844), there was a great persecution of Buddhism in China; monks were harassed and castigated, and temples destroyed. Beomil had no place to hide. However, with the help of the River God and the Mountain Spirit, he found a secluded place on Mount Shangshan where he practised meditation all alone, managing to survive on wild berries and spring water. He finally returned to Silla in the eighth month of *Jeongmyo*, the sixth year of Huichang (14 September - 12 October 847). On his return to his homeland, he sat in meditation on Baekdalsan mountain until the first month of the fifth year of Dazhong (851) when Governor Gim of Myeongju (now Gangneung) invited him to reside at Gulsansa temple. He stayed there for over 40 years. Three successive kings tried to appoint him a national preceptor: King Gyeongmun in the 12th year of Gantong, third month (25 March-23 April 871), King Heongang in the first year of Guangming (880) and King Jeonggang in the third year of Guangqi (887). But each time Beomil stubbornly refused to take the post. He died on the first day of the fifth month of *giyu* year, the second year of Wende (3 June 889) at Gulsansa temple at the age of 80. His funerary name was Great Master Tonghyo, and his stupa was called Yeonhwi.

What transpires from the above record is the fact that Beomil was neither a national preceptor, nor a military hero who won a victory against the invading Japanese army. He was in fact a Buddhist sage, who attained enlightenment through meditation. However, he commanded the great respect of the masses for his saintly behaviour, and in the popular imagination, became a *guksa*, the title that he persistently declined to take in his lifetime. Some people also confused him with the monk Hyujeong (1520-1604) who led the army consisting of 1,500 Buddhist monks against the invading Japanese army at the advanced age of 73 in 1592. Hence they bestowed upon Beomil not only the title of *guksa*, but also the glorious status of a national military hero.

What is significant for our present discussion, however, is the fact that Akiba, who meticulously recorded all the minute details of what he heard and saw in the field, appears to have been ignorant of the legends of Beomil[11] and his wife. He does mention Beomil Guksa and his "magical repulsion of the invading Japanese army" (1954/1993: 200). He (ibid.: 197) also records the story of the Jeong family's daughter being carried away by a tiger, but according to him, it was believed that the tiger had been sent by the Mountain Spirit, because he had been angry. As a consequence, the ritual procedures that he witnessed and recorded seem to differ considerably in detail from those described by Im (1971) and what I observed in 1998. Before discussing its implications, we will examine the Danoje ritual procedures of today.

The Rituals of Gangneung Danoje

Gangneung Danoje can be roughly divided into two parts; the preliminary rituals that are held before Danoje, and Danoje proper held from the fourth until the seventh of the fifth lunar month on the site specially set up for the festival in the city. The first of the preliminary rituals is the brewing of wine for the gods and spirits. I was informed by the officials concerned that the date of the ritualized wine-brewing was the fifth day of the fourth lunar month (30 April in 1998). However, Akiba (1954/1993: 194) states that the spirit wine was brewed on the twentieth day of the third lunar month. The same information is carried forward by Im Dong-gwon (1971: 213-224), who writes that Danoje thus lasted over 50 days. This discrepancy in the dates recorded by earlier scholars and the current date is in keeping with the simplification of the rituals in general, and particularly in shamanistic rituals.

On the 15th day of the fourth lunar month, a ritual is held at the Daegwallyeong mountain pass to make sacrificial offerings to the Mountain Spirit and to welcome and escort the Most Revered Guardian Spirit of Daegwallyeong (Guksa Seonangsin) to Gangneung. The custom of the government officials and *mudang*, accompanied by the inhabitants of the city and visitors from far and wide, going up to the mountain pass, which is described by Nam Hyo-on in *Chugang naenghwa* (1477), still remains. Most people nowadays travel to the Daegwallyeong mountain pass by car, and buses from the downtown are provided by officials for the convenience of the participants without cars. The shrines dedicated to the Mountain Spirit and Guksa Seonangsin are situated some 1km into the mountains from the main road, with a newly constructed Buddhist

---

11. He merely states that Beomil Guksa was one of the 12 spirits enshrined in the shrine.

temple next to them.

The offerings are made first to the Mountain Spirit. The ritual begins with a simple Confucian type offering of libation by three distinguished residents of Gangneung, including the mayor, followed by a simplified shamanistic ritual performed by *mudang*. Then the ritual party moves to the shrine dedicated to Guksa Seonangsin, and similar rituals are performed.

There then follows the most important ritual act of the day, the choosing and cutting down of a tree on which Guksa Seonangsin descends. The tree is considered to embody Guksa Seonangsin, and placed on the main altar of Gangneung Danoje site. A *mudang* climbs a little way up the mountain amid loud music and the great excitement of a large crowd of participants, including numerous reporters, and recites incantations to Guksa Seonangsin to descend. When the tree trembles, it is believed to be a sign of his descent. It is then carefully cut down with an axe, and reverently decorated with five long pieces of various coloured cloth. The tree is brought back to the shrine, and *mudang* performs another short ritual.

There follows what is termed *bonganje* ("laying in state ritual"). The tree is put in the back of an open lorry, and after a drive through the town, is taken to be reunited with Guksa Yeoseonangsin at her shrine situated in downtown Hongje-dong. There hangs a portrait of Guksa Yeoseonangsin, who is generally believed to be the afore-mentioned maid of the Jeong family inside the shrine. She is portrayed as a young woman, dressed in a traditional Korean costume of a full red skirt and a short yellow top. Next to her is a picture of a tiger, which it is believed to have carried her on its back to Guksa Seonangsin on the same day, a long time ago. In front of the portrait is an altar, where two spirit tablets are placed, each bearing the name of Guksa Seonangsin and Guksa Yeoseonangsin, respectively. The tree, representing the male spirit, is placed against the wall next to the portrait. They are then left in peace and privacy to enjoy each other's company until Dano Day. The re-enactment of their wedding day and honeymoon carries strong implications of their sexual union.

On the same day (the 15th day of the fourth lunar month), in the village of Gangmun, on the outskirts of Gangneung, offerings are made to their male and female village guardian spirits, and also to *jinddo baegi*, which is a high pole with three birds perched at the top, commonly known as *sotdae*[12]. The bird pole is believed to protect the village from the disasters of wind, fire and flood.

During the evening of the third day of the fifth lunar month (the 28th of May in 1998), the Confucian officiants and *mudang* climb up to the shrine of the female guardian spirit, and perform a short ritual, which is similar in length and form to the ones performed three weeks before. They then escort the divine couple, or to be more precise their spirit tablets which represent them and the tree, to the main altar at the Gang-neung Danoje site situated on the banks of Nam Daecheon (The Great South River) in town, in a spectacular lantern procession through the city. At the head of the procession is the tree carried by a man dressed in a Joseon dynasty military costume. Five long pieces of different coloured cloth are tied to the tree, the ends of which are carried by five men simi-larly attired. A man in a government ministerial robe of the same period, carrying the spirits tablets, escorts the tree/Guksa Seonangsin just ahead of the tree. All the dignitaries of the town join the two-hour long proces-sion, each carrying a paper lantern. Masked dancers and other partici-pants in Danoje, who will perform at the festival site from the next day march along behind the tree/Guksa Seonangsin. They give a preview of their performances to the spectators who line the streets to watch them, interacting with them, and generally making merry.

Shortly after they leave the female guardian sprit's shrine, the group makes a stop at her natal home. That year the Jeong family home was no longer occupied by the Jeongs, the present (as of 1998) owners being the Choe family. The head of the family, Mr. Choe Gyudong was a prominent businessman in Gangneung, and deputy president of the Gangneung Chamber of Commerce. His large house was located in spa-cious grounds, where he and his wife offered a shamanistic ritual (*gut*) to the divine couple. The libation and prostration that the Choes offer were very reminiscent of the Confucian style *jesa* (ancestral sacrifices). It was as though they had formed fictive kinship ties with the female de-ity. What was interesting was that Mr. Choe, the head of the family, was wearing mourning clothes of yellow hemp. When I asked Mr. Choe why he was wearing mourning clothes on such a happy day as their ancestor's

---

12. Almost identical high poles with birds perched at the top are also found among various peoples of Siberia, although the number can vary. Some examples, collected by the late Prof. Gim Taegon are on display at the Folk Museum of Gyeonghui University in Seoul.

marriage to a deity, he just smiled and could not find an answer. My interpretation would be that the mourning clothes were originally worn by the Jeongs, in memory of their daughter, who had been taken by a tiger, i.e. died on that day. The Choe family must have adopted the tradition as their own. They told me that it was a family tradition, and that they owed their personal good fortune to the protection of these two important spirits. The same tradition seems to have been well established by the 1970s. Im (1971: 220) writes that the original Jeong family home was large and its grounds spacious, and the then occupants were the Choe family who were also considered wealthy and prominent. The Jeong family originally offered the *gut*, which was carried on by the Choe family. An old lady told him that it was all thanks to their devotion to the most revered guardian spirit of Daegwallyeong (Guksa Seonangsin).

After the *gut* at the Choe family home, the procession continued through the city centre. It was already dark by the time it reached the Gangneung Danoje site, which was ablaze with colourful lights. A huge crowd gathered at the site to welcome the divine couple, and escort them to the main altar.[13] Fireworks lit up the night skies to celebrate their arrival.

When the tree and two spirit tablets were enshrined at the altar, ritual offerings were made to the couple, first in the Confucian style by government officials, then in the shamanistic style by *mudang*.

Every morning from the fourth day until the seventh day of the fifth lunar month, offerings are made to the divine couple by prominent citizens of Gangneung to pray for the well being, peace and prosperity of the city. This ritual is called *jojeonje* (early morning ritual), and performed in the Confucian style.

The Dano *gut* proper is held continuously for four days (from the fourth to the seventh of the fifth lunar month: 29 May to 1 June in 1998) from 10.30 a.m. to 8 p.m. A large marquee is set up over the shrine of Guksa Seonangsin and his wife, to accommodate the large audience, who come and go during the *gut*. The *mudang*, being of the hereditary type, neither experience ecstasy/trance nor practise *gongsu* (messages

---

13. In 1998, Dano Day fell just before the local election, and at the entrance of the site, the cronies of a prominent candidate took advantage of the opportunity to address the crowd, using it as part of their political campaign. To my disgust, the crowd was almost coerced to applaud the candidate, who after delivering his political address with a phoney smile disappeared immediately afterwards, without accompanying the party to the main altar.

sent by spirits through the possessed *mudang*), but perform a series of shamanistic singing and dancing, accompanied by lively music performed by male musicians, called *yangjung*. The *yangjung* from the east coast of Korea forms an integral part of the Important Intangible Cultural Property No 13.

While the *mudang* perform the *gut*, Gangneung residents and visitors pray to the divine couple at the altar, offering money and incense. The *mudang*, who await their turn to perform *gut*, burn pieces of paper with the propitiators' personal details written on them. This is the heart of Danoje, and the so-called "*mudang* tent" is the largest and most popular in the festival arena.

The procedure of the *gut* is as follows:

1) *Bujeong gut*: Purification of all the evil spirits with water, fire and *sin kal* (spirit knives)

2) *Jeongjwa gut*: Inviting all the spirits and settling them down.

3) *Hahoe gut*: According to Gim Yeongsuk, "*hahoe*" is a dialect for "*hwahae*," which means "reconciliation." Thus this *gut* is for the reconciliation of everybody, particularly those who normally have strained relationships.

4) *Josang gut* (ancestor *gut*)

5) *Sansin gut* (the Mountain Spirit *gut*)

6) *Sejon gut* (The Honourable Buddha *gut*)

7) Chilseong *gut* (The Seven Stars Spirit *gut*)

8) *Jisin gut* (The Earth Spirit *gut*)

9) *Seongju gut* (The House Tutelary Spirit *gut*)

10) *Chugweon gut* ("Blessing" *gut*)

11) Sim Cheong *gut*: Reciting the story of Sim Cheong, the filial daughter of the blind man, Sim. A popular folk tale, Sim Cheong sells herself to the fishermen as a live sacrifice for the Dragon King, to raise money for making her father see again. There have been various theories about why this story is recited at this particular *gut*, but nothing convincing, and certainly nothing conclusive, has been presented. The religious connec-

tion, i.e. live sacrifice of a young virgin, and the heroine who is a paragon of filial piety, may have made this story particularly attractive to *mudang*.

12) *Gunung janggun gut* (The Military Hero *Gut*)

13) *Sonnim gut*: Smallpox Spirit, called "*sonnim* (guest)" is invited and entertained. *Sonnim gut*, which at one time, was one of the most popular *gut* everywhere (Akiba 1950: 87) is now defunct, with the eradication of smallpox. However, one can detect traces of it in a small part of a community *gut*, such as this one.

14) *Jemyeon malmyeong gut*

15) *Ggonnorae gut* (Flower song *gut*)

16) *Baennorae gut* (Boat song *gut*)

17) *Deungnorae gut* (Lantern song *gut*)

18) *Songsin gut* (Seeing off the spirits)

On the last day, *daemaji* (testing through the pole) *gut* is performed to find out whether Guksa Seonangsin, the most revered guardian spirit of Daegwallyeong, enjoyed the *gut*. It is believed that if the *gut* is to his full satisfaction, he makes the pole held by the *mudang* shake, upon her reciting the ritual blessing.

When the Dano *gut* is finished, a ritual sending off and escorting the divine couple to their respective resting-places, called *songsinje*, is performed. The spirit tablet of Guksa Seonangsin is returned to Seonghwangsa (his shrine) in Daegwallyeong, whereas that of his wife is placed to rest at her shrine in Hongje-dong in Gangneung, until next year.

When all the Danoje rituals are over, the officials and *mudang* reverently burn all the ritual paraphernalia, such as the paper flowers, lanterns, the huge dragon boat, and so on.

Comparisons of the Old and New Traditions

In this section, I will compare the ritual procedures recorded by Akiba in the 1950s, those by Im in the 1970s, and those that I witnessed in 1998. We will see how the traditions concerning Gangneung Danoje have evolved and been reinvented over the last few decades. Since a similar phenomenon can also be detected in other rituals/festivals in contemporary Korea, it can provide a paradigm for folklorization of religious festivals, which are shamanistic in essence.

There are considerable differences between the contemporary Danoje rituals and those described in detail by Akiba (1954/1993: 193-200). Akiba (ibid.: 196) also describes the cutting down of a tree which trembled when a *mudang* prayed. But in his days the Mountain Spirit, Daegwallyeong, was believed to have descended on it. It was also escorted into the town centre on the 15th day of the third lunar month, its procession being more or less the same as that of today. The procession made a stop at the house of "so-and-so," who offered the spirit rice cakes and libation. The purpose of this sacrificial offering was apparently to appease the Mountain Spirit, who, having been offended for an unspecified reason, had sent a tiger to carry the Jeong maiden away on its back. He does not link her death to the Guardian Spirit in any way, treating it as a disparate incident. Next Akiba describes a ritual offered to the Mountain Spirit at the female guardian spirit shrine. After a tour of the town, the procession arrived at the great guardian spirit shrine at around midnight on the same day. Inside the shrine were the tablets of the 12 spirits, which included the male spirits, such as General Gim Yusin, Beomil Guksa, Songak Mountain Spirit, and Isabu, and the female spirits, such as Gangmun Buin, Chodang Buin, Yeonhwa Buin, Seosan Songgye Buin.[14] The divine branch was placed in the centre. For the following 21 days until the sixth day of the fifth lunar month, the officials and *mudang* paid a courtesy visit every morning.

What is totally absent in Akiba's detailed ethnography of the day is the union of the male and female guardian spirits. His omission can be explained for two reasons. Firstly, it could be a genuine slip on his part. He does mention that he occasionally came across a hostile reaction to his enquiries because some people tended to regard all men in western suits as oppressors (Akiba ibid.: 199), and hence he was not told properly about all the details of the ritual procedures. Second, the legend of the male and female guardian spirits of Daegwallyeong and their union is a relatively modern invention of tradition. The first reason is difficult to accept, since most of his ethnographies describe all the details very

---

14. Akiba writes that he failed to identify all 12 spirits, owing to the lack of available information. According to him, the 12 spirits tablets were burned by reformers during the Gabo (1894) Gyeongjang (Reform).

accurately. It can, therefore, be deduced that the second is a more likely explanation. Another piece of evidence that supports the second theory is that Mr. Choe, the head of the family who lives in the house located on the site of the Jeong family home, wore mourning clothes during the *gut* offered to his female ancestor. That could be a remnant of the earlier rituals, which, according to Akiba (ibid.: 197), were held to appease the Mountain Spirit who in his anger had caused the girl's death. In that case, the occasion being the untimely death of his adoptive ancestor, Mr. Choe's mourning clothes are most suitable.

Records claiming that General Gim Yusin became the Mountain Spirit of Daegwallyeong after his death, exist in *Samguk sagi* and Heo Gyun's *Seongso bubu go*. However, the celebration of the sexual union between the Most Reverend Beomil Guksa and the Jeong maiden appears to be a recent invention of tradition. When exactly and by whom that tradition was invented is difficult to prove, but it can be fairly safely assumed that it occurred between Akiba's time (1950s) and Im's (1970s).

Why did they link the spirit of a celibate Buddhist monk and the tragic young virgin who was taken by a dreaded tiger? That intriguing question can be answered through the basic principles of *musok*. One of the most important functions of Korean shamanism is to disperse people's *han*, which can be roughly translated into English as unfulfilled desires or grievances. It is generally believed in traditional Korean society that sexual inexperience is one of the gravest *han* that a person can bear to the grave. In the case of Beomil and the Jeong maiden, they both died without experiencing sexual fulfilment, the former having been a consecrated Buddhist monk, and the latter an unmarried young woman. The celebration of their union is therefore a form of spirit marriage, which is still performed by some families of unmarried dead men and women in Korea. By joining them in marriage, it is believed that Beomil Guksa will be pleased and therefore will bring about good fortune to the inhabitants of the city, and the Jeong maiden will not wreak havoc among her former fellow residents of Gangneung.

Whenever it happened, the re-enactment of their sexual union is now firmly established as a tradition, which has become one of the most important ritual procedures of Gangneung Danoje. Aided by the writings of folklorists such as Im, various governmental publications and even a web site[15], this recent invention of tradition will continue to be an indispensable part of the Festival.

Secular Aspects of Gangneung Danoje

Games, plays and other forms of entertainment are integral parts of a festival, and competition is an important element. In Gangneung Danoje, traditional forms of Korean entertainment definitely outweigh western-derived games, which feature prominently in modern Korean (especially young) people's everyday lives.

Some of the plays and competitions have been designated as national or regional Important Intangible Cultural Properties by the government. For example, the farmers' music (*nongak*) competition is the Important Intangible Cultural property No 11-4; Haksan Odok Ddegi is the Gangwon-do Intangible Cultural Property No 5. Both these events are supported by members of their respective preservation societies. One of the best known Korean folk plays, previously performed by the local government owned slaves, called *Gangneung gwanno gamyeon geuk* ("Gangneung Government-owned Slaves' Masked Dance Play")[16], also has a special society formed for its preservation, and its members include the students at the Gwandong University and Gangneung University.

Gangneung gwanno gamyeon geuk is said to have virtually ended after the Gabo Reform (1894), when the government-owned slaves were liberated. After Japan's annexation of Korea, the Japanese authorities abolished it altogether (Bak Jintae 1990: 233). Im Donggwon wrote a detailed report on Gangneung Danoje and *Gangneung gwanno gamyeon geuk* in 1966[17], based on the information supplied by Gim Dongha (b. 12 January 1884) and Sin Hyeongwon (b. 5 September 1890).   As a result, *Gangneung gwanno gamyeon geuk* was designated by the Korean government as an Intangible Cultural Property, together with Gangneung Danoje. A detailed analysis of *Gangneung gwanno gamyeon geuk* is beyond the scope of this paper. However, since it forms an important part

---

15. Its URL is http//tano.hanter.co.kr/

16. For a detailed description of this masked dance play, see Im (1971: 234-236). Incidentally Im (ibid.: 234) writes that the play had disappeared completely by the early part of the nineteenth century, but was revived according to the wishes of the inhabitants of the area. However, Akiba (1954/1993: 201-202) briefly describes the same masked play.

17. Published as a book in 1971, pp 211-236.

of the festival, being a popularized and dramatized ritual of an apotropaic nature, it deserves a brief description here.

Today's performance of the masked dance drama is more or less based on Im's (1971: 234-236) descriptions. The dramatis personae are (1) *yangban*: a dignified but philandering nobleman, (2) Somu Gakssi (also known as Somae Gakssi or So *mudang*) – a pretty young woman of uncertain marital status, (3) two Jangjamari: fat caricaturized rich men representing wealth and good luck, who carry sticks to beat off malevolent forces, and (4) two Sisiddakddagi frightening meddlers with pock-marked faces, representing the Smallpox Spirit who interferes with people's happiness.

The play roughly consists of four scenes. In the first scene, two Jangjamari enter, dance around, fool around with the audience, clear the space for the drama, and generally interact with the audience. This part corresponds with the initial purification performed in *gut*. The second scene depicts the courtship between *yangban* and Somu Gakssi. After a brief resistance, the woman yields to *yangban*'s advances, and they dance together. In the third scene, a pair of Sisiddakddagi enter and interfere with the couple. They forcibly take away the woman from *yangban*, and dance with her. Outraged, *yangban* tears her away from them in anger. The woman pleads her innocence, but *yangban* still shows his displeasure with her. Feeling wrongly accused since she was merely dragged by them, she attempts suicide by winding *yangban*'s long beard around her neck. *yangban* takes pity on her and forgives her, but she is already dead. He carries her body and exits. In the meantime, the two Sisiddakddagis dance around. In the final scene, *yangban* and Somu Gakssi are reconciled, and everybody dances around, some members of the audience joining them.

This simple story depicts the existence of ubiquitous and ever-present malevolent spirits who constantly threaten people's happiness, and the triumph of man (represented here by *yangban*) over them. Although the woman dies, she reconciles with her lover through her dying act. At the end she revives and dances with everybody.

Other popular competitions include 1) Chinese poetry writing, 2) *shijo*[18] reciting, 3) folk song, 4) *juldarigi* (tug-of-war), 5) wrestling, 6) *geune* (swing), 7) obscene talk, 8) Gangneung dialect, 9) archery, 10)

---

18. A special form of traditional Korea poetry, favoured by Confucian scholars.

duho (a kind of quoits played with arrows shot into a bottle, which was popular among the *yangban*, and 11) *janggi* (Korean chess). Of those, the swing competition for women and wrestling for men seem to attract the most media attention. The prizes for the winners of the wrestling competition, cows and oxen, in particular, are prominently displayed, attracting many would be Hercules of the area.

What is interesting about the games and plays performed during Danoje l is the fact that many have been forgotten by the young Koreans of today, who are more familiar with western games and sports, such as baseball, football and tennis. Through this type of folk festival, traditional games and plays are transmitted to the next generation.

The vast Danoje arena is also crammed with various stalls which sell everything under the sun, forming a vast open market. This commercial aspect of the festival is said to contribute greatly to the local economy. Some stalls are fixed, while others are mobile, allowing the vendors to move around the site.

On 29 May 1998, on just one corner of the arena I came across a traditional Korean pumpkin toffee (*hobak yeot*) seller who sang and danced to the accompaniment of traditional Korean-style scissors, several make-shift restaurants selling traditional Korean market fare, such as cow's head soup, *dongdongju* (coarse rice wine), *surichwi ddeok*, a circus with tiny monkeys, a portrait painter, a fortune teller, a shooting gallery, a horticultural stall, and several clothing stalls. What was apparent to me was the fact that most of these stalls sold traditional Korean foods and other items, some of which are difficult to obtain in modern markets and department stores in Seoul and other large cities. Many items sold seemed to emphasize the unique Koreanness of the festival, and many of the stall holders specially donned themselves in traditional Korean clothing. The participants' pride in and enjoyment of the now-disappearing traditional Korean culture could be detected ubiquitously. I saw a vendor of Korean national flags doing a roaring business, as if to prove the point.

Conclusion

The folklorization of various traditional cultural heritages is frequently found in many non-Western countries, where the Western-oriented global homogenization of culture has taken place. There is a sense in which such phenomena are directly linked to the national identity and cultural nationalism.

The folklorization of the shamanistic heritage, in particular, occurs frequently, in places where shamanism has existed, often syncretized with Buddhism or other world religions. For example, Spiro (1967) describes a *nat* festival where shamans feature, and more recently, Epstein and Wenbin (1998: 120-138) present an ethnography of a revived folk ritual called *luröl* (*glu-rol*, literally "music" or "musical festival"), which is strikingly similar to Gangneung Danoje. *Luröl* is said to have been celebrated for more than 1,000 years, around the sixth Tibetan month. Although it was banned as the "backward remnants of the old feudal society" around the Cultural Revolution in 1966, *luröl* was revived after 1978 with a shift in the Chinese government's policy towards religion.

In Korea, where there has always been a strong shamanistic tradition, the shamanistic folk festivals, such as Gangneung Danoje have always featured importantly in people's lives. A huge number of people participate in, and greatly enjoy, these shamanistic festivals, where the shamans occupy the centre stage, bearing witness to the fact that shamanism is an integral part of the Korean culture, and is closely linked to the Korean national identity. With the onset of Westernization, modern Korean people (particularly the young) have been losing touch with their traditional cultural roots. Against the backdrop of global cultural homogenization, ancient folk rituals are revived and reinvented with changed ritual procedures and meanings to make them more appealing to the masses. This I have called "folklorization." As an example, we have seen how Gangneung Danoje has been revived and reinvented as one of the foremost folk festivals in contemporary Korea, attracting visitors from all over the country and even overseas.

Part 8

THE DAN-GUN MYTH AS AN INVENTION OF TRADITION, AND ITS SIGNIFICANCE IN KOREAN SHAMANISM

Introduction

This paper analyzes the Dan-gun Myth in relation to Siberian shamanism and Korean *musok*, and how Korean people including *mudang* perpetuate the Korean national identity and nationalism through it. It also addresses the issue of whether it is the "creation of a nation" through a creation myth by applying a historical perspective.

Many Korean scholars who study Korean shamanism trace its beginning to the Dan-gun Myth, since it contains many elements which are also found in Siberian shamanism (Yi Neunghwa 1927/1991; Yu 1975; Gim Yeolgyu 1977; Cho 1983), while Dan-gun as a shaman is generally refuted by Western scholars, e.g. Clark (1932/1961: 176). In this paper, 1 will discuss whether the Dan-gun Myth can be said to have its origin in ancient times, or is an invention of tradition compiled by the monk Ireyon. The questions that I pose will be 1) Why was it presented to the public in a written form for the first time by the monk Iryeon at that specific historical moment, and not before? and 2) Why was it presented in that particular form? I will go on to discuss how the Myth evolved after its publication, and by what process it came to provide the Korean people with the rationale for the Korean national identity and its perpetuation.

Dan-gun, whether he existed historically or not, plays a significant role in the modern history, ideology and everyday lives, of the Korean people. (Gim Heonseon 1994: 12) He also plays an important role in Korean shamanism, as one of the most important shamanistic deities. I shall conclude by discussing Dan-gun's role in contemporary Korean shamanism and its reasons.

The Dan-gun Myth

The Dan-gun Myth contains many elements which are also found in classic Siberian shamanism and also contemporary Korean shamanism. First of all, the name Dan-gun has a very similar sound to the Mongolian "*tengri*," "*tengeri*" of the Buryat, "*tanger*" of the Volga Tatars, "*tingir*" of the Beltir, "*tangara*" of the Ya*gu*t, etc. which all mean "sky" or "heaven. (Yu 1975: 34) The Koreanization of the word may have occurred to include "*gun* (prince)." Thus Dan-gun denotes "the prince from heaven," i.e. *cheonin*, which is a term for the shaman priest in ancient Korea.

The sacred tree, as the *axis mundi*, is a common motif in shamanism. (Eliade 1951/1964: *passim*) The Siberian shamans are believed to ascend to the sky through the *axis mundi*, which is often represented as a pole or a tree. The cosmic mountain linking the earth and the sky is also a prevalent concept. (Shirokogoroff 1935; Edsman 1967; Diószegi & Hoppál 1978/1996; Hoppál 1984)[1]

Hwanung's ministers of wind, rain and cloud, and 3,000 followers can be paralleled to the shaman's guardian and helping spirits respectively. Also his ministers of "wind, rain and cloud" suggest that his chief function was to ensure plenty of rainfall, which is the main requisite for agriculture. It is an interesting co-incidence that one of the most important functions of the shaman everywhere is to bring rain. (Lan 1985;Hogarth 1999: Chap 1 & 7) Hwanung's 360 kinds of work is similar to what modern Korean *mudang* attempt to do, i.e. curing disease, preserving long life, ensuring a good harvest, punishment where it is due, distinguishing right from wrong, etc.

The importance of the number "three" in shamanism has been observed by many scholars.(Hogarth 1999: Chap 3 & 7) What is significant is that "three" also features strongly in the Dan-gun Myth; Hwanin,

---

1. For a detailed discussion on this subject, see Hogarth 1999: Chap 1 & 7.

Hwanung and Dan-gun form the Trinity; Hwanin gave Hwanung three heavenly seals; Hwanung had three ministers; he taught humans 360 (multiples of three) kinds of work; and the bear became a woman after three times seven days (Note it is not written 21 days).

The bear's metamorphosis into a woman was accomplished only through adhering to the ritual restrictions, which involved eating prescribed ritual food and avoiding light. Light is generally thought to symbolize life. The prescribed food, i.e. 20 pieces of garlic and some bitter mugwort for such a long period of time, is tantamount to a starvation diet. In other words, the bear's trial is similar to a Siberian shaman's initiation experiences of the symbolic death and resurrection. (Hogarth 1999: Chap 2) Incidentally it is interesting to note that mugwort is also considered sacred by other peoples of the world. For example, among the Chumash it is called the "dream herb," and the shamans use it as a hallucinogen to enter trance states (Drury 1989). In contemporary Korean *musok*, rice cake made of mugwort (*ssuk tteok*) is an indispensable item for the *gut* table.

The union of gods and earthly women is also a common theme in Siberian shamanism.(Hogarth 1999: Chap 2) According to Sternberg's (1924: 476 ft.) interpretation, the nature of the relationship between the spirits and the shaman is primarily sexual.[2] He presents various evidence to support his argument. Shirokogoroff (1935) reports that a shamaness experienced sexual feelings during her initiation ritual; the Goldi shaman's ritual dance also had sexual connotations; in the Yakut folklore studied by Troschansky, there is constant reference to young celestial spirits descending to earth and marrying mortal women. (Eliade 1951/1964: 73-75) The union of Hwanung and the bear woman is a familiar shamanistic theme.

The zoomorphic character of the shaman's guardian spirits originating from totemism is a common feature of Siberian shamanism.[3] The Evenki shaman's cult of the bear, which, according to Anisimov (1958)[4], originates from the totemic source, is an interesting co-incidence. Ap-

---

2. In contemporary Korean *musok*, although the sexual relationship between the spirits and *mudang* is certainly not the primary element, it is reported from time to time. (Gim Taegon 1981: passim).

3. Basilov in Hoppál (ed.) 1984.

4. Cited by Basilov in Hoppál (ibid.).

parently Evenki shamans are prohibited to hunt the bear or eat its meat, since for a totemist, totemic animals are his blood relations. Among the Tuvans, of all the guardian spirits the bear spirit was considered the strongest, and only a "powerful" shaman could own it.[5] Also among the Yakut and Dolgan, the "animal mother" is considered the most important.[6] The shaman has an ie-kyla (animal mother), a sort of mythical image of an animal helper. A powerful shaman has a bear or an eagle as his animal mother. (Eliade 1951/1964: 89-90) A remarkable parallel can be found in the existence of a zoomorphic guardian spirit in the form of a bear-mother in the Dan-gun Myth. Guardian spirits are so fundamental in shamanism that "without the belief in helping spirits shamanism cannot be spoken of Vajda (1964: 272)," and "the ecstatic who attains the other world without the help of his guardian spirits is certainly no shaman Hultkrantz (1978/1996: 14)." Then Dan-gun with his powerful bear-mother as his guardian spirit can be said to be an archetypal shaman.

Is the Dan-gun Myth an invention of tradition?[7]

To understand why the Dan-gun Myth has had such a great impact on Korean people, despite the existence of many other creation myths (e.g. Bak Hyeokkeose, Gim Aljji, etc.), a historical perspective is required. The Dan-gun Myth first appeared in *Samguk yusa* (*Memorabilia of the Three Kingdoms*), compiled by the monk Iryeon (1206-1289) in the late 13th century.[8] Iryeon complied orally transmitted tales and descriptions of historical events, anecdotes and legends from the Three Kingdoms Period in the book. Although it is an important book for a study of the ancient folkways and institutions of that period, there has always been controversy surrounding the "scientific authenticity" of the book itself. *Samguk yua* states that the story appears in *Gogi* (古記: literally "the Old Chronicle"), which is somewhat ambiguous. It is mentioned neither in

---

5. Vajnštjn in Hoppál (ed.) 1978/1996: 169).

6. Hultkranz in Hoppál (ed.) 1978/1996: 14).

7. I use the term "invention of tradition" in Hobsbawm's sense. To quote him: "'invention of tradition' is taken to mean a set of practices, normally governed by overtly or tacitly accepted rules and of a ritual or symbolic nature, which seek to inculcate certain values and norms of behaviour by repetition, which automatically implies continuity with the past (1983: 1)" The same concept can be applied to a myth.

8. Although the exact date of Samguk yusa is not known, it is estimated to be the seventh year of King Chungryeol's reign (1281). (Choe Byeongheon 1994: 157).

Samguk sagi (1145)[9], which was written about a century earlier by Gim Busik, a scholar and a court historian, nor in Wiseo (魏書), an ancient Chinese chronicle, mentioned in the myth.

Some Japanese scholars therefore maintained that the Dan-gun Myth had been created during the Goryeo period (Mishina Shouei 1971; Inoue Hideo 1974).[10] A similar view was expressed by a few Korean scholars (e.g. Mun 1985). Circumstantial evidence indeed suggests that Dan-gun is a creation of Iryeon. He might well have written it, combining an old Korean myth with a myth of Mongolian or other central Asian origin.

Why then is such great significance attached to such a myth? To find the answer, it is important to examine the political and social circumstances in which Iron wrote his book.

Groryeo in the 13th century was a precarious nation, with military courtiers in revolt, peasant and slave uprisings and repeated foreign invasions to the north, first by the Khitans, and ultimately by the Mongols to whom Goryeo in all reality lost her sovereignty.

Under Yuan rule, there emerged newly powerful pro-Mongolian officials[11], who amassed private estates, eroding the state land resources and severely depleting state revenues. They threatened Groryeo political stability, causing the disaffection of a large section of the elite of the pre-Mongol period.

Throughout the 13th century, many literati were pushed out of their government posts by military men, who had previously occupied a lower status. These disfranchised people retired to remote mountain villages and lived out their lives in literary pursuits. The genre developed by these people was the prose tale, ranging from humorous tales personi-

---

9. "Korea's oldest extant history in annals form with separate chronological tables, treatises, and biographies, it reflects an aristocratic point of view and adopts a Confucianist histriographical perspective—that is, it is a frankly didactic work that evaluates the actors and event of Korea's early history from the viewpoint of Confucian moralism" (Lee Ki-baik et al 1990: 103).

10. Mishina Shoue 1971, **Kenkoku shinwas no sho mondai** (Problems in Creation Myths). Inoue Heido, 1974, 'Chosen no kenkoku shinwa (The Creation Myths of Joseon)' in **Sinra shiki so kenkyu (An Elementary Study of the History of Silla)**, pp 494-498. Cited in Seo Yeongdae (1994: 59).

11. These people gained power through offering services to Yuan, and include Mongolian language interpreters, military agents, etc.

fying ordinary objects, and a concoction of anecdotal material, poems and stories, and casual commentary. The enhanced national identity and nationalism, elevated by the trauma of repeated foreign invasions, was reflected in these tales. Semi-legendary founders and heroes were created based on oral legends, and eulogised in long epic poems to reinforce the national identity and instil nationalistic sentiment in the face of the pervading Mongolian influence. The Dan-gun Myth may well have been one of the most celebrated of those tales.

We may well ask a few vital questions. Why did it make its first appearance in that particularly distressed time in Goryeo history? Why did it not feature in *Samguk sagi*, which includes many other mythical tales of founders and heroes? Why was it not mentioned in works dealing with the progenitor of the Korean nation written in the previous century? Why is one unable to trace it in the ancient Chinese chronicle, to which it refers? Why was that particular myth, imbued with shamanistic elements, chosen? Why are there so many elements that can be traced to Mongolian or other north-eastern and central Asian sources? To provide answers to these questions, we must examine the political and social circumstances of the period in which the myth was compiled:

First, it was a period when the perpetuation of the Korean nation was under threat. A succession of Goryeo kings were forced to take Yuan princesses as their primary consorts, and their sons as legitimate heirs ascended the throne. The racial similarities between the two nations meant that there was a danger of the Goryeo people being biologically absorbed into the Mongolian nation.

Second, after 30 years of military and political invasion, Goryeo was now subjected to the Mongol's cultural colonization. Instigated by the newly emerged powerful pro-Yuan families, some of the elites were forsaking traditional Goryeo culture in favour of Mongolian costumes and hairstyles. The shock was even greater, since the Goryeo people had previously considered the Mongols "barbarians."

Third, Goryeo achieved peace on humiliating terms, agreeing to present annual tributes to Yuan. That in turn meant the opening of cultural exchanges between the two nations. The people of Goryeo therefore gained access not only to Mongol customs and culture, but also the myths and legends of the central Asian peoples.

The circumstantial evidence leads me to formulate the hypothesis: 1) the monk Iryeon "invented" the Dan-gun Myth to reinforce the Korean national identity and instil a nationalistic sentiment in the Goryeo people facing a national crisis, and 2) he may have written it combining an ancient Korean creation myth with a Mongolian or possibly some other north or central Asian myth.

To support the "invention of tradition" theory, there is some evidence to suggest that Dan-gun as the national progenitor did not exist before Iryeon's *Samguk yusa*. As mentioned earlier, it did not feature in *Samguk sagi* written a century earlier. Apart from that, before *Samguk yusa*, there were two books dealing with the progenitor of the Korean nation, which did not mention Dan-gun. One is *Dongmyeong Wang pyeon* (Section on King Dongmyeong) by Yi Gyubo, who wrote after reading *Dongmyeong Wangbon-gi* (the Original Chronicle of Dongmyeong Wang), in *Gu samguksa* (Old *Samguksa*). He said that "I realized that Dongmyeong Wang was not an illusion (*hwan*), but sacred (*seong*)," and that he wrote it "to let the world know that our country is originally a nation of sacred people."[12] He clearly saw King Dongmyeong (58 BC - 19 BC) as the Goryeo people's progenitor. Dan-gun was not mentioned at all. The other is a verse, entitled "Samdobu," written by the military courtier, Choe Ja (1188-1260) to celebrate the history of Pyeongyang. He wrote:

> When Seodo (Western Capital, i.e. Pyeongyang) was first
> created, an emperor called Dongmyeong came down from
> heaven.[13]

He did not mention Dang-un, who according to Iryeon's Dan-gun Myth, precedes Dongmyeong by a long period of time, i.e. about 23 centuries. This suggests that before Iryeon, the Dan-gun Myth did not exist in its present form.

My hypothesis that the Dan-gun Myth may not be a "pure" Korean myth, is obliquely supported by Sin Chaeho (1948/1983)[14] who did not think that it is a pure traditional Korean myth, but as containing many Buddhist elements. I would suggest that as well as the Buddhist elements, it contains many shamanistic elements. That provides an explanation for questions asked by some scholars concerning the reason why it contains such archaic concepts such as the bear woman (Mishina Shouei

---

12. Cited by Seo Yeongdae (1994: 66).

13. Cited by Seo Yeongdae (1994: 68).

14. Cited in Yi Pilyeong (1994: 9).

1971:429[15]; Choe Namseon 1988:12). We must take into consideration the fact that shamanism and myths containing shamanistic elements were prevalent among the peoples in Siberia, Mongolia and other parts of north and central Asia well into the nineteenth century. That suggests that the Dan-gun Myth may well have been based on a myth of Mongolian or other north or central Asian origin.

What is interesting is that the "mythical" (or what I call "shamanistic") elements are eliminated in the Dan-gun Myth which appeared in *Jewang un-gi* (1287) by Yi Seunghyu. In it Dan-gun's three ministers, Pungbaek (Wind), Usa (Rain) and Unsa (Cloud) are omitted, and Dan-gun is shown to be the son of Dansusin and Danung's granddaughter, instead of the son of Hwanung and the Bear Woman.[16] In other words, Yi Seunghyu eliminated some of the non-indigenous Korean elements. Since it is most likely that Yi Seunghyu was aware of Iryeon's work, which came earlier, the differences between the two versions of the myth can be interpreted as Yi's deliberate attempt to emphasize the historical aspect of Dan-gun as the progenitor of the Korean nation, to reinforce the Korean national identity.

The "invention of tradition" theory is often vehemently refuted by Koreans. As evidence that Dan-gun actually existed. Lee Ki-baik (1988: 64) writes about a stone depicting a story similar to the Dan-gun Myth. It was found in the family shrine of the Mu clan in Shan-tung Peninsula, China, and apparently can be dated to the second century A.D. However, to my mind, it does not constitute definitive evidence of Dan-gun's historical authenticity, the vast discrepancy in the time-scale still posing problems.

I am inclined to come to the conclusion that the Dan-gun Myth was created by Iryeon, or somebody/some people and compiled by him, to instil a sense of nationalism in the Goryeo people.[17] Nationalism is

---

15. Mishina Shouei writes (1971: 429): "It is incomprehensible why an ancient mythical element such as the bear woman should exist in a myth compiled at such a late period (i.e. 13th century)." In Mishina Shoue, 1971, *Kenkoku shinwas no sho mondai* (*Problems in Creation Myths*). Cited in Seo Yeongdae (994: 53-55).

16. Iryeon's reputation was widespread and he was designated Kukjon (National "sage" by King Chungryeol in 1283 (the ninth year of his reign). So it is highly probable that |Yi Seunghyu was famila with *Samguk yusa*.

17. By this, however, I am not refuting the existence of Go Joseon. Archaeological and other evidence suggests the existence of an ancient country in Korea. I am merely questioning the view that Dan-gun was its definitive founder.

a principle of political legitimacy (Gellner 1983). Therefore, nationalist sentiment is most aroused if the political unit is ruled by rulers who belong to a nation other than that of the ruled (Lan 1985). Under such circumstances, demands for a national hero become strong. Dan-gun was an ideal figure to meet such demands, enabling the Goryeo people to declare Goryeo's autonomy and supremacy through claiming their sacred and ancient blood line. Thus the Dan-gun Myth can be said to be an invention of tradition by the illustrious Zen monk Iryeon[18] (more exactly created by somebody/people and compiled by him) to provide the Goryeo people with the rationale for the national identity, and unity and solidarity of the Goryeo nation. Whether Dan-gun historically existed or not[19], the Dan-gun Myth has served a vital function since its first appearance in *Samguk yusa*, and is still of great significance to the Korean people.

The significance of Dan-gun to the Korean people

The Dan-gun Myth quickly found favour with the Goryeo public, and by the reign of Gongmin Wang, it would appear that it was generally known and accepted (Yun 1994: 718). Historical documents record the Dan-gun shrines nation-wide where sacrifices were officially offered to Dan-gun, most often together with his grandfather Hwanin, and father Hwanung.[20] Some of these sacrificial rites continue to this day.

In the sixteenth century, the awareness of Dan-gun decreased, and during the dominance of the Confucian literati (Yi Eulho 1994: 287), who tended to doubt his authenticity, Dan-gun was not frequently mentioned. However, in the 17th and 18th centuries, with the social changes on the international front, new reforms were called for and Dan-gun began to be put under the spotlight again (Yun 1994: 720). Towards the end

18. Anderson (1983/1991: 75)points out the role that various writers and artists play in creating an "imagined community."

19. According to the North Koreans' claim, they discovered Dan-gun's tomb in Pyeongyang in the autumn of 1993. Based on the age of the bones found inside the tomb, they maintained that the year of the foundation of Go Joseon was 3011 B.C., instead of the more generally accepted 2333 B.C. But No (1994: 35) argues that the tomb is more likely to be that of the Three Kingdoms period. There is a tendency among Korean scholars to view Dan-un as a historical figure, and Go Joseon as a historical nation, and hence they discuss its boundaries, political and other social structures, etc. (Yun 1986, 1992 & 1993) However, as No says, too much abstraction and ambiguity exits in the study of Dan-gun and his "nation," because of the dearth of historiographic materials.

20. For details, see Yun (1994: 393-544).

of the Joseon dynasty, the social and political unrest generated many new religions based on Dan-gun, such as Dan-gun-gyo (Dan-gun Religion) and Daejonggyo (The Great Religion) (Jeong 1995: 44-51).

Under Japanese colonial rule, Dan-gun took on a fresh significance for the Korean people, particularly for the Korean patriots fighting for independence in Manchuria. After independence, the newly born nation-state, the Republic of Korea, officially adopted the calendar called Dan-gi, calculating its first year as 2333 B.C., which was based on Iryeon's statement in the myth. It had already been used unofficially by the *Gwoneop sinmun*, the newspaper published by the independence fighters abroad. Dan-gi was officially used between 1948 and 1961, but after Park Chung Hee's military *coup d'etat* in 16 May, 1961, it was abolished. In 1949 the government proclaimed the third of October (by the western calendar) an official holiday to celebrate Gaecheonjeol (National Foundation Day).[21] On that day and also all through October, sacrifices to Dan-gun are offered on famous mountains nation-wide.

Today the Dan-gun Myth is so well-known that there does not exist a Korean who is not familiar with it, regardless of age, sex and class. Its pervasiveness in contemporary Korean society is manifested in a large number of Dan-gun-related new religions, research groups and other societies. According to Cho Hung-youn (1994: 338-342), as of April 1992, there were 33 religious groups, 12 research groups and 8 societies, in which Dan-gun plays the primary role. He reckons there are possibly also another 20 or 30 groups in existence.

Systematic studies of Dan-gun began in the 1920s by Choe Namseon, and since then a large body of work, numbering over 200 have been published (Seo 1994: 48). These studies have been conducted from historical, religious, folkloristic, archaeological and psychoanalytic perspectives.

Now that the reunification of the two Koreas constitutes a major task facing the Korean people, Dan-gun has been brought into relief once again. With the long-standing division of the country, the people of the north and the south have diverged in many ways under different ideologies and foreign influence. It is generally believed that Dan-gun is the most important factor (and some believe the only factor) to reawaken the solidarity and unity of the Korean people as "one nation" (Yun 1994:

---

21. It literally means "Commemoration of Heaven Opening."

passim; Gim Heonseon 1994: 12). If and when reunification is achieved, Dan-gun will once again play an all important role in reuniting a people, long separated by circumstances beyond their control.

Dan-gun's role in Korean shamanism

Dan-gun also plays an important role in Korean shamanism, as one of the most important shamanistic deities. It is generally believed that he forms Samseong (the Holy Trinity), together with his father, Hwanung, and grandfather, Hwanin (Cho 1990: 176), and is always depicted as an old man in Taoistic costumes accompanied by, or mounted on, a tiger. In many contemporary shamanistic shrines, the Holy Trinity of Hwanin, Hwanung and Dan-gun, are installed. For example, at *Musok* Bojonhoe, a training school for neophyte *mudang*, run by Bak Ino, three spirit tablets representing them are placed at the centre of the *beopdang* (altar).

It is difficult to say when Dan-gun started to occupy such a key position in Korean shamanism. Documental evidence suggests that Dan-gun, as the founder of the Korean nation, perhaps had not existed before Iryeon made it popular in the 13th century. For example, he is not mentioned in Yi Gyubo's *Nomu pyeon*[22]. Yi Gyubo names some prominent shamanistic spirits, such as Heavenly Jeseok (The Buddha Emperor), Chilwon (the Seven Stars Spirits) and Guyo (the Nine Stars Spirits). However, neither Dan-gun nor Samseong is mentioned.

Yi Gyubo refers to the Heavenly Being as "Jeseok (the Buddha Emperor)." Iryeon calls Hwanin (Dan-gun's grandfather) by the same name. Thus Iryeon seems to have diversified Yi Gyubo's Heavenly Being into Samseong (the Holy Trinity), i.e. Hwanin, Hwanung and Dan-gun. Samseong features in historical documents mostly dating back to the Joseon period. Frequent mention is made of the shrines dedicated to them and sacrifices offered, usually in October. (Yun 1994: 393-522)

In *Mudang naeryeok,* the pictorial instruction book in colour for *mudang* written during the Joseon dynasty, Dan-gun is clearly recorded as a deity, and sometimes referred to as Seongjo (the "Sacred Ancestor") (Yun 1994: 52). It can then be deduced that *mudang* specifically included Dan-gun as "the Sacred Ancestor" after he was popularly established as the national founder. *Musok*, in any case, includes all founders of successive Korean dynasties in its pantheon. It is natural that Dan-gun should

---

22. For details, see Hogarth 1999: Chap 7.

feature as an important shamanistic deity. Whether Dan-gun was introduced to *musok* at a later period or not, he is considered the apical ancestor of the Korean people by *mudang*. He is one of the deities who most often descend on a neophyte at his or her initiation ritual. A neophyte often "opens wordgate" with "I have come here by the order of Grandfather Dan-gun. I want to become a *nara mansin* (national shaman)."

In October, when Dan-gun is believed to have founded Go Joseon ("Old Joseon"), sacrifices to Dan-gun, called Dan-gunje, are offered throughout South Korea on major mountains. The oldest of these rituals appears to be that performed on Mani-san (Mt. Mani) situated on Ganghwa Island. It appears to be an old practice, since in Goryeosa, the location of Dan-gun's heavenly altar is clearly indicated ("Jiriji Ganghwa-hyeon," in *Goryeosa gweon 56*).

On a selected auspicious day in the tenth lunar month[23], Daehan Seunggong Gyongsin Yonhaphoe (the Korean Spirit Worshippers' Association for Victory over Communism) organizes a "security and unity convention and Dan-gunje." Members of the association meet at the shrine, situated near the top of Mai-san, and make offerings of wine, a slaughtered whole pig, fruits, rice, etc. The recipients of the sacrifices are not only Hwanung and Dan-gun, but also some of the past heroes of Korean history. The figures deified in this shrine are national heroes, who contributed to the nation's security at one time or another. These "great patriots" are honoured without fail every year by *mudang*, who forgo their income for the day. October, being a particularly busy month, their financial sacrifice can be considerable.

Apart from these official rallies, when they get together to pray for the security and unity of the Korean nation, *mudang* pray for the reunification and general welfare of Korea in private as well. I have often observed *mudang* praying for Daehan Min-guk (the Republic of Korea) during their *jinjeok gut*. Praying for the reunification of the Korean peninsula on South Korean terms can be satirically interpreted as *mudang* praying for their own survival. However, the tradition of *mudang* praying for national security and welfare goes back to ancient times, when shamans had political and jurisdictional, as well as religious, power.

---

23. It is held on the third day of the tenth lunar month, if possible, but not necessarily. I attended two Dan-gun-je; one was held on 10 October 1997, which was 9 September in the lunar calendar that year, and the other on 11 November 1993, which was 28 September that year.

In contemporary Korean society, in terms of politics, *mudang* do not feature as prominently as do the Kaffa shamans. However, they exert their influence on the preservation of traditional Korean culture, which is fast disappearing. The homogenized global culture, evolved from western culture, is threatening to take over the lives of the Korean people, particularly, urbanites and young people. Against that backdrop, *mudang* are carrying on "traditional" Korean culture through their religious activities. Therefore some of them have been designated human cultural treasures by the government, in recognition of their value as great repositories of traditional Korean culture.

It is no surprise that as self-appointed champions of Korean nationalism, contemporary Korean *mudang* should consider Dan-gun as the most important figure. In Korean shamanism as elsewhere in Korean culture, Dan-gun is used as one of the most powerful symbols of Korean national identity, together with *taegeuk-gi* (the flag), *mugunghwa* (the Korean national flower) and the crater of Mt. Baekdu. Hence the pictures of those symbols can invariably be found on the walls of *mudang*'s private shrines and also in shamanistic ritual halls.

Part 9

INSPIRATION OR INSTRUCTION?
SHAMAN-TRAINING INSTITUTES IN
CONTEMPORARY KOREA

Introduction

The predictions by various researchers of shamanism (e.g. Shirokogoroff 1935: 402) in the earlier part of the 20th century that shamanism would disappear completely with the advancement of science and technology, have not come true. On the contrary, there are signs that it has been re-emerging in various societies in recent times [Diószegi & Hoppál (eds) 1978/1996; Heinze 1991; De Rios 1992; Joralemon & Sharon 1993].

As of November 2001, the Royal Anthropological Institute library in London lists 386 books on shamanism in European languages, a large proportion of which are in English, but also in German, French, Spanish, Hungarian, etc. What is surprising is the fact that of those about 240 books (about 62%) were written in the 1990s, and some in this millennium. That suggests the global existence of active shamanistic practices in the contemporary world.

Shamanism, which is essentially an archaic socio-religious phenomenon, has always reflected the social structure and ethos, adapting its practices to social change. How then is it maintained and transmitted to the new generation of shamans in today's rationalized scientific world?

9. Inspiration or Instruction? Shaman-training Institutes in Contemporary Korea

143

More to the point, how does the shaman get recruited? Does modern technology have a new bearing, if at all, in the way shamanhood is initiated and maintained? Does advanced information technology mean that anyone can become a shaman through learning shamanic techniques?

It is an axiom that there are two ways of recruiting the shaman, namely by heredity and by "divine election" or "call from the spirits," which is manifested through various visions, illnesses and misfortunes. It is also generally accepted that once prospective shamans have decided to accept their destiny, they receive help from the spirits who actively give them clear guidance through visions, dreams and also by spirit possession (Shirokogoroff 1935; Eliade 1951/1964; Halifax 1982; Hoppál & Sadovszky 1989; Drury 1989; Vitebsky 1995; Diószegi & Hoppál 1978/1996).

However, this initial selection does not automatically qualify a person for shamanhood. In societies with a long established shamanistic tradition, a lengthy period of vigorous training under a teacher shaman called spirit mother/father is a prerequisite for attaining shamanhood (Eliade 1951/1964: 116 & *passim*). A classic example of van Gennep's "liminality" (1909/1960), this apprenticeship is often described by aspiring shamans as painful and arduous. The Korean shamans, collectively called *mudang*, traditionally go through a similar period of training under a teacher shaman called *sin eomeoni/abeoji* (literally "spirit mother/father") (Yi Neunghwa 1927/1991; Akamatsu & Akiba 1938; Akiba 1950/1987; Yu 1975: 281 & *passim*; Harvey 1979; Gim Taegon 1981: 62 & *passim*; Hwang 1988: 23; Kendall 1985: 58-60 & *passim*; Kendall 1988; Vitebsky 1995: 67).

Is this method of attaining shamanhood still relevant in contemporary South Korea, which has undergone a complete metamorphosis from a hierarchical agricultural society into a democratic industrialized nation-state? It is inevitable that changes should take place in the method of attaining shamanhood as in other aspects of shamanistic practices. It is therefore to be expected that the traditional method of serving a long arduous apprenticeship under an experienced *mudang* in virtual servitude, has undergone some form of modification. My research reveals that there are signs in some quarters that individual apprenticeship is gradually being replaced with group lessons in a classroom environment.

Murayama (1932: 157-164)[1], a Japanese colonial government officer who studied Korean shamanism during the Japanese colonial rule, mentions the existence of a training school in the southern provinces for hereditary *mudang*[2]. However, Choi (1991: 59) claims that such schools no longer exist in contemporary Korea, although she mentions an institute which offers four-week courses to interested laymen and some "advanced *mudang*." My research refutes Choi's claim, since I have visited three institutes which specialize in training neophyte *mudang* in Seoul. Two of them, in particular, are solid establishments with veteran shamans as teachers and a fair number of registered students who regularly attend the lessons.

Does the existence of *mudang*-training institutes mean that anybody can become one by merely attending classes? On the one hand, it seems possible. Some of my informants have told me in the field that anyone can become a *mudang*, if you associate with them long enough and if the conditions are right (Hogarth 1998: 138). Indeed many of my family and friends have expressed a concern, albeit jokingly, for the possibility of my becoming a socially lowly and despised *mudang* while researching Korean shamanism. They have repeatedly asked me: "Aren't you afraid that the shamanistic spirits may choose you to descend on?"

On the other hand, various scholars have noted that even when heredity is involved, not everybody can attain shamanhood. Apparently a prospective shaman has a certain inherent predisposition; he/she is often sickly, psychologically unstable, introspective, moody, solitary, anti-social, and is prone to prophetic visions and dreams from early childhood. Akiba (1950/1987: 65) also writes that even in families of shamanic lineage, some people can never become *mudang*, however much they want to, or try to be. Spirits apparently only descend on a person with certain psychic orientations, which enable him/her to mediate between them and the humans. We will try to find out which is closer to reality through analyzing my field data collected through participant observation.

In sum, this paper analyzes the results of my research into the con-

---

1. Cited in Choi 1991: 59.

2. There exist mainly two types of **mudang** in Korea, the inspirational type called **gangsinmu** ("god-descended shaman") and the hereditary type called **seseummu** ("hereditary shaman"). The former is the norm north of the River Han and some parts of the east coast, whereas the latter are prevalent in the south. For more details see Hogarth 1998 & 1999.

9. Inspiration or Instruction? Shaman-training Institutes in Contemporary Korea

145

temporary shaman institutes in Seoul, to divulge how much of a shaman's abilities are acquired through learning, as opposed to spontaneously bestowed inspiration, which I will call "the gift," in contemporary Korea.

Sources of Shamanic Abilities

Does the shaman acquire his/her special psychic abilities in later life, or are they inherent in him/her? Existing studies on shamanism reveal various results.

Cross-culturally there are basically two methods of recruiting the shaman, namely through divine election and heredity. However, since even in the latter case, the spirits "elect" those with a certain shamanic predisposition, being out of the ordinary, often sickly, solitary and introspective (Shirokogoroff 1935; Eliade 1951/1964; et al). They have visions and dreams in which they have direct contact with the supernatural world. Therefore the boundaries between the two are often blurred.

It is also more or less universally found that a prospective shaman's journey through life is fraught with difficulties, most notably the loss of loved ones, health, employment and other financial resources (Akiba 1950/1987; Choe 1978; Harvey 1979; Gim Taegon 1981; Kendall 1988; et al). This is generally interpreted by those involved as the spirits' way of forcing him/her to serve them, offering no alternatives.

My research among the Korean *mudang* reveals that they are without exception unfortunate people who have suffered great adversities in their lives. Since there are many people in similar situations who do not become *mudang*, what emerges is the fact that shamans are people with a strong character as well as inherent psychic abilities. Only those who have surmounted all the troubles and tribulations usually accompanying the spirit descent succeed in attaining shamanhood (Halifax 1982).

If the shamanic abilities are inherent in people, is there a need for their apprenticeship? Some, for example, Gwon, claims that they do not need any special training, since all they have to do is to follow the instructions of their tutelary spirits (Hogarth 1998: 120). Indeed in the early stages of their profession, when the most important task that they have to perform is fortune-telling or to give advice to their clients about their future, all that they have to do is to consult their tutelary spirits for guidance. However, through its long history Korean shamanism (generally called *musok*) has developed into such a highly artistic and intricate form of religion that it is not possible to rely on direct inspiration from the spirits alone. Rather like musicians, who have to master the techniques before exercising their power of inspiration, the *mudang* have to learn the techniques involved in their chosen profession.

As Eliade said, shamanism is the "technique of ecstasy," which is multifaceted and culturally patterned. In most cases, entering into states of trance/ecstasy requires little instruction for prospective *mudang* who already possess such abilities. However, what should be learned is the socially accepted method of reaching such a state, and formalities surrounding it. Since the mode of instruction varies according to social change, we will first examine the changing structure of the Korean shamanistic community.

Changing structure in the shamanistic community in Korea

The Korean shamanistic ritual, called *gut*, is the most important element of Korean shamanism. It would not be too far-fetched to say that without mentioning it, Korean shamanism cannot be discussed. Since the *gut* is the manifestation of the human devotion to the spirits, it is highly labour intensive, as well as extremely expensive.[3]

In pre-modern Korea, *mudang* relied entirely on the help of their spirit sons/daughters and close relatives, in preparation and management of *gut*. That is still to a large extent true, but there have been many changes.

These days, Korea is a newly industrialized and urbanized modern nation-state with great technological advancement. Modern conveniences, such as electrical appliances, are readily available. Butchers and supermarkets deliver sacrificial drinks and food, as well as other paraphernalia needed for *gut*. Neophyte *mudang* often have cars now, which means that they can prepare ritual food in advance in their well-equipped modern kitchens, and transport it to the ritual place in plastic containers. *Gut* are also most often held in commercial ritual halls, which provide food and render much assistance for a fee.

These days, many neophyte *mudang* are reluctant to serve arduous apprenticeship under spirit mothers/fathers, being able to make quite a lot of money since they are thought to have more psychic powers,. Therefore they become independent much sooner than in previous

---

3. For a detailed discussion of the reciprocal relationships between humans and the spirits, see Hogarth 1998.

9. Inspiration or Instruction? Shaman-training Institutes in Contemporary Korea

147

times. For example, Bak Ino, a veteran Seoul male shaman (*baksu*[4]), with a large number of students (also called his spirit sons/daughters), has a quick turn-over of them, since many of them leave after only a few months. Several of them confided to me that they did not want to serve under him, since they could only expect a tiny income, although it was they who "booked" the *gut* for their own clients through divination in the first place.

Being financially independent early on is all very well, but after a while many of them realize that their skills are woefully inadequate, and that they have much more to learn about *gut* and its technicalities. Since they do not want to give up their newly-found freedom thanks to financial independence, the ideal solution for all concerned appears to be a training institute. It has many advantages. The neophyte *mudang* can keep their independence whilst training, and they can benefit through easier networking and pervasive community spirit. It also provides them with social occasions, through sharing food and conversations and other forms of relaxation during and after class. When a fellow student has an initiation ritual (*naerim gut*), they have an opportunity for hands-on practice by performing a part in it. Teacher *mudang* also benefit, since they get regular extra income and respect due to them as teachers, as well as a sense of achievement.

In the next section we will examine the three *mudang*-training institutes to gain insights into the psychic and social makeup of *mudang* in contemporary Korean society.

Three Shaman-training Institutes in Contemporary Korea

Currently the best organized and most active society of Korean *mudang* is Daehan Seunggong Gyeongsin Yeonhaphoe (the Korean Spirit Worshippers' Association for Victory over Communism), the largest of the three officially registered societies of *musok-in* (*musok* people)[5]. Founded by an ex-politician called Choe Nameok in June 1970,[6] it cur-

---

4. **Mudang** and **baksu** are direct terms referring to Korean shamans, but carry derogatory connotations because of the long existing prejudice against them. **Mansin** is a more polite term, but is not so universal a term. I use **mudang,** since it is the most generally used term for Korean shamans, and I personally think that the stigma attached to the **mudang** will diminish in time.

5. Literally meaning '**musok** people,' it is a term of self-address preferred by **mudang**.

6. However, the society was officially registered in January 1971.

rently boasts over 40,000 registered members, with some 183 provincial branches (For a detailed discussion of the societies of shamans, see Hogarth 1998: Chapter 6.). It is based on the ideology of anti-communism, as shown in the inclusion of "Seunggong (Victory over Communism)" in the name[7]. All *mudang* regularly go on a pilgrimage, called "*san gido*" (literally "mountain prayer")[8], to high mountains to supplement and strengthen their spiritual/psychic powers. Since *mudang*'s rituals mainly take place on remote mountains, which are favoured sites for North Korean agents' covert activities, they have had plenty of opportunities to spot and help capture the latter. Since its foundation, the society has been awarded many commendations and prizes by the government for contributing to the capture of North Korean agents. It seems quite clear to me that the situation is that of exchange, i.e. there exist reciprocal relationships between the South Korean government and *mudang*, the former giving a seal of official approval to the latter, in return for which the latter contribute to maintaining national security. Capturing North Korean agents also serves the purpose of self-protection for *mudang*.

The *mudang*-training institute, which first had the official sanction of Daehan Seunggong Gyeongsin Yeonhaphoe is called *musok* Bojonhoe ("*Musok* Preservation Society"), run by one of the vice-presidents, Bak Ino, a veteran male shaman from Seoul. It is situated in the basement of the three-storey building which contains the offices of Daehan Seunggong Gyeongsin Yeonhaphoe. The number of students fluctuates between 20-40, their ages ranging from 20 to 50. The classes begin at 7 p.m. and finish around 10 p.m. The hands-on practice sessions consisting mostly of singing and dancing last about two and half hours, with the last 30 minutes allocated to the theory of *musok* and questions. According to Bak Ino, all the students have experienced spirit descent, some having already done *naerim gut* (initiation ritual) and some being on the verge of doing it. However, they still had to learn the basic skills for performing *gut*. As of 1993, the fee was around W 70,000 per month, with some fast learners mastering the arts in three to four months. What is amazing is that even *gongsu* (the spirits' messages sent through the possessed

---

7. For a detailed account of the society's activities, see Jang Hogeun (2000).

8. Shamans in other societies are also said to reinforce their powers through visiting mountains and rivers. For example, shamans in northern Peru (Joralemon & Sharon 1993: 28).

9. Inspiration or Instruction? Shaman-training Institutes in Contemporary Korea

149

shamans) is also learned and practised. Apparently although the contents of *gongsu* are sent by the spirits, the format, i.e. the vocabulary and the tone of voice, etc., have to be learned. Mr. Bak sits at the front facing his students, and sings and dances with them. That way he and his more advanced students lead the less experienced ones, who by copying them improve their own instrumental and vocal skills.

Mr. Bak also uses a textbook which he wrote, entitled *Jeontong Hanyang Gut Geori* (*Traditional Seoul Gut Procedures*). In the introduction of the book (Bak 1990: 6), he succinctly sums up the reasons why there is a need for such an institute: "Although the spirits give us inspiration and insights, the ways and means of putting them into practice must be learned." The book gives the novices a clear guidance as to the correct way to practise *musok*. It describes the basic principles of *musok* as venerating and paying proper homage to the Heavenly, Earthly and Human gods, ancestor worship, abandonment of self and emptying of one's mind,[9] and the ancient Chinese cosmology of *ohaeng* (The Five Elements). It explains various shamanistic practices such as fortune-telling, ritual procedures including dance movements. It also contains the transcriptions of usually orally-recited *mudang* songs, such as the Ballad of the Abandoned Princess (Bari Gongju *muga*)[10].

I first visited Mr. Bak's institute in 1993, and have made similar calls on a number of occasions since. What hits me each time I visit is the changing faces of the students, which suggests that a long apprenticeship under the same teacher *mudang* is perhaps slowly coming to an end. What is interesting is the continuing existence of the fictive kinship system, the students calling Mr. Bak, *abeoji* ("father") and referring to one another as sin *donggi* ("spirit sibling").

In 1993, I also visited a much smaller-scale, albeit possibly older, institute in Seoul, run by a musician called Gim Jongdeok. Although not a practising *mudang*, being of shamanistic lineage, he was well versed in all aspects of *musok* practices. He used a textbook written by himself for *mudang*, called Hanyang Seon geori (1989), which includes a history of Korean shamanism, classification of the gods and spirits, fortune-telling methods, *gut* procedures and transcriptions of the Ballad of the Abandoned Princess. However, it is not written in any systematic or organized way. On

---

9. This concept clearly suggests a strong influence of Buddhism on Korean shamanism.

10. For a complete English translation of this ballad, see Hogarth 2002: Chap. 6.

the day when I visited his institute in a seedy room situated in a ramshackle part of central Seoul, he had a Korean traditional musician called Gim Jonghui (b. 1918) who gave me some interesting comparisons between shamanistic music and other forms of Korean traditional music.[11] Gim Jongdeok, however, did not appear to possess the social skills of Bak Ino, and that day there was only one middle-aged lady student present, who just stayed for a short while. The fact that he is not a practising *mudang* who can actually show them what to do may have something to do with his lack of success as a teacher. After the visit, I lost contact with him, and do not know whether he still runs his institute or not.

The more successful *musok* Bojonhoe (*Musok* Preservation Society), however, recently seems to have lost the full approval and backing of Daehan Seunggong Gyeongsin Yeonhaphoe, because of Mr. Bak's fall from Mr. Choe's favour, following a minor financial scandal involving the former. Mr. Choe's current favourite appears to be Hong Gwangun (b. 1958), a veteran Seoul male shaman, who possesses great dancing, singing and social skills. He is a good example of the newly-emerging generation of better-educated dynamic *mudang*, and even has an email account. He often officiates in public shamanistic rituals praying for rain and the reunification of the two Koreas.

In January 2001, he opened a new institute called Jeontong Minsok Wiwonhoe (Traditional Folklore Committee) in eastern Soul, which has long been an area where *mudang* reside. The students ranged from 20 to 50 years of age, proportionally younger than those of *musok* Bojonhoe, and generally better educated. Mr. Choe told me that most of Mr. Hong's students held a high school diploma.

In the next section, we will examine the most recently opened *mudang*-training school in Seoul.

Jeongtong Minsok Wiwonhoe (Traditional Folklore Committee)

Can shamanhood be entered through instruction alone? An extended evening that I spent at Mr. Hong's institute as the sole invited guest and participant observer provided me with an excellent opportunity to try to find an answer to that question. Let us first briefly examine the events that took place that evening.

It was Friday, 12 January 2001, a bitterly cold day with the day-

---

11. For details, see Hogarth 1998: 40.

9. Inspiration or Instruction? Shaman-training Institutes in Contemporary Korea

151

time temperature hovering around -17°C. It had been snowing heavily for the previous few days, and Seoul took on the look of a city in Siberia. Despite the gloomy arctic conditions outside, the room inside was warm, clean and bright, the institute having been opened only a few days before. The lessons took place in a well appointed room with mirrored walls, and decorated with the usual symbols of contemporary Korean shamanism, such as the Korean national flags, calligraphy of the Chinese character '*bul*' (meaning the Buddha)[12], long strips of *osaek cheon* (long strips of five-different- coloured cloth), etc.

The students arrived more or less on time, around 7 p.m. There were 18 students in all, predominantly female with only four male students, making the female:male ratio 78:22 . Interestingly enough that is consistent with Gim Taegon's rough estimate and also with my previous research results (Hogarth 1998: 100).

To my surprise and delight, one of them, in fact the oldest member, turned out to be Gim Huisu (b.1949), the ex-wife of Jo Jaryong (real name, Jo Yongjin: b. 1946), an ex-vice president of Daehan Seunggong Gyeongsin Yeonhaphoe. Apparently, they had got divorced following Mr. Jo's affair with one of his spirit daughters, and his wife had experienced the spirit descent soon afterwards and had become a *mudang*. During my two previous visits, I was unable to make contact with her, but promised myself to track her down in one way or another. Oddly enough I wrote in my book (Hogarth 1998: 121-122) that she had a distinct shamanic predisposition, but did not practise as a *mudang*, mainly because she was involved in it anyway through her husband. Mr. Jo often said that she would have become a *mudang*, if he had died of blood cancer in his twenties as the doctor had predicted. As it happened, with the help of the spirits, he had miraculously recovered from his terminal disease, and had "employed[13]" the spirits ever since[14] After their separation and subsequent divorce, she suffered the usual fate of a prospective shaman, illnesses, loss of fortune, etc., which forced her to become a *mudang*. She

---

12. The Buddha which is represented in various forms is one of the most important symbols in Korean shamanism. For a detailed discussion of the extensive syncretism of Buddhism and shamanism in Korea, see Hogarth 2002.

13. Mr. Jo prefers to use the term "**sin-eul burida**" which literally means "use/employ/manage the spirits," instead of the more generally used phrase "serve the spirits." In other words he insists that he is the master of the spirits, rather than vice versa.

14. For details of Jo Jaryong's biography, see Jo 1996a, 1996b

was fascinated to hear that I had actually written about her shamanic predisposition in my book. She also seemed to be overjoyed to see me, and confided to me that she decided to attend Mr. Hong's classes, because she wanted to improve her dancing and singing skills as well as learn more about the theories.

The students got dressed in red *dopo*[15] and sequinned red *gat*[16], the costume normally reserved for the Mountain Spirit. According to Mr. Hong, he made them wear proper costumes, since it made them feel as though they were participating in a real *gut*, thus making the practice more effective. The class was assembled in several rows, rather like a dancing class, with the wall facing the students entirely covered with mirrors. Mr. Hong positioned himself at the front, where he gave lectures, demonstrated various dances and also played the hour-glass drums, to the accompaniment of which most dancing took place.

Many of the students already knowing the basic dance steps, the lessons consisted of mainly rehearsal-like practice sessions. What I call "possession dance," which is a frenzied dance involving twirling and jumping up and down immediately prior to the spirit descent, was repeatedly practised. The dance was followed by *gongsu*, the spirits' messages through *mudang*, which usually begins with '*eo ut ja*' in the Seoul area *gut*. However, the practice ended with that phrase, since apparently the rest of the *gongsu* was the domain of the spirits, and need not be learnt.

Mr. Hong's classes differed from Mr. Bak's in that the former concentrated on the dancing practice while Mr. Bak combines dancing, singing and playing of the instruments in more or less equal measures. Rather like a ballet teacher, Mr. Hong gave individual attention to his students, going around the room, pointing out students' mistakes and correcting them. Every so often they all sat down, and Mr. Hong explained some of the dance movements or other aspects of *musok* practices. About half way through, the students had a break with snacks and drinks brought in by some of the senior members.

After another long session of group dancing practice, three ladies demonstrated the routine choreographed by Mr. Hong. They had

---

15. A traditional formal outer wear for gentlemen, it is often used as costumes for gods.

16. A gentleman's headgear resembling a top hat, it is secured with two pieces of string tied under the chin. It is usually made of horsehair and comes in black. Red ones are only used for **gut**.

9. Inspiration or Instruction? Shaman-training Institutes in Contemporary Korea

153

been chosen to perform at the *gut* to be held on the 30th of March on top of Nam-san[17], to pray for the reunification of the two Koreas. Gim Huisu[18], Jo Jaryong's ex-wife, was one of the group, being the eldest and considered to be one of the best of Mr. Hong's students. To the uninitiated, this shamanistic dance programme closely resembled any traditional Korean dance. The other students had a rest, while watching the chosen trio rehearse the fairly long and intricate dance routine.

I soon noticed that Choe Bokhui, one of the most experienced *mudang* of the group, was performing a similar dance, albeit her own creation, right behind the group. She was an excellent dancer, almost every bit as good as the trio. When I asked a male *mudang* sitting next to me what she was doing, he told me that it was Ddok-Suni (literally "Smart Suni," Suni being a popular girl's name) who was dancing, not Ms. Choe. He went on to explain to me that Ddok-Suni was a bright little girl spirit who ran errands for Ms. Choe, often conveying messages to the *mudang*'s tutelary spirits. It struck me as amusing that Ms. Choe, who was not included in the trio of chosen dancers, should join them unofficially on the side with her impromptu free-style dance, but nobody seemed to care. It seemed to me that a mild grudge that Ms. Choe possibly bore about having been excluded, might have played a part in the sudden descent of Ddok-Suni on her. Displaying her dancing skills to the onlookers might well have helped alleviate her disappointment.

The class ended when the trio finished their rehearsal at around 10.30 p.m., and a few packed up their bags and went home. However, about a dozen of them stayed behind for an after-class party, to which I was most warmly invited. Despite the lateness of the hour and the treacherous road conditions outside, I was persuaded to stay, particularly after Ms. Choe told me that Ddok-Suni wanted to play with me and show me how well she could sing.

What followed was an informal jolly party with plenty of food and drink. After an evening of exertion, the students relaxed completely sharing rice wine, soft drinks, cold roast pork, nuts and other snacks, as well as various banter and jokes. When the atmosphere became very mellow, there was the inevitable round of singsongs. One of the first to volunteer to sing was Ms. Choe, or to be more precise Ddok-Suni. "The little girl

---

17. Literally South Mountain, which is situated on the centre of Seoul.

18. Korean women traditionally keep their maiden names even after marriage.

spirit" sang very well, interspersing her songs with various short dialogues with Ms. Choe whom she called "my Mummy."

Suddenly a neophyte shaman in her thirties, called Yi Sunok, jumped up and started talking in a little boy's voice. Being one of the youngest of the group and a new *mudang*, she had stayed right at the back and had been almost invisible, except for the fact that she was a strikingly pretty woman with regular features, smooth skin, and a tall slim figure. 'The little boy spirit (*dongja*)[19],' who so suddenly descended on Ms. Yi, started playing around with Ddok-Suni, playfully arguing with the little girl spirit, chipping in with 'his' childish songs, etc. The little boy spirit's sudden descent on Ms. Yi can be said to be a parallel to that of Ddok-Suni on Ms. Choe. Being a junior in terms of age and experience, Ms. Yi would have had to wait for a long time before her "proper" turn came. Her subconscious wish to join in the fun as soon as possible might well have caused the little boy spirit to descend on her, enabling her to chip in almost immediately.

After that all order and "propriety" vanished. On one corner another *mudang*, started dancing to their songs. The whole thing was spontaneous and natural, and everybody present took it as a matter of fact. While all this was going on, the rest of the group continued to eat, drink and converse. It looked as though the party would continue throughout the night, but I had to leave this fascinating scene at around 1.30 a.m.

What I witnessed that evening confirmed my view that shamanhood cannot be attained merely through learning. As we saw earlier, all the students have already experienced the spirit descent in one way or another before registering at the institutes. Nobody teaches them how to contact the spirits. What they learn is merely the technique involved such as singing, dancing and the mode of speech, etc.

Conclusion

South Korea, one of the few places on earth where shamanism has been continuously practised over the centuries, has recently undergone dramatic changes in her social structure. Almost completely vanished is the rigid social hierarchy with little social mobility. Good educational opportunities exist for most people, which enable them to escape from the

---

19. Dongja is one of the spirits that most frequently possess *mudang* these days. It is often said to be the spirit of the *mudang*'s close relative, such as her dead son or nephew.

9. Inspiration or Instruction? Shaman-training Institutes in Contemporary Korea

155

social class into which they were born.

Strangely enough, however, *mudang* are people who still believe that they cannot escape their destiny. Despite the breakdown of the rigid social class system, the stigma that has long been attached to *mudang* persists, and they are still socially shunned and marginalized. *Mudang* themselves, especially older ones, are often ashamed of their profession, and do not reveal their true identity to their neighbours, and in extreme cases even to their relatives, especially their in-laws. What Akiba's *mudang* informants said is still true in contemporary Korea: "Nobody wants to engage in this profession which is so despised by people. One is obliged to do it, because to disobey the spirits means certain death (Akiba 1950/1987: 65)."

Conversely, not anybody can become a *mudang*, since the most vital element in shamanhood is "the gift," i.e. special abilities that enable one to enter another reality, which is neither seen nor felt by ordinary people (Siikala 1978; Winkelman 1992; Merkur 1992; Joralemon & Sharon 1993; Hines 1993; Gray 1997; et al). Harner (1973, 1980) seems to believe that another reality exists and claims that anybody can practise shamanism with appropriate training and help, such as group coaching and hallucinogens. However, I cannot say that such a reality actually exists, since I have never experienced it. On the other hand, I cannot absolutely deny its existence, just because I am personally incapable of getting in touch with it. What I can say for certain is that only those born with such abilities can attain shamanhood. Whether such a gift is born out of sensory deprivation or extreme stress, or a mere psychopathy is also hard to say categorically. My experience suggests that despite the existence of *mudang*-training institutes in contemporary Korea, a person who can competently mediate between humans and spirits is born with the gift. Since in Korea two of the most important means of this mediation are singing and dancing[20], a person who is to become a great *mudang* is also naturally gifted in those areas.

As Jo Jaryong, a veteran male shaman, said (1996b: 20-21), no amount of learning can create true *mudang*, but studies are necessary for them to interpret the divine messages correctly and convey them to the humans in a socially accepted manner.

---

20. The Chinese character for 'shaman' is '*mu*,' which depicts two people (人人) linking heaven (ˉ)and earth (_) through dancing.

Part 10

DRUMBEATS IN THE KOREAN SHAMANISTIC RITUAL: "MUSICAL MAGIC" OR "MAGIC OF NOISE"?

Introduction

Drumbeats form the basis of the shamanistic ritual cross-culturally. According to Eliade (1951/1964: 174) the original function of the drum in the shamanistic ritual is enabling the shaman to enter a state of altered consciousness in which it is possible for him/her to communicate directly with the spirits. Therefore the shamanic drums are imbued with rich symbolism, which signifies their role as a means of communication or transport between the human and spirit worlds. That is why in traditional Siberian-type shamanism the drum is sometimes described as the "shaman's horse" or the "stag," being a vehicle for the shaman to be transported to the realm of the spirits (Eliade ibid.: 173-174). In other words, according to him, drumbeats in the shamanistic ritual represent "musical magic."

On the other hand, according to early scholars of shamanism, such as Lehtisalo (1937) and Harva (1938), the shamanic drum was originally used to drive away evil spirits. In other words, the drumbeats are "magic of noise." However, Eliade (ibid.: 174) interprets Lehtisalo and Harva's ethnographic evidence as examples of alteration in function.

This paper attempts to find the answer through analyzing the Korean shamanistic ritual (*gut*). The indispensable hourglass drums, called *janggu*, will take centre stage, but the significance of the presence of several other percussion instruments used in *gut* will also be discussed.

Although the same basic principles of the Siberian-type shamanism apply to *gut*, complications arise in that the Korean shaman (generally known as *mudang*) invites the spirits down to this world to join the human company rather than making a trip to their world. Therefore this paper also addresses the questions: "Does this basic difference have any bearing on the role of the drum in *gut*?" and "If so, in what way?"

The pivotal role of the drum in the shamanistic ritual

It is a truism to say that the shamanistic ritual is unthinkable without the presence of the drum. It is generally acknowledged that the drumbeats help the shaman to enter an altered state of consciousness in which he/she makes direct contact with the spirit world. Much research therefore has been done into the shaman's drums, especially symbolism represented in shapes, materials used, decorations and inscriptions. The common theme is the drum as the shaman's vehicle to transport him/her to the spirit world, hence its description as the shaman's horse, stag or a canoe for crossing the sea that separates this world with the other (Shirokogoroff 1935: 297). Among Siberian peoples, the drum is traditionally made with birch wood, which is considered the *axis mundi*, or the world tree, that links the two worlds. The skin used for the drum must be only that of a male reindeer. It is often decorated with animal figures such as reindeer, bear, tiger, dragon, and various birds, i.e. the shaman's guardian power animals which help him on his journey to the realm of the spirits, thought to be up above the skies. The frequently found round shape of the drum is said to represent the sun, and celestial motifs such as the stars and the moon can also be found. The drum's role in aiding the shaman's flight to the upper world is also symbolized by feathers which are sometimes attached to it. Among other decorations are animal bones and metal discs symbolizing them, signifying the drum itself becomes the shaman's spirit helper (Howard 2002: 68). The drum is sometimes oval, in the shape of an egg, symbolizing the rebirth of the shaman as a supernatural being capable of making direct contact with the spirits. In Scandinavia, the drum takes the shape of the figure eight, signifying motherly fertility (Howard 2002: 67), again a symbol of the shaman's rebirth. This shape is also echoed in the hourglass drum most popularly used in the Korean shamanistic ritual, which we will discuss later.

The inherent power of the drum to help a person to reach another reality has been demonstrated by a renowned anthropologist Michael Harner (1980) who runs an experimental shamanic workshop to cure various psychological ailments and/or physical illnesses. According to him, "Simply by using the techniques of drumming (sonic driving, a monotonous percussion sound), people from time immemorial have been able to pass into these realms which are normally reserved for those approaching death, or for saints."[1]

But complications arise, since in many shamanistic rituals, such as the Korean *gut*, the shaman does not take a trip, but the spirits descend on the human company through possession of the officiating shaman. In that situation then, does the role of the drum change, and if so, how? Before we address that issue, it is necessary to examine different types of shamanistic rituals that exist in spatial and temporal variety.

Two types of shamanistic ritual based on "trance" or "possession trance"

Although theoretical debates continue to rage as to what shamanism is among scholars, most would agree that one of the most important features of shamanism is the utilization of an altered state of consciousness for the purpose of making direct contact with supernatural entities [e.g. Shirokogoroff 1935; Eliade 1951/1964; Underhill 1965; Harner 1980; Rogers 1982; Hoppal (ed) 1984, 1989; Drury 1989; Heinze 1991]. Altered states of consciousness are institutionalized in many societies ancient and modern, although in differing forms. Bourguignon (1968, 1979) classifies altered states of consciousness as "trance" and "possession trance," linking them to differing levels of societal complexity and, ultimately, to types of subsistence economies. To Bourguignon, "trance" is typically, though not always, utilized by men, and "possession trance" by women. "Trance" involves interaction with supernatural beings through hallucinations, visions or dreams, often by sending the subject's soul on a journey, so that he sees, hears, and interacts with the spirits while retaining his identity. "Possession trance," on the other hand, involves an

---

1. In interview with Nevill Drury, in the magazine Nature and Health 9/2, cited in Howard (2002: 69).

10. Drumbeats in the Korean Shamanistic Ritual: "Musical Magic" or "Magic of Noise"?

159

impersonation of the spirits, the trancer, in amnesia, becomes the spirit. "Trance" is generally induced by hypoglycaemia, brought on by fasting, sensory depravation, isolation, mortification, or hallucinogens (Harner 1973), while "possession trance" is usually induced by drumming, singing, dancing, crowd contagion, or more rarely drugs. "Trance" is a private experience, reported from memory to the community. "Possession trance" is a public performance, to be observed by all present, and it requires an audience.

Bourguignon bases her initial discussion on a comparative study of 488 societies, later whittled down to 84. She concludes that "the greater the societal complexity and the higher the level of subsistence economy the more likely the society is to employ 'possession trance' rather than 'trance.'" "Trance" is prevalent in the Americas and among predominantly hunting societies, while "possession trance" is usually found in agricultural societies in Asia and Africa. Types of altered states of consciousness are linked to patterns of socialization and stress, to different stages of life, and to culturally defined gender roles. "Trance" is associated with more independent and self-reliant males, with stress linked to young men pressured to achieve independence in hostile settings such as hunting, warfare, and sex. "Possession trance" is utilized by obedient and compliant women, stress linked to new marriage, moving from natal homes, and domestic conflict.

There is of course a discrepancy between Bourguignon's theory and shamanic techniques used to achieve an altered state of consciousness (Hogarth 1998b). In shamanism, where both types of trance can be utilized depending on the location, singing, dancing, and especially drumming are common techniques used by the officiating shaman in almost all rituals. Memory and the degree of control exercised by the shaman during an altered state of consciousness also challenge Bourguignon's view (Kendall 1985: x). For example, although the Korean shaman has no knowledge of what the spirits will say through him or her before "possession trance," the oracle is clearly remembered afterwards. However, Bourguignon's perhaps too simplistic theory can be applied to classification of multifarious shamanistic rituals into two basic types, i.e. the shamanistic ritual where the shaman takes a trip to the spirit world, and the one where the spirits join the human company on earth by possessing the officiating shaman. For brevity I shall call the former "T-type" and the latter "PT-type" shamanistic ritual.

Her theory is also linked to the evolution of human society, i.e. "trance" is the prototype institutionalized altered state of consciousness, since it is more prevalent among simpler societies, while "possession trance" is a later development, prevalent in more advanced ones. Therefore, her theory is also useful in tracing the changing roles of the drum in the shamanistic ritual.

The functions of the drum in *gut*, a "PT-type" shamanistic ritual

Most of the existing studies on the shaman's drum, which we examined earlier, are concerned with the "T-type" shamanistic ritual. Much of it also applies to the "PT-type" ritual, since the shaman still enters an altered state of consciousness for possession to occur. The only difference is that it is the spirits, not the shaman, who take a trip.

Then is the drum considered as a means of transport through which the spirits travel to this world, in the same way it is for the shaman? There is very little indication of that, in the symbolism of the shapes, materials and decorations, etc. of the drums used in the "PT-type" shamanistic ritual. A possible and logical explanation for that could well be that it is generally believed that the gods and spirits can fly or float around freely to go wherever they wish, hence do not need tangible means of transport to travel between the two worlds in the way that shamans, after all mortal beings, do.

However, the drum still plays vital roles in the "PT-type" shamanistic ritual. As well as sending the shaman into an altered state of consciousness, it has taken on various other functions. An analysis of the Korean shamanistic ritual well demonstrates various roles that the drum plays in this type of ritual.

The most indispensable percussion instrument in contemporary *gut* is the hourglass shaped double-headed drum called *janggu* (or *janggo* in Sino-Korean). *Janggu* which is also called *sheyo-go* (narrow-waited drums) date as far back as Han and Wei China, but is generally said to have been imported to Korea during Goryeo (918-1392) dynasty from Sung dynasty China (960 – 1278). *Janggu* is usually beaten with a narrow bamboo stick on the right-hand side while the left hand side is beaten with the bare hand. However in Korean shamanistic ritual both sides seem to be beaten with sticks, although the left-hand side is beaten with a stick with one end covered with cloth to produce a softer muffled sound. The reason why *janggu* got so firmly established as an indis-

10. Drumbeats in the Korean Shamanistic Ritual: "Musical Magic" or "Magic of Noise"?

161

pensable prop in *gut* may be because of its shape which is imbued with various symbolism. As we briefly discussed earlier, the hourglass shape, the female form, symbolizes the birth of the shaman as a being with supernatural powers which enable him/her to mediate between humans and spirits. The two drum heads at the opposite ends symbolize the two opposing worlds of humans and spirits with the narrow part in the middle implying the difficult journey that lies between the two. Various other drums also feature, such as *buk* (barrel drums) and *sogo* (small drums).

As well as different kinds of drums, other percussion instruments, are also employed, the most important being the brass cymbals, called *jegeum* or *bara*, which make a louder and more piercing noise than the drums. The brass cymbals are used for more dramatic moments such as those of the spirits' entrance or when the evil spirits are chased out of the room. A bunch of small brass bells are used to maintain the shaman's altered state of consciousness. Gongs of various sizes, called *jing*, *ggwaeng-gari*, etc., which produce noisy regular beats. The gongs are favourite instruments in *nongak* (farmers' music), because of their exuberant sounds, and therefore have naturally been incorporated into *gut* in agrarian communities, particularly community *gut*. The influence of the farmers' music on provincial *gut* is also reflected in the style of beating the drums, which is faster, wilder and fiercer than in Seoul *gut*. In the Seoul area, since they tried to emulate court music (according to Bak Ino, a veteran Seoul male *mudang* in a private conversation), the music is slower and more refined. In Jindo, an island off the south coast of Korea, where shamanistic traditions are very much alive, a unique percussion instrument, called *jeongju* is played by *mudang*, during Jeseok *gut* (*gut* for the Buddha Emperor). It is a small brass rice bowl-shaped instrument with a string attached through the hole in the bowl, beaten with a deer-horn stick. What is interesting is a small piece of deer horn used as a stick for beating it, which symbolizes a flight up to heaven, the concept of which is also prevalent in many Siberian tribes. In this simple instrument one can detect the syncretism of Siberian-type shamanism, the ancient Korean worship of heaven, and Buddhist elements (Hogarth 2002).

At the beginning of a *gut*, *mudang* notify the spirits of the commencement of the ritual and invite them down to join the human company (Yi 1927/1991; Akamatsu and Akiba 1938; Akiba 1950/1987; Gim Taegon 1981; Hwang 1988; Kim Geumhwa 1995: 288-289). *Janggu* is beaten slowly to accompany the shaman's monotonous recitation of the personal details of the sponsors and beneficiaries of the *gut*, such as the names, the addresses and the dates of birth. Those details are often written on a piece of paper, which is fastened onto the strings holding the two sides of the drum together. The chief officiating *mudang* then calls all the spirits and invite them to join the *gut*, not forgetting the spirits of those who cannot receive proper offerings from their descendants through ancestral rites, owing to their "bad deaths." This part can last quite a long time.

After that, chasing away undesirable evil spirits and purifying the ritual place takes place. In the "T-type" ritual it is the shaman who goes far away to the realm of the spirits, the ritual place remains secular, hence there is no great need to purify it, although a degree of sacredness is required. In the "PT-type" ritual, on the other hand, the ritual place must be prepared so that it is suitable to receive the sacred guests who descend on it. Therefore, great care is taken to cleanse and sanctify the ritual place. In the case of Korean shamanism, preparations can start days before the actual ritual, and take on various forms, such as covering the ground with yellow soil, cordoning the area off with rope to stop unclean people entering and polluting it, etc. (Yi 1927/1991; Akamatsu and Akiba 1938; Akiba 1950/1987; Gim Taegon 1981) At the beginning of the ritual, a tray with small bowls containing salt, water, sometimes ashes or red pepper powder, a small knife, etc. is carried by a shaman over every corner of the room and the front yard, before being scattered into the air, to eliminate the unclean elements. Paper is burned as a symbolic gesture of purification. These ritual gestures are accompanied by deafening noises produced by the fast furious beating of all the percussion instruments used for a particular *gut*, ranging from the hourglass drums to brass cymbals. In Seoul area *gut*, all the participants except for the shamans directly involved in this part are asked to leave the room, in case they are hit by the dangerous "darts (called "*sal*")" which are thought to be shot indiscriminately by the evil spirits out of spite as they flee the room. [2]

Then follows the main part, which comprises of 12 sections, called "*geori*," each dedicated to a particular god, ancestor or spirit. The number 12 is a symbolic one, in that it represents the wholeness rather than the exact number (Yu 1975). Hence it can contain many more then

---

2. For details of the purification procedure, see Hogarth 1998a, 1999.

10. Drumbeats in the Korean Shamanistic Ritual: "Musical Magic" or "Magic of Noise"?

163

12 sections. Each *geori* starts with the invocation of the spirit to which it is dedicated. A *mudang* dressed in the particular costume representing a spirit, enters a trance state through the monotonous but rapid loud beatings of the drums and cymbals before getting possessed by a spirit and speaking on its behalf. There is also a theory that the spirits recognize their costumes and descend on them (Yu 1975). Once possessed, he/she uses the brass rattles to maintain the trance state.

The final part of the *gut*, called *dwitjeon*, is performed to feed all the nameless sundry hungry ghosts in the spirit of the obligation of the haves to give to have-nots prevalent in traditional Korean society (Hogarth 1998a). This is a long part, in which the *mudang* calls all the names of the sundry ghosts that are known at the time of the good. The invocation of the spirits is done with the accompaniment of the monotonous drumbeats, rather like at the beginning, but with less ceremony. The *mudang* performing this part often changes into her/his everyday clothes, ready to go home as soon as this part is over.

The percussion instruments then have various functions in *gut*. First of all, the drum is used to call and invite the spirits. Secondly, they send the shaman into the state of trance/ecstasy, thereby inducing possession. The wild but rhythmic beating of the drums and the cymbals accompanying the shaman's frenzied dancing, is a prelude to possession, at the beginning of each part. It is a common theme in most societies in which shamanism is practised. Unlike many peoples who use hallucinogens for achieving ecstasy, the highly developed music and dance are all that the Korean shaman needs to achieve it. Thirdly, it is believed that the tremendous noise they make frighten away evil spirits, which wield noxious influence, causing illness and misfortune on the living. More precisely, noise, like fire and water, is a purifier. According to Freedman (1967: 17-18), that is why at a traditional Chinese wedding, during the procession of the bridal sedan chair, firecrackers are let off, while bands play loud music. In sum, the drumbeats in *gut* are both "musical magic" and "magic of noise."

Conclusion

Eliade (ibid.: 174) maintains that originally the indispensable drumbeats in the shamanistic ritual are "musical magic," which sends the shaman into an altered state of consciousness. According to him, their other function of driving the evil spirits away, i.e. as "magic of noise," is a later development or the alteration in function.

His theory is along the similar lines of Bourguignon's theory of the institutionalized altered states of consciousness based on "trance" and "possession trance." They both seem to suggest that the "T-type" ritual where the shaman takes a trip to the realm of the spirits is the prototype, whereas the "PT-type" is a later development. We might add that since purification and elimination of the evil spirits is of paramount importance in the "PT-type" ritual because of the actual presence of the sacred beings in the ritual place, the drumbeats took on an additional function of purification.

However, that neat theory is problematic since Lehtisalo and Harva, who suggested the role of the drum as "magic of noise," conducted their field research in "T-type" societies, where the shaman takes a trip upwards. Also the concept of the noise being capable of driving the evil spirits away has been present since ancient times, as shown in ancient Chinese customs, such as letting off firecrackers at a wedding.

The contemporary Korean *gut* is a "PT-type" ritual, with its officiating shamans predominantly female. The drum plays multiple roles, and also various other percussion instruments are added to create different moods and symbolisms which are deemed to be meaningful to the participants at a given time. However, there is some evidence to suggest that it might originally have been a "T-type" ritual with male shamans who also held political and jurisdictional power in society (Kim Taegon 1990; Hogarth 1999). Elsewhere I have maintained (Hogarth 1999: 252) that there still remain traces of the shaman's flight to the upper world in the "possession dance" of the contemporary *mudang*. For example, the sleeves of some of the costumes are extended with long white kerchiefs, giving the impression that they appear to be trying to fly when they dance the "possession dance," flapping their arms up and down in front of them. In the ancient times, then were the drums used solely for the purpose of sending the shaman into a trance state, or were they also beaten furiously to chase away the evil spirits? In the absence of systematic detailed records of *gut* over the ages, it is impossible to know for sure. Therefore, we cannot categorically ascertain that the drumbeats were originally "musical magic," and later took on an added function of "magic of noise." All we can say for sure is that the drums fulfil both functions in contemporary *gut*. The concept of the noise frightening the evil spirits away as well as "sonic driving, a monotonous percussion sound" putting

10. Drumbeats in the Korean Shamanistic Ritual: "Musical Magic" or "Magic of Noise"?

165

people in a trance, have existed from ancient times. In view of the fluid and dynamic nature of the shamanistic ritual, where impromptu ideas are put into practice as and when the officiating shamans deem necessary, it would not be too far-fetched to say that the drumbeats in the shamanistic rituals have long fulfilled the dual function of inducing trance and eliminating unclean elements, including evil spirits. It would not be possible categorically to state that the former is the original function and the latter an "alteration."

Part 11

ESCHATOLOGY AND FOLK RELIGIONS
IN KOREAN SOCIETY

Introduction

Eschatology is best represented in practices of various folk "religions" as well as mortuary rituals in Korean society. This paper analyzes three of the most important Korean folk "religions," namely shamanism, ancestor worship and geomancy, in relation to the Koreans' tripartite view of the human soul.

The concept that a human being possesses three souls is prevalent in traditional Northeast Asian societies (Shirokogoroff 1935: 52,134; Eliade 1951/1964: 216). In some of these societies it is believed that after a person's death, his/her soul diverges into three; one soul goes to the other world, a second floats about in the air near the home of the dead person, and the third stays in the grave.

This paper examines whether modern Koreans also share the tripartite view of the human soul after death. Earlier literature on Korean religions (Gifford 1892; Clark 1932/1961) seems to confirm that a similar view existed in Korea. For example, Clark (ibid: 113) states categorically that "Koreans believe that everyone has three souls." More recently, however, the concept of three souls seems to be less universally known and believed. For example, Janelli and Janelli (1982: 59) appear to doubt the existence of such a belief in contemporary Korean society. According to them, it lacked both "conviction and consensus" in a small Korean village where they conducted fieldwork. Their view is also reflected, albeit obliquely, in other books and recent articles dealing with Koreans' view of death and what happens to a human soul after death (O 1978; Gim Taegon 1981; Jang Cheolsu 1995; Choi Joon-sik 1996; Lee Hyun Song 1996). My own field research would also indicate that many modern Koreans are not even aware of the concept of three human souls.[1]

I was therefore interested to come across an overt display of "three human souls" in a *gut* (Korean shamanistic ritual) held for a man in his prime who died of a heart attack in his sleep. The *gut* was officiated by a group of *mudang* (Korean shaman) from Gangwon-do, headed by a veteran called, Gwon Mallye, a long-term acquaintance and informant of mine. An analysis of this *gut* will be the starting point for interpreting the meaning of three souls to contemporary Korean people.

First I will examine the eschatology reflected in *musok* (Korean shamanism), based on comparisons with mortuary *gut* from various regions. Next a comparison will be made between *gut* and mainstream mortuary rituals. Finally I will discuss how the concept could be linked to other seemingly unrelated folk practices, such as ancestor worship and geomancy. I will conclude by addressing the question why the concept of three human souls does not appear to be so prevalent in contemporary Korean society.

A Gangwon-do[2] *Gut* for the Victim of a Sudden Death

Mudang from Gangwon-do claim that their *gut* are the most "orthodox" of all. Although such boastful remarks are common among all Korean shamans, *gut* from this province seem to retain many traditional features, which have largely disappeared in rituals of other regions. A *gut* performed for the dead (*jinogi gut* or *ogu gut*)[3], particularly one held for

---

1. During my fieldwork, three souls were not usually mentioned voluntarily by my informants without my prompting. It is only when I venture to suggest the concept that many of them would tell me that there is such a notion.

2. -do is a province.

3. There are basically two kinds of **gut** for the dead. One is held soon after a person's death, and the other some time afterwards. The former is called **jin jinogi gut**, and the latter, in the case of Gangwon-do **gut**, **josang haewon gut** (**gut** for dispersing ancestors' grudges). As we shall, see later, the names, as well as the ritual procedures, have regional variations.

the recently dead, called *jin jinogi gut*, contains paraphernalia and procedures which clearly reflect Koreans' popular views of death, dead souls
and afterlife.

I attended a classic *gut* of that kind on Thursday, 23 April 1998,
held in Samgoksa, a commercial ritual hall (*gut dang*) situated on top
of a mountain in Seoul. It was sponsored by the family of a 48-year-old
man who had been found dead on early Sunday morning (12 April). He
had been perfectly fit and well until the night before, when he had enjoyed convivial conversations over beer with his son who had been on a
weekend home visit. His son was in the army, doing his national service.
Unlike most other *gut* which are attended by mainly female members
of the family, most of the close cognatic relatives of the dead man were
present.[4] Playing the central roles in the *gut* were the 72-year-old father,
21-year-old son, 44-year-old wife of the deceased, in that order in terms
of hierarchy. His mother had passed away some years before. Other
participants were his wife's mother[5], his wife's elder brother's wife,
his wife's sister, his wife's younger brother, his elder brother's wife, his
younger sister and her young son, and his father's sister.

The *gut* was performed by the chief officiating *mudang*, Gwon
Mallye (b. 1950), together with other *mudang* called Ham Okja (b.
1934), Min Sun-geum (b. 1946), Gim Chunja (b. 1956) and Bak Okja (b.
1946).

The order of the *gut* was similar to that of other cognate *gut* from
various areas.[6] It consisted basically of: (1) purification of evil spirits
and unclean elements (*bujeong*) and the invitation of all the spirits to the
gut, (2) entertainment and direct interactions with the Village Guardian
spirit (Seonang), the Mountain Spirit (Sansin), the Seven Stars Spirit
(Chilseong), the ancestral spirits (*josang*), the dead man's spirit, the
Death Messenger (Saja), The Official Spirit (Daegam) and the General
Spirit (Janggun), and finally the dead man's spirit again, (3) sending off
the spirits and the final tearful farewells between the dead person and his
family, and (4) finally feeding of the sundry ghosts.

The *gut* conformed to the usual pattern, but with a few extra

---

4. Most **gut** are instigated and attended by women. Men sometimes take part, but usually
   with extreme reluctance and awkwardness.

5. His wife's father is dead.

6. The order varies from **gut** to **gut**. For details, refer to Hogarth (1999: Chapter 4).

parts. After purification and invitation, the sponsors lit candles and joss sticks, offered wine to the spirits, and reverently kowtowed to them several times. A brief discussion about the order of parts took place among the *mudang* at this point. The *mudang* then prepared the symbol of the dead man, which was the most interesting part of the *gut* for the current discussion. A small rectangular straw mat[7], measuring about 1.8 by 2.5 metres, was used to make the symbolic representation of the dead man. A new set of traditional Korean clothes was placed on it, on top of which Gwon put three white paper cut-out men, with the name and the date of birth of the deceased written on each of them. The father and the wife of the dead man (his son arrived later) in turn poured spoonfuls of raw rice over each paper man, chanting "thousand, ten thousand, million sacks of rice." Similarly, rice grains (or more rarely pearls) are put into the mouth of a corpse in Jeju-do and other areas. Go (1990: 174) interprets it as a symbolic gesture to stop the dead man reporting to the king of the underworld about the living. However, I would interpret it as a gesture to give the dead man a means of spreading largesse on his difficult path to the other world, and obliquely to wish that he would bring great wealth to his surviving family in reciprocation. For the same reason, several W10,000 notes were also deposited on top, after which the mat was rolled and tightly bound with three white pieces of cloth. Three pieces of white paper folded into triangular shapes were inserted through the binding cloths. Everything was done in threes, or in the triangular form, which confirms the importance of the number three in Korean shamanism.[8] The colour used in connection with the dead was all pure white, which symbolizes "west," or heaven.[9] The prepared mat looked as through it had a corpse inside it, and was used throughout the *gut* to represent the dead man.

Then the spirits arrived in the order of the Village Guardian spirit (Seonang), the Mountain Spirit (Sansin), the Seven Stars Spirit (Chilseong) and the ancestral spirits (*josang*). The ancestral spirits who appeared through Min were those of the dead man's great grandfather, his grandmother, his grandfather and his mother. The scenes enacted

---

7. Poor folk used to roll up a corpse in a straw mat for burial in the old days.

8. The number three has the same significance in shamanism in general, and in Northeast Asian people's cultures (See Covell 1986; Hogarth 1998: 27).

9. For colour symbolism in Korean shamanism, see Hogarth (1998: 29-30).

between the living and the dead were reminiscent of psychoanalytic sessions. For example, his grandmother's spirit repeatedly attributed his untimely death to the family's regular eating of dog meat. His mother's spirit was severely rebuked by his still distraught father for "having so heartlessly taken her own son away." She defended herself against her husband's wrongful accusations, and they finally forgave and blessed each other. After venting all their grievances, grief, resentment and unfulfilled desires, and such sentiments, everybody was reconciled with one another, and the spirits invariably ended up giving their promises of help to the sponsors.

After the ancestral spirits, the dead man possessed Min, who fainted on the ground in the front yard and was carried indoors by fellow *mudang*. When in the room, Gwon castigated the spirit (the possessed *mudang*), "You unfilial person, how could you go so far away before your own parent?" The first thing "he" did, however was turning to "his" wife and asking for "his" wallet and passport. His wife replied, "Didn't we send them all off to you by burning them?" "He" then knelt in front of his father, with "his" head touching the ground and sobbing uncontrollably. His father asked Gwon who it was, and the *mudang* explained that "he" was lost for words, because he had passed away so suddenly and unexpectedly. When the old man realized who it was, he burst into a rage, and shouted at "him," "You bad wicked creature! The most unfilial wretch! How could you, how could you die before your own father!" The old man continued to call "him" all sorts of names with tears streaming down his cheeks. The most ironic profanity that he throws at his son's spirit was "*i jugil nom*," which literally means something like "You rascal, you shall be killed!" This particular phrase, which is equivalent to "Damn you!," is employed by a person only on the greatest provocation, which bears witness to the importance that Koreans put on life. The dead spirit could scarcely face his father, and finally left the possessed *mudang*, who indicated the spirit's departure by jumping up and down with the rolled mat ("the body") held high over her head. The wife then took the "body," stood at the altar holding it for a few minutes, and placed it there.

Then Ham, the old *mudang*, recited a few passages from the Buddhist Scriptures, beating the wooden gong. Another *mudang* rotated a glass of wine and a pair of small knives (*sinkal*) around everybody in the room. The two *mudang* walked around the widow, beating the gongs loudly and waving lighted joss sticks all around her. The Buddhist Scriptures are believed to have the power to keep the evil spirits at bay, and wielding knives and making loud noises, to frighten and chase away the evil spirits which have gathered around the widow.

Death is believed to be not only "pollution" in itself, but also highly contagious, hence anybody who comes into contact with it is touched by its potently dangerous forces. The most vulnerable is the closest relatives of the deceased, particularly his/her spouse who is believed through their horoscope to be responsible for the death. In other words, the death occurred because a person is destined to be a widow/widower. The deceased spirit descended on the *mudang* several times, and talked to the other members of his family, sharing greetings, tears, and food. There followed the *mudang*'s prayers for the wellbeing of the deceased spirit and the family. Ham chanted the prayers, which comprised passages from the Buddhist Scriptures and her own impromptu prayers.

Then the reciting of the Ballad of Bari Gongju/Beridegi (the Abandoned Princess) took place. Min recited the story of the Abandoned Princess, the unwanted seventh princess of the King, who later owes his life to her. The princess, the epitome of unconditional absolute filial piety, is an ideal guide of the dead on their difficult journey to the other world.[10] Towards the end of the long recitation of the Bari Gongju epic, the dead man's son arrived, and took his seat where his grandfather had sat before. A tender scene between the "father" and son took place, the former giving various words of advice to the latter. The most emphatic advice was not to eat "dirty things," i.e. dog meat. He said that his death was caused by his family eating it so often.

Now that the encounter between the dead man and his all-important son and heir had taken place, the former was ready to go on the long journey to the other world. Gwon performed the distribution of the "three souls" of the deceased. With the father, son and wife of the dead man seated on the floor around the "dead man" mat, Gwon unrolled it. A paper sailboat decorated with colourful paper cut-outs was brought in, and she put a large candle, a bowl of water, three triangular folded pieces of paper and some paper flowers into it. She lit some joss sticks, and proceeded to transfer the money from inside the mat into the boat, using

---

10. For full transcriptions of a Seoul area version, see Hogarth (2003: 251-266). The Gangwon-do version has some variations, but is essentially the same.

a pair of chopsticks, chanting "Jijang Posal (Kshitigarbha-Matrix of the Earth: the Guardian Bodhisattva of the Dead)." She then picked the three paper men with chopsticks one at a time, dropping one each on to the lap of the father, the son and the wife of the deceased, in that order. After that she picked the paper cut-out men with chopsticks and burned them on the candle flame, one at a time. The ashes were placed in the bowl of water, and the family were told to water a flowering bush with it later.

This part eloquently reflects Koreans' views of the dead soul and its journey into the next world. A boat of the dead suggests that the other world is far away from this world, separated by a huge watery obstacle such as a river or sea. Its path is pitch dark, hence a large candle to light it. A bowl of fresh drinking water is essential to keep the journeying soul alive. Paper money and flowers are needed to bribe the Death Messenger and many dangerous savage creatures that the dead soul will meet on the way.

More importantly, here we see clear manifestations of the three souls, which are symbolized by three white paper cutout men. The three paper men can be interpreted as symbolizing three human souls, representing heaven, man and earth respectively. One is given to the father, who is often analogized to heaven according to Korean folk beliefs. It could be interpreted as suggesting that one soul goes to the other world, which is often vaguely represented by heaven. The second is given to the son, the human heir who will carry on with ancestral offerings to the dead man. The second soul then could be interpreted as going into the ancestral tablet. The *mudang* gives the third to the wife, who personifies earth as in "earth mother."[11] Interestingly enough, my interpretations coincide in principle with Clark's view (1932/1961: 113).

At long last, the time had come for the dead man to leave this world, but his spirit did not want to embark on his long difficult journey to the other world. He bid a final farewell to his relatives, one by one, lamenting pitifully: "The path in front of me is so very lonely, and so sad. Do I have to go alone? I feel so sad I can't go. They say if I cry, the road

---

11. Gwon told me that the third paper man would have been given to the dead man's mother, had she been alive. But I think the wife would have still received it. In contemporary Korean society, a man's wife seems to feature more prominently than his mother on occasions like a funeral, particularly a shamanistic ritual for the dead. Also a man's wife seems to take on the role of his mother in due course. In fact, one often comes across a man calling his wife, 'Mum.'

to the other world is even darker, so I won't cry." The extreme reluctance of the spirit to leave this world made this part very long. The spirit made all sorts of excuses to linger on. He even offered to sing for his father for the last time, and sang a song. His sister was startled to hear the song, which she claimed was the only one that her dead brother could sing reasonably well while alive. Apparently the *mudang* possessed by his spirit had not been told about it. This incident is an example of mysterious coincidences that often occur in Korean shamanism.

Gwon performed various "purifying" acts, such as tearing five different coloured pieces of cloth and hemp to purify of all sorts of evil spirits and forces. She also wielded a pair of small knives, symbolically "killing" all the evil spirits around those present. Finally, the Death Messenger (*Saja*) arrived to take the dead spirit away to the other world. Gwon personified the Death Messenger, wearing a hemp cloth headband, and carrying a dried fish and three pairs of straw shoes. The dried fish apparently symbolize the dead; three pairs of straw shoes[12] imply the long journey that he has to face ahead. The clothes bought for the dead man were taken outside in the yard and burned. It is believed clothes and other possessions of a dead person are sent to him/her through burning them.

There followed a more cheerful part featuring fun-and-money-loving Daegam (The Official Spirit), which is the caricature of the Joseon dynasty corrupt official, prone to taking bribes. This part eased the tension of the previous more serious parts, helping the sobbing relatives to dry their tears by briefly taking their minds off their tragedy.

Gim was then possessed by a series of general spirits, which on this occasion included the spirit of Admiral Yi Sunshin[13]. She smoked three cigarettes simultaneously, when possessed by general spirits. What is inexplicable is that in the ordinary state of consciousness, she cannot normally even bear cigarette smoke.

Next, a prediction of the next reincarnation took place. Three bowls, each piled high with raw rice, were brought in, and Gwon declared that the deceased would be reincarnated into a bird, after examin-

---

12. Sometimes three straw shoes, rather than three pairs, are used. Some claim that it is because there are three Death Messengers (See *Gut* Series 17: 28).

13. Strictly speaking, Admiral Yi, but the Korean word, *janggun*, does not differentiate between generals and admirals. Strangely enough, despite Yi's high profile in Korean history and society, he usually features neither separately nor prominently in *gut* (See Hogarth 1998: 83-87).

ing the patterns made on the rice.

Finally, having dispersed all the grudges and grievances of the deceased through open dialogues and gifts, they were ready to send the dead spirit away. Amid loud lamentations of the dead spirit (possessing Gwon) and the surviving family, Gwon tore through a long piece of hemp cloth, which symbolizes the dead man's journey to the other world. The cloth represents the bridge over the great river which is believed to separate this world and the next.

The mortuary *gut* from Gangwon-do, described above, contains elements which clearly suggest the existence of the concept of three human souls after death. But before going on to discuss how a similar concept is reflected in the other two folk "religions," it is necessary to present a comparative study of regional variations, lest I get accused of basing my argument on an isolated case study.

Korean eschatology reflected in mortuary *Gut*: regional comparisons

Today mortuary *gut* constitute the most important part of shamanistic rituals in Korean society, as Hwang (1985: 76) observed. With the advancement of modern medical technology, healing, which used to be the raison d'être of *gut*, is no longer the main reason for performing *gut*. Since inexplicable illnesses are often attributed to the recently dead or the victims of past disasters, mortuary *gut* often take the place of the classic healing *gut*. Death generates so much grief in the bereaved that when they face with it, particularly when it occurs unexpectedly, as well as performing the usual elaborate mortuary rituals, they sometimes turn to *gut* to seek consolation or explanation.

At a financially insecure time such as the one following the sudden collapse of the Korean economy in late 1997 (popularly dubbed "the IMF Age"), the most frequently-performed *gut* seem to be the mortuary rituals. During my stay at the Academy of Korean Studies between September 1997 and August 1998, these were the *gut* that I was most frequently invited to attend. What is interesting is the fact that during my previous research trip (from September 1993 to April 1994), mortuary *gut* only accounted for less than 20% of the *gut* that I was invited to attend,[14] although it was the most consistently performed *gut* with the

---

14. For details, see Hogarth (1998: 62).

least seasonal fluctuations (Hogarth 1998: 62). Whilst rituals praying for good luck or community *gut* were noticeably less frequently held, in the event of a loved one's death, particularly an unexpected one, people did not seem to begrudge the huge expenses involved. The importance of mortuary *gut* is well represented in the series of books published by Yeolhwadang (1983 - 1993).[15] Of 20 books describing various regional *gut*, eight (40%) deal with mortuary *gut*.

It is considered fairly axiomatic that there are two types of *mudang* (Korean shamans), namely inspirational type called *gangsinmu* and hereditary type called *seseummu*. The main difference between the two types of *mudang* is the spirit possession/descent, which the former experience, while it is absent in the latter. However, since the basic principles underpinning the ritual practices of both types do not differ greatly, I have maintained that there is no need to differentiate the two, or ignore one type in favour of the other, in discussing the basic ideology of Korean shamanistic rituals. (Hogarth 1998, 1999) I shall therefore put emphasis on the underpinning principles, rather than specific behaviours *per se* of the *mudang* in *gut*.

Although I have attended and recorded various *gut* from different regions, for the sake of objectivity, in this section I shall analyze the material contained in the eight books dealing with mortuary *gut* in the Korean *Gut* series published by Yeolhwadang. Four books (vol. 5 *Pyeongan-do dari gut*, vol. 8 *Hamgyeong-do mangmuk gut*, vol. 17 *Hwanghae-do jinogi gut*, vol. 20 *Seoul jinogi gut*) portray *gut* officiated by *ganginmu*, and four (vol. 4 *Suyongpo sumang gut*, vol.6 *Jeolla-do ssitggim gut*, vol. 7 *Jejudo muhon gut* and vol. 14 *Tongyeong ogwi saenam gut*) deal with those performed by *seseummu*.

All *gut* start with the purification of evil spirits and unclean elements, but it is considered particularly important in mortuary *gut*, because of the implication of pollution and danger connected with death. *Mudang* enact various ritual gestures of purification on and around the bereaved several times throughout the *gut*. Malignant spirits are generally anthropomorphized, hence the substances that cleanse, disinfect, repel or kill humans, such as water, fire (in the form of ashes), salt, ground red pepper, arrows (see 14: 52) and sharp knives, are employed to chase

---

15. Although this series of books largely consist of photographs, they give readers vivid pictorial records of the **gut** performed in contemporary Korean society.

away or kill them (see 4: 18-19; 5: 35, 79; 6: 33-35; 7: 19; 8: 42-43; 17: 50-51,56-57; 20: 30-31). Loud noises and joss sticks are also believed to be effective in chasing away unclean spirits and purifying the ritual space. In the case of Hwanghae-do *gut*, officiating *mudang* stuff their mouths with *hami/hamae* (a piece of white paper folded into a triangle), to prevent *bujeong* ("impurities") escaping or entering through the mouths (see17: 79).

The soul container, i.e. the symbolic dead person, takes various forms in mortuary *gut*. The modern trend is simplifying it as a large paper cutout ball resembling a brain, or a series of paper cut-out men (often three in number). The paper cutout soul sometimes resembles a Confucian-style ancestral tablet (see 5: 78). Paper cut-outs are sometimes tied onto a pole and placed on top of raw rice in a rice container for the spirit descent. A close relative holds down the pole, and it is believed that when the dead person's spirit descends on it, the pole shakes (see 7:29, 34-35, 106,108; 8:44-45, 86). As we saw in the Gangwon-do *gut* earlier, in some areas, a symbolic dead body is made with a straw mat with the dead person's clothes rolled inside it (see 14:38-49). In Jeolla-do, instead of a straw mat, straw is used to form a shape of a man, (see 6: 31-33), and is called "*yeongdon mari*" (Hwang 1985: 87), and in Tongyeong it is called "*yeongduk mari*" (Jeong Byeongho 1989: 91). A paper soul house, or a basket containing the paper cut-out "soul," is also used in conjunction with various other representations of the dead person (see 6: 35-37, 69; 14: 26- 30, 54-58).

The shape of the symbolic "soul," which resembles the brain tissues, suggests that the human soul is believed to dwell in the brains and leaves the body after death. The straw figure or the straw mat, which contains clothes, the "soul" (or the three souls in the Gangwon-do case), money and rice, represents the mortal body. The impure "body," which has suffered a highly "polluting" death, has to be cleansed before joining the sacred world of the spirits and ancestors. This concept is dramatically enacted as repeatedly washing the symbolic body with water and herbal water in the *gut* from the Jeolla-do and adjoining areas (see 6:33, 64-65; 14:42-45), hence the name *ssitggim gut* (cleansing *gut*).

The most important part of any mortuary *gut* is the direct encounter between pole held firmly by a member of the sponsoring family, which is commonly called "*daenaerim*," i.e. the spirit descent through the pole (8: 44-45, 86; 17: 29,34-35, 107). Sometimes the spirit of the dead person is supposed to descend on a lotus flower (5: 54-55). The meeting and venting of all the pent-up feelings of all those concerned has a highly healing effect through catharsis, which has a parallel to psychoanalysis. This psychotherapeutic aspect of *gut* has been dealt with by many scholars, and beyond the scope of this paper (Rhi 1970, 1977, 1978, 1983, 1985).

The most universally found concept is the bridge over the watery boundaries that separate this world from the other world. In most mortuary *gut*, if not all of them, there exists a part enacting this concept. The bridge is usually represented by a length of hemp or cotton cloth, which the *mudang* cuts through. Sometimes the representation of the dead person, such as a doll or a soul container, is slowly pushed up and down the bridge, symbolizing the dead person's journey to the other world (see 4: 68-71; 5: *passim*; 6: 36-37, 68, 101; 8: 57-61, 89). Money is put on the "bridge" for the dead person to "spread the largess" ("*injeongeul sseuda*").

Money, which preoccupies most modern Koreans, is thought to be needed for the dead souls to pay their way out of difficulties encountered on the way to the other world (Im Seokjae 1985: 86, 88).[16] High-denomination notes, usually W10,000 notes, are placed everywhere, not only on the "bridge," but also on ritual foods, artificial flowers, paper cut-outs, the five flags representing the five directions, musical instruments, fans, etc.[17] The ubiquity of these bank notes makes them appear to be essential props in contemporary *gut*. They are even stuck on *mudang*'s brows, cheeks and chins, held by their hat strings, when they get possessed by the Spirit General (Sinjang) and the Government Official Spirit (Daegam) (see 20: 24-27). The Death Messenger also wears them around their headband and other places (see 20: 52-23).

The Death Messenger appears in most *gut* performed by *gangsin-mu*. The dramatic sketch involving the Death Messenger trying to snatch the dead person from his protective family can be said to be a means of reconciling them with the inevitability of the death that has already taken place. Also by means of lavish gifts of money and food, the family hope that the dead soul has a comfortable journey to the other world (see 5: 48-50; 17: 20-22, 28; 20: 52-55).

Mun gut ("door" *gut*) is sometimes performed near the gate

---

16. For a discussion of the role of money in *gut*, see Hogarth (1998: 66-67).

17. Pictures featuring money are in all the books mentioned (*passim*).

of the house, particularly for ones held for victims of accidents away from home (4: 33-35; 8: 54, 55,87; 14: 28-32). Its purpose is to allow the person to return home one last time, and also signifies the opening of the door to the other world. According to Im (ibid: 85-86), this part takes place to clear the way to the other world so that s/he could have a comfortable journey. What is interesting is the fact that in mainstream Korean society, the body of the person who died away from home is not admitted inside the household lest it should bring in highly polluting malignant spirits.[18]

The *han* (unfulfilled grievances, resentment and desires) of the dead is often represented as a series of knots made with a length of white cloth, called *"go."* Unravelling the knots (called *"go puri"*) represents dispersing the *han* that is thought to nestle like a large bundle of knots. *Go puri* is conducted for ancestral spirits in all *gut*, but it is considered the most important in mortuary *gut* to dispel the *han* of the recently departed (see 6: 27-29, 59-62).

Paranormal acts performed by *mudang* to display the powers of the spirits are essential in *gangsinmu*'s *gut*. They take the forms of running a sharp blade on the tongue (5: 35-37; 17: 78), standing barefoot on sharp twin blades (17: 80-83) or having the lower lip stuck on a large earthen rice steamer (5: 39-41), etc. Incidentally, *seseummu* just imitate *ganginmu*'s acts, such as briefly biting the rim of a basin before letting it go (see 4: 56). The latter also test the spirits' satisfaction by standing an animal part (or a whole carcass) on a trident (see 5: 43; 17: 71, 20: 29), called *sasil/saseul se-ugi*.[19]

Reincarnation, which has been derived from Buddhist *samsara* (the Eternal Wheel of Death and Rebirth, called *yunhoe* in Korean), is another frequently encountered concept. Many mortuary *gut* include a part in which the *mudang* interprets the dead man's reincarnation through examining the patterns made on a pile of raw rice (see 17: 47-49; 20: 61-62). Most frequently the person is fated to be reincarnated as a bird, butterfly, a baby, or a snake. The snake reincarnation is abhorred, and another *gut* is often recommended to alter the dead person's fate. However, the rein-

---

18. I have witnessed it several times. When a death occurs in hospital, the coffin is not allowed inside the house, but on the way to the burial site, they take it to the house and let the dead person have a look at his/her home one last time.

19. For details of **sasil se-ugi** and its meaning, see Hogarth (1998: 49, 170).

carnation represented in *gut* is not in any way linked to the dead person's merit in this life, which reflects the non-judgemental nature of Korean shamanism.

Burning is considered a means of sending tangible objects to the dead. In most mortuary rituals, dead people's clothes and personal belongings are burnt at the end (See 5: 72-72; 6: 39, 70-71; 8: 64-66; 14: 72-73; 17: 96).

Although mortuary *gut* is no longer universally performed by modern Koreans, the shamanistic view of death and afterlife still exerts great influence on general Korean eschatology (Choi Joon-sik 1996: 11). Conversely Korean eschatology can be said to be directly reflected in *musok*, by virtue of the latter's long history and significance in the ideology governing the Korean way of life. Since the essence of *musok* is the belief in the existence of the spirits, the mortuary *gut* which is performed at the point of division between the living and the dead, has always featured strongly.

In sum, first of all, death is universally accepted as final and separating. This world and the other are separated by vast watery boundaries over which there is a bridge of no return that the deceased have to cross. The passage to the other world is sad, dark, lonely, long and difficult, therefore often symbolized by an arch called "the Thorny Gate (*gasi mun*)."

Second, death is viewed as pollution. It deprives a community of one of its established members, disturbing its equilibrium. Also since life is valued above all else, the dead do not want to go to the other world, but wish to linger on in this world. Their envy of the living may cause them to wield a noxious influence on their descendants. The closest relatives of the newly dead are believed to be the most vulnerable. To avoid such harm, the newly dead should be safely guided to the other world to join the ancestors. Special arrangements are required for victims of "bad deaths" who harbour *han* (unresolved grievances and grief, unfulfilled desires, etc.). "Bad deaths" are all manners of untimely deaths, other than "good deaths" of aged people who lived and died peacefully, and have left behind legitimate male descendants, thus becoming benevolent ancestral spirits. Victims of "bad deaths" are believed to cling to this life, and yield a noxious influence on the living out of pure jealousy for them. It is therefore considered important to perform a *gut* for them, during which everybody present lends a sympathetic ear to their venting of *han* and coax them to leave the living and enter the world of the dead. If there is any hindrance to their becoming ancestral spirits, it should also be removed by arranging a spirit wedding with another dead spirit whose horoscope is compatible.

Third, death is not viewed as the extinction of an existence. Although separated from this world, the dead are believed to "live on" in their own realm and have close interactions with their living descendants. Their spirits return to this world from time to time to receive *gut* and ancestral offerings. They also let their descendents know of their displeasure or discomfort by inflicting misfortune on the living. Therefore the living must make sure that the dead come to terms with their new state, and console and keep them happy though feeding and watering them at regular ancestral rites, choosing comfortable dry gravesites and entertaining them at occasional *gut*, if deemed necessary.

Eschatology reflected in the mortuary rites in mainstream Korean society

In discussing mortuary rituals in Korean society, it is important to remember that shamanism is practised only by a specific group of people, mainly women, and often covertly. Therefore it is necessary to compare *gut* with what is more-widely accepted "traditional" mortuary rituals performed in contemporary mainstream Korean society. They are based on Confucian ideology, which puts emphasis on this-worldliness and continuation of a person's life only through his agnatic descendants. Human souls after death were beyond the scope of the original Confucianism. Confucian famously dismissed the idea of the existence of dead spirits. He allegedly rebuked his students for asking questions about afterlife, when they had so much to learn about this world. When asked about ancestral rituals, he remarked that one should merely act as though the spirits existed (Choi Joon-sik 1996).[20]

However, traces of folk beliefs, manifested in *gut*, can be traced in mainstream mortuary rituals. First of all, in a ritual called "*bok*" or "*chohon*" performed immediately after a person's death, a close relative carries the dead person's jacket to the roof top and waving it about, says his/her name three times to call his/her soul (Han 1981: 140; Jang 1995: 150). Calling the name of a newly-dead person three times is significant in that it suggests a belief in "three souls." Second, a body is ceremoni-

---

20. In *Lynyu* (*Analects*), cited by Choi Joon-sik 1996: 23.

ously washed after death, using three separate bowls of scented water, which again suggests the same belief (Han ibid.: 148). Third, a pearl or a bead is placed in the mouth of the deceased (Han ibid: 154), together with a ceremonious pouring of raw rice into the corpse's mouth with a willow wooden spoon (Jang ibid: 153), while reciting, "Thousand, ten thousand and hundred thousand sacks of rice!" Sometimes money is put there as well. I have already discussed the significance of these ritual acts while discussing the Gangwon-do *gut*. Whether this act originated in *gut* or *gut* adopted it from the mainstream mortuary ritual is difficult to say categorically. However, it is fairly safe to say that the ideology underpinning it is of a shamanistic nature. Fourth, a coffin is usually placed behind a screen, which signifies the separation of the worlds of the dead and the living. Fifth, a brief ritual to the Mountain Spirit is usually performed as part of the funeral procedure (Jang ibid: 156, 158). Sixth, a grave geomancer is usually employed in choosing an auspicious gravesite (Jang ibid: 156).

Conclusion

There is much phenomenological evidence to support Clark's remark (1932/1961: 113): "At the funeral time, one soul stays in the dead body and goes into the grave; one goes into the prepared tablet, and the last one goes off to the realm of the shades...."

In Gangwon-do *gut*, we see clear manifestations of the concept of three souls, which are symbolized by three white paper cut-out men, each representing heaven (realm of the shades), man (ancestral tablet) and earth (grave) respectively. The three paper cut-out men are given to the father of the dead man (representing heaven), the son (responsible for the ancestral tablet), and the wife ("earth mother")[21].

Korean eschatology is thus closely linked to the concept of three souls, and manifested in the three of the most important folk religions, namely shamanism, ancestor worship and geomancy of the gravesite. One soul goes to heaven, i.e., the other world, thus falls in the domain

---

21. Gwon told me that the third paper man would have been given to the dead man's mother, had she been alive. But I think the wife would have still received it. In contemporary Korean society, a man's wife seems to feature more prominently than his mother on occasions like a funeral, particularly a shamanistic ritual for the dead. Also a man's wife seems to take on the role of his mother in due course. In fact, one often comes across a man calling his wife, 'Mum.'

of shamanism. A second resides in the ancestral tablet, the emblem of ancestor worship[22]. The third soul is believed to reside in the bones of the dead in the grave. Therefore it is important to keep the dead person comfortable and happy. Geomancy, which originally determined the auspiciousness of the location of a building or a room, has been developed further and applied to the gravesite.

Nevertheless, it is true that there is neither "conviction" nor "consensus" among modern Koreans as to whether the concept of three souls exists. I would argue that the main reason is the fast disappearance of traditional Korean culture in the face of globalization, or more specifically westernization. Today, especially in urban settings, even family elders and mortuary specialists are not sure what the traditional funeral procedures are, hence books giving detailed instructions on the "correct" procedures for the rites of passage are published (e.g. Han 1981: 140; Jang 1995: 150). However, the concept of three souls is clearly and overtly displayed in some *gut*, which often serve as a receptacle of Korean traditional culture.

---

22. In traditional Korean society, ancestral tablets were housed in a special room of a household, and food and drinks were regularly offered them by the descendants. Even today, in some households, particularly in rural settings, male heads regularly pay tributes to the tablets, and even report their daily events to them, as though they were talking directly to living lineage elders. Mun (1998: 156-157) describes how a man, who has just been dismissed from his job, reports the unfortunate event to his ancestral tablets: "In spite of your benevolent caring, it was my own shortcomings that brought my dismissal...."

Part 12

BUDDIST ELEMENTS
IN KOREAN SHAMANSIM

The influence of Buddhism on Korean shamanism (*musok*) is immediately apparent to any casual observer of *gut*. By nature, shamanism is all inclusive and fluid on account of the lack of the holy founder with authoritative instructions and systemized written scriptures. It is therefore natural for *musok* to absorb various elements of Buddhism, which was the most important foreign religion to Korean people for a long period of time before the introduction of Christianity.

I will first discuss how the Buddhist influence on *musok* is phenomenally manifested through examining the human participants, i.e. *mudang* and their associates, the spirits, the ritual procedures and paraphernalia. Since the songs that *mudang* sing during *gut* best represent the ideology of Korean shamanism, we will also examine three representative ballads to see Korean *mudang*'s interpretation and adaptation of Buddhist ideology.

Mudang and their associates

In their earlier lives, *mudang*[1] often practised another religion, such as

---

1. I am referring to **gangsinmu**, the "god-descended type."

Buddhism and Christianity. A majority of them come from the Buddhist background, many continuing to visit Buddhist temples, particularly to attend various festivities. On the other hand, ex-Christian *mudang* sever all ties with the Christian church once they start their new profession, mainly because of the latter's general condemnation of Korean shamanism as a "devil worship."

This close association with Buddhism surfaces more prominently in the cases of lesser *mudang*, who make a living mainly by fortune-telling, although some of them also perform *gut*[2]. The female *mudang* of that kind are generally called, by their clients and also among themselves, as *bosal* (bodhisattva) (Figure 2.1), and the male *beopsa* (a Buddhist priest/Dharma teacher). Their places of practice are often named rather like a Buddhist hermitage (*-am*), such as Chilseong-am, Yaksa-am, Yaksu-am, etc. The Buddhist symbol "*man* (卍)" is usually displayed on the signboard outside their houses where they usually receive their clients (Figure 2.2). Such ubiquitous signboards testify to the proliferation of *mudang* of that type in many areas of Seoul.

Fig. 12.1   Fig.12.2

Most *mudang* dream of owning a commercial ritual hall of their own, many actually realizing their dream. These halls are often situated on the remote mountainside, where the air is pure and the scenery serene and spectacular. They are named like proper Buddhist temples (*-sa*), such as Yonggung-sa, Hwangnyong-sa, Daegeum-sa, etc., although they are usually modest-sized private houses in large grounds. *Mudang* refer

---

2. Gim Taegon (1989: 144) also noticed a similar phenomenon.

to those halls as "*uri jeol* (our Buddhist temple)." The largest room in the building is allocated as a shrine where *mudang* place the pictures and statues of all their tutelary spirits. The building has cooking and washing facilities, and accommodate and cater for a large number of people, who sometimes attend *gut*. These halls are also rented to other *mudang* for a fee, and as *mudang* advance in age, they often live on the proceeds, occasionally performing a small part in their friends' *gut*.

What is interesting is that there are usually Buddhist temples in the neighbourhood (Figure 2.3). Their co-existence appears to be mostly peaceful; *mudang* and their associates frequently visit the temples and participate in special festivities such as the Buddha's Birthday celebrations on the eighth day of the fourth lunar month. Buddhist monks, on the other hand, very rarely visit the shamanistic halls, and often deny any connection with their *mudang* neighbours.

Fig. 2.3: A Buddhist monk and a shaman client bow to the statues of Buddha and the Mountain Spirit. Note their sizes and positions; the former is huge while, the latter is much smaller and placed in the lower position.

Many *mudang* belong to an organization called Daehan Bulgyo (The Republic of Korea Buddhism) (Figure 2.4), and have a signboard prominently displaying the name of that organization outside their homes/practices. They are often less well-known *mudang* who still feel uncomfortable with their calling *vis à vis* those in mainstream Korean society, the source of most of their income from fortune-telling. One of my *mudang* informants told me it was because Buddhism commands more respect than *musok* in Korean society. She then added quickly, "after all

Buddhism and *musok* are the same thing." It seems to me that on account of the still persisting social stigma attached to *mudang*, they are hiding behind the shield of more socially accepted Buddhism.

Fig. 12.4   Fig. 12.5

Jeong Wonhae (b. 1932), an important *mudang* informant of mine, is a typical example of Buddhist-oriented *mudang*. She often confided in me that she hated being called "*mudang*," and that she was different from other ordinary *mudang*. Her home shrine in the centre of Seoul emulates a small Buddhist hermitage, without a myriad of shamanistic paraphernalia which are usually displayed at the private shrine of a *mudang*. A row of Buddhist brass bells are hung above the small altar, and on the wall hangs the only portrait of the deity, that of Dan-gun[3].

A similar atmosphere of simplicity also prevails in the small shrine room of Yi Jehwan (b. 1934) who has a high level of education for a *mudang*. His tutelary spirits are not represented in the usual colourful shamanistic paintings and statues, but as Chinese calligraphy on strips of paper hung on the walls. On the floor in front of the altar is a small table on which a *moktak* (a wooden gong) is placed. Mr. Yi strikes it rhythmically while praying, rather as a Buddhist monk does in meditation and prayer. (Figure 12.5)

More commonly found are one or more Buddha statues of various kinds amid a dazzling array of shamanistic paintings and statues of the gods and spirits, and other paraphernalia. Huge gilded statues of The Buddha Triad can often be found, but most *mudang*'s private shrines contain at least one small gilded statue of Gwaneum Bosal (Avalokiteśvara), the God/Goddess of Mercy. Another popular Buddha is Yaksa Yeorae (The Supreme Physician), with whom *mudang* share a close affinity. It is because from time immemorial the chief function of *mudang* has been healing of the mind and body.

The Venerable Triad (*Seokga Samjon*) Figure 12.6-12.9

Fig. 12.6: Ms Choe Seongja's private shrine
-Buddha Sakyamuni in the centre
-Bodhisattva Manjusri (*Munsu Bosal*: "Transcendent Wisdom") to his left
-Bodhisattva Samantabhadra (*Bohyeon Bosal*: "Universal Kindness") to his right

Fig. 12.7: Private shrine of Jo Jaryong (Jo Yongjin)
-Sakyamuni (centre)
-Bodhisattva Manjusri (left)
-Bodhisattva Samantabhadra (right)

Fig. 12.8: Bak Ino in *Jeon-ssi gutdang* in Seoul
-Buddha Sakyamuni (centre)
-Buddha Amitabha (right)
-Bodhisattva Manla ("The Supreme Physician") (left)

Fig. 12.9: Ms Yi Sanghui 's shrine
-Bodhisattva Manla, (The Supreme Physician) to the right of the Buddha.
- A medicine bottle in his left hand
- More popular with *mudang* because of his healing powers

Buddhas and Bodhisattvas of various kinds, particularly Gwaneum Bosal (Avalokiteśvara), are often *mudang*'s tutelary spirits. For example, Ha Bubang (b. 1953) cites Gwaneum Bosal with one thousand arms as her chief guardian spirit (Figure 12.12). According to her the Goddess of Mercy with so many arms which enable her to spread her compassion, is her ideal role model. She told me she strived to emulate her in her chosen profession and help as many desperate people as possible.

Bodhisattvas (Bosal) worshipped as popular shamanistic gods

Fig. 12.10: Manla - popular Bodhisattva (Medicine bottle in his left hand) in Yi Sunui 's shrine.

Fig. 12.11: Gwaneum Bosal (Avalokiteśvara), the God/ess of Mercy
("The Lord who looks in every direction")
-One of the most popular Buddhist "gods" in *musok*
-Symbol: rosary / -Colour: white / -A statue in Daegeumsa, Gangwon-do

Fig. 12.12: Avalokiteśvara with ten thousand arms (Cheonsu Bosal)
Ha Bubang (b.1953) at her shrine
Her main tutelary spirit

Clients of *mudang* are often Buddhists. To many of them, particularly less educated ones, the boundaries between Buddhism and *musok* are often blurred. Their main reason to go to Buddhist temples is to pray to the Buddhas so that a particular wish can be fulfilled. While visiting a temple, they would pray at the small shrine dedicated to the indigenous Korean spirits, such as the Mountain Spirit (Sansin) and the Seven Stars Spirit (Chilseongsin). Since many shamanistic ritual halls also contain large gilded statues of the Buddhas as well other similar objects of worship such as incense, they seem to feel fairly comfortable with the surroundings. The ubiquitous temple signs at *mudang*'s private shrines add to the familiar feeling for their Buddhist clients. The only difference is that the Buddhist temples have a seal of social approval, while *mudang* houses/*gutdang* (commercial shaman halls) are visited covertly. In fact they often tell their family and friends that they have been to a Buddhist temple when they secretly consult a *mudang* or sponsor a *gut*.

The Spirits Derived from Buddhism
<Jeseok>
Jeseok is derived from the Buddhist God, Jeseok-cheon (Skr: Śadra

Devānām Indra) who protects the Dharma, together with Beomwang, one of the twelve Heavenly gods, the guardian of the East. He is supposed to live in Doricheon which is situated at the top of Mt. Sumi. In *musok*, Jeseok is believed to be in charge of long life, grains, clothes and good fortune and misfortune.

<Jijang Bosal (Skr: Ksitigarbha)>
A Bodhisattva who guides the multitude of people in the world locked in Yukdo where there is no way out until the reappearance of Maitreya, at the request of the Buddha Śākyamuni. He holds a lotus flower in his left hand and jeweled stick in his right.

<Gwanseum Bosal (Skr: Avalokiteśvara)>
Usually a female Bodhisattava, she is a symbol of great compassion and great grief, who is most widely worshipped in Korea by Buddhists and shamanists alike. It is believed by the masses that if they devotedly recite her name in times of trouble, she listens to their prayer and saves them. She is believed to be the assistant of Amitabul in Pure Land, helping him with his teaching. Gwaneum manifests herself in various forms, and names vary depending on appearances, as follows:

- Cheonsu Gwaneum (千手 觀音): Avalokiteśvara with one thousand hands
- Sip-ilmyeon Gwaneum (十一面 觀音) : Eleven-faced Avalokiteśvara
- Baekui Gwaneum (白衣 觀音): White-clad Avalokiteśvara
- Madu Gwaneum (馬頭 觀音): Horse-Headed Avalokiteśvara
- Eoram Gwaneum (魚藍 觀音): Indigo Fish Avalokiteśvara
- Yeo-uiryun Gwaneum (如意輪 觀音) Avalokiteśvara with wheel-like intention

<Mireuk Bosal (彌勒 菩薩): Maitreya Bodhisattva>
Maitreya was an Indian, born into a Brahman family. He is the future Buddha, who is currently staying on Dosolcheon (Heaven), guiding the masses from there. He is believed to reappear in this world 5,670,000,000 years after the death of the Buddha Śākyamuni. He will then achieve Buddhahood under the *yonghwasu* tree in the garden of Seungrim-won, and become the saviour of the mankind. Also known as Mireuk Jajon,

Mireuk Bul, Mireuk Jwaju.

<Yaksa Yeorae (藥師 如來): Supreme Physician>
Also called Yaksa Yurigwang Yeorae (藥師 琉璃光 如來), this Buddha is
believed to save the suffering masses from *chil nan* (seven disasters) and
cure their diseases. He usually holds a medicine bottle in his left hand
and knots the stamp of *simuoe* (施無畏) with his right hand. He is the
head of the Eastern Country in the Pure Land, called Yuriguk (琉璃國).

<Jigong (指空) (? - 1363)>
An eminent Indian Seon (Zen) monk from Magadha. His real name is
Dhyānabhadra. He came to Goryeo through Yuan China during the reign
of King Chungsuk, and actively spread Buddhism. Later he returned
to China and passed on the tradition of Seon meditation to the Goryeo
monk Naong/Hyegeun.

<Muhak Daesa (Bak Jacho: 1327[3] - 1405[4])>
Born a son of a high government official Bak Inil in Samgi, he became a
monk at age 18, and received from Soji Seonsa (禪師)[5]. He studied the
Dharma under Hyemyeong Guksa (國師) and practised asceticism in Gil-
sang-sa (Temple) and Geumgang-gul (Hermitage) on Mt. Myohyang. In
1353 (King Gongmin 2) he went to Yuan (元) dynasty China, and studied
in Yeon-gyeong (燕京) under the Indian monk Jigong Seonsa and his
disciple, Naong/Hyegeun, and returned in 1356. In 1373, he learned the
Dharma under the monk Naong/Hyegeun who had become Wangsa (王師:
the Royal Teacher). In 1376, Naong/Hyegeun invited him to lead a Buddhist society at Hoeamsa, but he declined. In 1392, after the foundation
of the Joseon dynasty, he was made Wangsa, and was also given the title
of *Daejo gyyjongsa/seon-gyo dochongseop/jeon bulsim inbyeonjimuae
bujongsu gyohongri boje/dodaeseonsa/myoeom jonja* (大曺溪宗師 禪教
都摠攝 傳佛心印辯智碍 扶宗樹教弘利普濟 都大禪師 妙嚴尊者), and lived at
Hoeamsa Temple. The following year, he accompanied King Taejo, while
he was looking for a new site for his capital, and agreed with the king
in choosing Hanyang (now Seoul) as the new capital. In 1397, a stupa

---

3. Goryeo King Chungsuk 14.

4. Joseon King Taejong 5.

5. The title given to a great Seon (Zen) master.

was erected to pray for his long life in the grounds of Hoeamsa Temple. In 1402, he was appointed the head monk of Hoesamsa Temple, but resigned his post the following year to retire into Geumjangam Hermitage in the Diamond Mountains, and died there.

<Naong/Hyegeun (1320 - 1376)>

An eminent Seon monk, he wielded a great influence on Buddhism during the late Goryeo and early Joseon period. He was born in Yeonghae with the name, A Wonhye. His pen names include Naong, Gangwolheon, Seon-gak and Hyegeun. He was a *wangsa* during the reign of the 31st Goryeo King Gongmin. He learned the method of mind-control developed by the Indian monk Jigong (指空) in Seocheon (西天), China. He also excelled at calligraphy and painting. One of the Three Greatest Monks, together with Jigong and Muhak.

<Beomil (810[6] - 889[7])>

A Silla Buddhist monk whose lineage name is Gim. He became a monk at age 15. In 829 (King Heungdeok 4) after receiving the precepts, *gujokgye* (具足戒)[8], in Gyeongju, he went to Tang (唐) China to study and practise asceticism for six years. In 844 he came across the great persecution of Buddhism in China, and secretly engaged in mediation in Sangsan (商山). He returned home in 847 (King Munseong 7), meditated in Mt. Baekdal and spent 40 years in Gulsansa (Temple). He declined invitations to receive the title of *guksa* (National Teacher) from the three successive kings, Gyeongmun, Heon-gang and Jeonggang. He leaves a book entitled *Chodang jip*.

The ritual components and procedures

During the long history of co-existence, Buddhism has wielded a great influence on various as aspects of *gut* procedures and paraphernalia used in it. A *gut* is characterized by its lurid colours, loud noise, and frantic activities. The opposite is true of Buddhism which is essentially a religion of peace, quiet, austerity and non-action. The ultimate goal of Bud-

---

6. Silla King Heondeok 2

7. Silla Queen Jinseong 3.

8. The precepts for the Buddhist monks. There are 250 precepts for nuns (**bhikkhunī**) and 348 for monks (**bhikkhu**).

dhism is transcending *samsara* (the Eternal Wheel of Death and Rebirth), which starts with emptying one's mind of all worldly desires, etc. In *gut*, white represents the Buddhist ideals, i.e. "emptiness," which is why the Buddhist elements are often expressed in white in *musok*, the costumes and even the fan carried by the Buddhist spirits being usually white. During a divination session involving the picking of a flag out of the five which represent the five directions, the white flag usually symbolizes the Heavenly Spirit. However, when a potential *mudang* picks a white flag, it is interpreted as her tutelary spirit being Bulsa Halmeoni (The Buddhist Guru Grandmother), which suggests that among her/his kinsmen, affinal or consanguineal, there was a female member with a shamanistic propensity in the past, whether s/he was a practising *mudang* or not.

In Buddhism the cardinal sin is killing and thus eating meat is prohibited. In sharp contrast, in *gut* the most important offerings are uncooked animal body parts, such as a pig's head or a butchered and skinned whole pig, a bull's head, huge beef ribs or a pair of ox's forelegs complete with hoofs, depending on the size of the *gut*. Roasted or boiled chickens are often put on the table, while live chickens are immolated for ritual purposes at healing *gut*. I have interpreted its symbolic meaning as a residue of live sacrifice, in the bygone days, the traces of which still remain even in the Seoul area today. Various clients of *mudang* told me in the field that blood sacrifices used to be regularly practised in North Korea. One such client gave me the detailed descriptions of dogs being immolated and their blood scattered all around in her home town in Hwanghae-do, now in North Korea. There is also evidence to suggest that the original animal sacrifice may have included hunting for the sacrificial animal. For example, *Samguk sagi* (Gim Busik 1145/1984 : 704) contains the statement that in Goguryeo, every year on the third day of the third lunar month, men gathered around on a mountain, hunted wild boars and deer, which were offered to Heaven and Mountain and River Spirits.[9] What is interesting is the fact a number of the *gut* which I attended, contained a part called *tasal gut* (hunting *gut*). I also saw shamans appear dressed in a hunting costume, carrying a bow and arrow, even when there were no such specific parts.[10]

---

9. The hunting scenes are depicted in tomb murals dating back to the Goguryeo period. See Figures 31 and 32 in Part 2.

10. See Figures 33 and 34 in Part 2.

The Buddhist influence on Korean shamanism is an important reason for the gradual disappearance of blood sacrifice, or hunting for the animal offerings. In Hwanghae-do *gut*, which have preserved much of the original features, a live ox is brought into the *gut* in a lorry, and the officiating *mudang* "teases" it with a trident and pretends to stab it in several places, before sending it to the nearby abattoir to have it humanely and expertly killed by a butcher. One *mudang* told me that they could not possibly kill a living being near the presence of the Buddhas.

The parts dedicated to the Buddhist-derives deities, such as Jeseok (The Buddha Emperor), Chilseong (The Seven Stars Spirit), Bulsa (The Buddhist Guru Grandmother), Sambul (The Three Buddhas), are "played" by *mudang* in Buddhist monk costumes of flowing white or grey robes with a white peaked cap, carrying a wooden gong, a string of beads, small cymbals, etc. During these *geori* (parts), or *nori* ("plays"), the animal heads or other joints, are covered with a large piece of paper (preferably white) or cloth, lest the sight of blood and butchered flesh should offend the Buddhist gods, who are strongly opposed to any killing. The atmosphere turns more solemn, reverential and devout, the use of lurid colours becoming somewhat subdued, with even some fans carried by Bulsa Halmeoni being plain white, instead of the colourful versions with various pictures, which are more frequently used. The background music also reflects the serene atmosphere which prevails in Buddhist settings.

In Jindo, an island off the south coast of Korea, where shamanistic traditions are very much alive, a unique percussion instrument, called *jeongju* is played by *mudang*, which deserves special mention. It is a small brass bowl-shaped instrument with a string attached through the hole in the bowl, beaten with a deer-horn stick. It is used only during Jeseok *gut* (*gut* for the Buddha Emperor), possibly because of its clear serene sound, which is reminiscent of the world of the Buddha. (Han-guk Munhwa Yesul Jinheungwon 1980) Jeseok is also the Harvest Spirit, responsible for bringing a good harvest of rice, which is represented in the rice-bowl shape of the instrument. What is interesting is a small piece of deer horn used as a stick for beating it. Jeseok is also identified with the Heavenly Spirit, and the deer symbolizes the flight up to Heaven, the concept of which is also prevalent in many Siberian tribes. In this simple instrument one can detect the elements of Siberian-type shamanism, the ancient Korean worship of Heaven, and Buddhist elements.

Shamanistic paintings, which adorn the walls of the ritual hall, include various Buddhist saints, and the shamanistic spirits are frequently depicted as Buddhas. Apart from the ubiquitous statues of Sansin (the Mountain Spirit), Janggun (the General), three gilded statues of Buddhas, representing, Śākyamuni, Yaksa Bosal (Medicine Bodhisattva) and Amitabha, are placed in many shamanistic shrines, both private and commercial.

Korean *mudang* and their clients also celebrate many Buddhist festivals, such as Sawol Chopa-il (the eighth day of the eighth lunar month, which is the Buddha's Birthday) (Figures 13, 14, 15 & 16), *bangsaengje* (Liberating Life Ritual). The latter is sometimes called Yonggung *Gut* (Dragon Palace Ritual) by the shamans and their clients, who mix indistinguishably with Buddhists, performing the act of releasing fish or sometimes turtles, into the sea or river, for merit-making, on the third day of the third month in the lunar calendar (Figure 17). I witnessed such a ceremony on 13 April, 1994, (3 March in the lunar calendar) at the Yonggungdang (Dragon Palace Shrine), at Gwangnaru Pier on a bank of the River Han. There were, however, no outward signs of shamanistic activities, everybody I talked to denying vehemently that they had anything to do whatsoever with *musok*. It was later confirmed again by my *mudang* informants that bangsaengje and Yonggung *Gut* are one and the same, only different terms applied by the Buddhists and the shamanists.

The Buddha's Birthday celebrations (Figure 12.13-12.17)

(from left to right)
Fig. 12.13: a Buddhist temple with lanterns inscribed with prayers
Fig. 12.14: a private shaman shrine with the same

Fig. 12.15: congregation at a Buddhist temple on the Buddha's Birthday

Fig. 12.16: clients at a private shaman shrine on the same day

Fig. 12.17: Bangsaengjae (Life-liberating ritual)

In some *gut*, particularly in the southern variety, male shamans, called *beopsa*, chant long incantations for chasing the evil spirits away. Many parts of *gut*, particularly those featuring Buddhist-derived spirits, contain the actual chanting of the Buddhist Scripture, called *dok gyeong*, often accompanied by the wooden gong, used by Buddhist monks. Less frequently, the chants take on a similar tone to that heard at the Confucian ancestral rite, particularly in mortuary *gut*, *Gyeong/-gyeong* primarily means "scripture," such as the Buddhist Sutra, or the Confucian classics. However, since people believed that these sacred texts carried "magical" powers to exorcise evil or malevolent spirits, *-gyeong* has come to mean "incantation or magic formula or words," against such evil powers. *Mugyeong*, the shamanistic incantations, are traditionally recited by *pansu*, blind male "shamans." These days, however, they are not only used by the blind *pansu*, but also by the male *mudang*, who are called various other names, such as *beopsa*, and also frequently by some female *mudang*.

There exist a vast number of books on *mugyeong*; some are in printed form, while others in handwritten form. Akiba and Akamatsu actually list three pages of different names of the books on *mugyeong*, collected from ten different areas in both South and North Korea (1938: 240-242). The contents of *mugyeong* include direct copies, paraphrases and imitations of the Taoist scriptures and the Buddhist Sutras, which reflects the syncretism of shamanism with Taoism and Buddhism. According to Akiba and Akamatsu (1938), the syncretism of Taoism and Buddhism might have happened during the Silla period.

The epic songs that *mudang* recite during *gut*, called *muga*, directly reflect the shamanistic ideology and cosmology, to such an extent that they have been called "the oral Scripture" (Gim Taegon 1981: 332). A great deal of research has been carried out about them, by some Japanese and Korean, and one or two Western scholars. (Akamatsu & Akiba, 1937; Yim & Jang, 1966; Gim Taegon, 1971, 1978 & 1980; Hyeon, 1992; Walraven, 1994). In the next section, I will analyze three of the most popular *muga*, to find out how *mudang* interpret the Buddhist ideology and incorporate into their world.

As stated earlier, exuberant dancing is an integral part of *gut*. However, Buddhist influence can also be felt in dancing in that during the part dedicated to the Buddhist-derived spirit, the pace of the dance becomes slower and more ponderous.

Some community *gut* contain masked dance drama, at the end of the ritual part, which is performed by *gwangdae* (village entertainers or performers). The most famous example, the masked dance drama, from a small village called Hahoe, is performed by village residents, frequently separately from community *gut* called *byeolsin gut* of which it is originally the final part. It was rediscovered by a group of young enthusiasts in the 1970's, based on the memory of Yi Changhui (b.1911), now designated a Human Cultural Treasure by the government. What is interesting about the Hahoe masked dance drama is the fact that it is a classic case of Gluckman's institutionalized safety valve (1963), in which the socially oppressed people (e.g. the Butcher, the Village Fool, the Servant Boy, etc.) poke fun at their masters. Through periodically relieving dissent and disaffection, and momentarily rejecting the authority of *yangban* (the ruling class) in their fantasy, their resentment was neutralized, thus maintaining the strict social stratification, which was so unfair to them. That is why the performance was actively encouraged, and even partly sponsored, by *yangban*, who of course would not dream of attending such a "vulgar" gathering. Another character in the play is a Buddhist monk who breaks his vows of chastity, after seeing the pretty young girl urinate on the mountain path. This type of humanization of the austere Buddhist monk is also frequently found in *mudang*'s epic songs, as we shall see.

Costumes and paraphernalia used in *gut* also reflect Buddhist influence. Buddhist monks' robes, in white, grey or charcoal, worn for Buddhist-derived spirits, such as Jeseok, Bulsa, Samsin, etc. The white robe is worn with long sashes over both shoulders, called *gasa*, which are either all red (in Seoul *gut*) or a red one over the right shoulder and green/blue one over the left. A white peaked Buddhist monk's hat is worn with this costume.

Fig. 12.18: Wooden Gongs (*Moktak*) - used by the Buddhist Monks to aid meditation, etc. Popular props for shamanistic rituals, private and formal.

Fig. 12.19: Intricate paper cut-outs used as *gut* prop
at Jo Jaryong's *jinjeok gut* on 5 April 1994.
Note the Buddha featuring prominently

Fig. 12.20: Bang Chunja at her *jinjeok gut*

Fig. 12.21: Jeong Wonhae at her *jinjeok gut*

(from left to right)
Fig. 12.22: Artificial illuminated fish at the Buddha's Birthday celebrations at a Buddhist temple
Fig. 12.23: an artificial fish as a decoration at a gut performance

Buddhist paraphernalia used in *musok* (Figure 12.18-12.23)

Muga: epic songs of *mudang*

Ortner (1970, 1973) presents a concept of "key scenarios," which she defines as "preorganized schemes of action, symbolic programs for the staging and playing out of standard social interactions in a particular culture." The point of the concept is that "every culture contains not just bundles of symbols and not just even bundles of larger propositions about the universe ("ideologies"), but organized schemas for enacting (culturally typical) relations and situations." She further argues that these schemas often take on an "ordering function," which is almost generally applicable to a variety of disparate social situations. Thus she shows how a scenario of hospitality is present in the structure of a wide variety of the Sherpa social encounters, such as getting a favour, shamanistic séances for curing the sick, rituals of offerings to the gods for community well-being, and so on. In all these social events, hospitality is an ordering schema, with Ego as the host. Alter as guest(s), and the party atmosphere with food and drink.

Along the same lines, Victor Turner (1974) shows the persistent force in various religious traditions, which he calls "root paradigms," for example, martyrdom in Christianity. Schieffeling (1976) explores a "cultural scenario" of reciprocity and opposition among the Kaluli of New

Guinea, showing the degree to which it orders a range of social and ritual interactions.

The idea of cultural schemas is also present in diachronic or historical studies, such as Geertz's *Negara* (1980) and Sahlins's *Historical metaphor* (1981). Their argument appears to be that historical events are also structured by cultural schemas in the same way as various social behaviours are in synchronic contexts. Thus cultural patterns of action, cultural dramas or scenarios reappear over time, and order the ways in which people deal with conventional and historically novel social encounters. Geertz (1980: 134) demonstrates that in the Balinese state, despite major shifts in political fortune, "the characteristic form seems to have reconstructed itself continually," and new courts are "but further transcriptions of a fixed ideal" over a period of nearly 600 years (between 1343 and 1906). Sahlins (1981: 17) shows that the Hawaiians acted according to a cultural script, embodied in myth and ritual, in dealing with novel historical events, such as Captain Cook's second visit to the Islands. He describes it as the replaying of "a cosmological drama."

Why then do cultural schemas have such durability that they seem to have? One of the reasons is that they "depict actors responding to, and resolving (from their own point of view), the central contradictions of the culture (Ortner 1989: 61)." Ortner shows that in the case of the Sherpa, there is a cultural schema in temple-founding stories, which describes a hero playing out and winning the fraternal and political rivalries that are recurrently reproduced out of the contradictions of the social/cultural order.

A cultural schema, or key scenarios, can also be found in the Korean case. I have elsewhere shown (1998) how the "cultural schema" of reciprocity orders a wide range of social and ritual interactions, though analyzing the Korean shamanistic ritual.

In the ballads that *mudang* sing during *gut*, there also exists a "cultural schema," which portrays the protagonist playing out, and triumphing over the conflict produced by the contradictions of the social and cultural order. This schema is based on the Buddhist ideology of the law of cause and effect. What is interesting, however, is that in the *mudang* songs, the result of one's action is usually manifested in this life, rather than in the next incarnation. That bears witness to the this-worldly nature of shamanism.

I will analyze three of the most popular ballads recited by *mudang* during *gut*, to establish that there exists a cultural schema that runs through them, which also applies to the cross section of Korean culture. Although the ballads that I analyze are those sung by Korean shamans, there is a close connection between shamanistic songs and oral literature in general in Korea.

One of the three ballads that I present, called the Ballad of Sim Cheong, in particular, is well known virtually throughout Korean society. The origin of the ballad has been a subject of much debate, some scholars claiming that it has been derived from the shaman song, while others maintain that Korean shamans adopted it from the orally transmitted tale.[11] More to the point for the present discussion, there are "key scenarios," which order these ballads, as well as most other folk tales, myths and orally transmitted tales. I will try to establish it by examining the three ballads in detail.

Three of the most popular ballads (*muga*) that *mudang* recite in various *gut* are the ballads of Bari Gongju (the Abandoned Princess), Danggeum Aegi, and Sim Cheong. The first, recited by the god-descended northern shamans (*gangsinmu*) as well as the hereditary southern shamans (*seseummu*) at mortuary rituals, is widely prevalent, *mutadis mutandis*, in almost all areas of Korea, with a few exceptions.[12] The second and the third ballads are only recited by *seseummu* to the south of the River Han and along the east coast of Korea. As we shall see, of the latter two, the ballad of Sim Cheong appears to be a later invention,[13] and is found less frequently, occurring mostly in coastal areas. Despite regional variations in their occurrence and contents, the three ballads have a common theme running through them. I will analyze the three ballads within this thematic framework, focusing on the Buddhist elements contained in them.

You can see the full texts of my English translations of the three ballads as sung by contemporary Korean shamans in my book, *Syncretism of Buddhism and Shamanism in Korea*. Several transcriptions of these three *muga* have been published in recent years, starting with Gim Taegon in the 1970s. Variations occur in the length of descriptions of a particular character or incident, the choice of words, and in some cases there are slight alterations even in the story. But the basic characteriza-

---

11. For a detailed discussion of this subject, see Walraven (1995).

12 For example, it does not seem to be recited in Jejudo **gut**.

13. According to one of the **mudang** reciting this ballad, Yi Geumok, the **gut** incorporating this ballad was first introduced around the twenties or thirties (Walraven 1994: 123).

tion of the main *dramatis personae* and the storyline remain the same.

In the above three tales, there is a common pattern, or a cultural schema, underlying the plot and characters as follows:

1) The protagonist is a young socially disadvantaged female through her birth or an unfortunate event in her life beyond her control.

2) The protagonist is of royal birth, or becomes loyal through re-birth.

3) The conflict in her life is produced through the ethos prevailing in society at the time of the tales.

4) The protagonist is forced to leave home or abandoned.

5) The protagonist survives through divine intervention.

6) After some time, the protagonist either returns to the fold, or reunited with the person(s) closest to her, who is (are) the main cause of the conflict.

7) In the end, the conflict is resolved and the protagonist is re-warded, being either deified or empowered.

The above "key scenarios" generally underpin the archetypal stories of apotheosis in Korean shamanism. A high-born, but disadvantaged person becomes deified or empowered after going through a period of life fraught with difficulties and conflict. What is interesting is that in the above stories, the protagonist is a marginalized young female, with problems produced by the society she lives in. But instead of being embittered by her unfair treatment and renouncing her society, she triumphs in the end by displaying the very virtues imposed by the society which persecutes her. The underlying principle is then undoubtedly shamanistic in nature, in the sense of "entertaining" the malignant spirits that cause harm, in the hope of receiving favours in return. (Hogarth 1998: 27-28)

The cultural schema here is in other words reciprocity, which is the basis of all social interactions in Korean society. Filial piety, which is considered the supreme human virtue in all Confucian societies (Lee Kwang Kyu 1977: 332; Choe Jaeseok 1982: 189-204), can also be said to be based on the concept of reciprocity (Hogarth 1998: 156-159, 191).

The underlying principles of reciprocity are essentially the same as those of the Buddhist law of causation (*in-gwa eungbo* in Korean). Put simply, they are along the lines of "As you sow, so you reap," as a popular English proverb goes. The general belief that there exists retributive justice in the universe, which is Buddhist in essence, is well reflected in these three ballads. In the case of Bari Gongju, her parents' terminal sickness is said to have been caused as a punishment for abandoning their flesh and blood. Despite this severe treatment she suffered as a baby for no fault of her own, Bari Gongju undertakes a dangerous mission to the nether world to save her parents. As a reward for her filial piety, she becomes not only reunited with her parents, but also ends up enjoying the highest status of a deity leading the dead to the netherworld for perpetuity. The old couple who raise the princess also get financially as well as socially rewarded, although their assistance is prompted by a higher power, i.e. that of the Buddha Śākyamuni. Everybody connected with the princess, including her husband and sons, reap handsome benefits. In the ballad of Danggeum Agi, the notion of filial piety is absent, but the law of cause and effect is evident throughout the song. Danggeum Agi, which literally means "a baby who is considered precious as silk imported from (Tang dynasty) China" often refers to a young maiden brought up with the utmost care. In sharp contrast to Bari Gongju, Danggeum Agi is the only daughter with nine brothers, hence regarded precious by her family. The destiny of her birth and her union with a Buddhist monk was predicted to her parents at the time of the choice of their house site. Her parents made a conscious choice (cause), which resulted in the predictions coming true (effect). Having already nine sons, one daughter is welcomed and considered precious. Danggeum Agi, whose reputation for her beauty and goodness reaches far and wide, is consciously chosen by the monk, a son of Jeseok, as the mother of his sons. Her conception is miraculous, although in some regional versions, such as the one that I translate below, an actual sexual intercourse between the two is hinted at. However, in most versions that I came across, she conceives by swallowing the three grains of rice that the monk leaves behind. Because of her pregnancy, which is socially unacceptable for an unmarried girl of a good family, she gets banished from her home. But as a result of giving birth to three sons, who are flesh and blood of Jeseok himself, she becomes deified as Samsin Halmeoni responsible for fertility and wellbeing of children. Her three sons also become Sambul (the Three Buddhas) or Samsin (the Three Spirits). Another incident of minor importance which only appears in some versions (for example in the translation given below), the monk, having fathered the three boys, has to renounce his monkhood and return to a secular life.

In the case of Sim Cheong, the law of causation is more evident. The protagonist is splendidly rewarded for her filial piety, which prompted her to sacrifice her own life for her father's sight. Although the main theme is the filial piety of the heroine, the devoted caring of her by her blind father in her early life is also emphasized. Instead of abandoning her to the care of a more suitable person to bring up a baby, Blindman Sim takes on the responsibility of raising his baby daughter single-handedly against all odds after his wife's death. Sim Cheong's filial piety, which she would still have practised, even if he had abandoned her, as in the case of Bari Gongju, is more reinforced as a result. His final reward of regaining his sight in other words is caused by his goodness of bringing up a motherless infant instead of abandoning her. Everybody who helped them in the time of deprivation is also rewarded in the end. The wicked characters such as Bbaengdeok's Mum and Blindman Hwang who run off with her, are punished in the end. What is interesting in this tale is the fact, the *dramatis personae* all make intentional choices regarding their actions, according to the merit of which they reap rewards. This concept is very Buddhist in nature, although in these tales, the benefits are accorded to the deserving in this life, rather than in subsequent rebirths. That aspect of the storyline is what distinguishes them from the stories that appear in the Buddhist Scriptures.

The moral code of conduct

Buddhism has provided *musok* with the moral code of conduct for everyday life. Underpinning the rules of everyday conduct is the law of causation (*in-ga eungbo*). The Buddist influence on shamanistic ethics is well reflected in the initiatory dreams of the *mudang* just before they receive the spirits. A good example is Jo Jajryong (real name: Jo Yongjin - b. 1946). While he was suffering from *sinbyeong* (possession sickness), he received three commandments from Yasa-Yeorae on Mr. Palgong as follows (Hogarth 1998: 110):

First, do not go near women.

Second, do not gamble

Third, do not drink alcohol.

These commandments are clearly based on the Five Precepts

(Hogarth 2002: Chap 1, 1.2.2.)

The following poem. which is displayed on a well of the house of Gim Geumhwa, the best known Korean *mudang* today, sumps up the moral code of conduct for contemporary Korean shamans and their clients. It clearly reflect the Mahayana Buddhist doctrine of *in-gwa eungbo* (retribution), merit-making, mind control, elimination of greed, anger and ignorance, the importance of harmony, love and compassion, and also filial piety and loyalty to country.

How to Control Myself

My happiness or unhappiness is all my own making.

It is never other people's fault.

Build good fortune on doing good for others, rather than myself.

All sins are derived from greed, anger and ignorance.

Always be patient, and be satisfied with little.

Face others with a smiling face and gentle true words.

Go with the flow in all things.

Remember my righteous life is for the good of my country.

Serve your parents as you cherish yourself.

Respect your seniors, and love your juniors.

Show warm love to your neighbours.

You inevitably receive a retribution for your sin,

or a reward for your good deed.

Live every moment without regret.

Part 13

TRANSVESTISM IN SHAMANISM: A REFLECTION OF FEMALE HEGEMONY IN THE PRIMEVAL ERA?

Introduction

Transvestism is a phenomenon frequently occurring in temporal and spatial diversity in shamanism (Yi Neunghwa 1927/1991: 17; Akamatsu & Akiba 1938: 259; Akiba 1950: 168; Eliade 1951/1964: 125, 168, 258, 351, 461; Beattie and Middleton 1969: 224; Hoppal 1984; Gim Geum-hwa 1995; Jo Jaryong 1996a, 1996b; Hogarth 1998, 1999, 2003). It is often interpreted by various scholars as representing a return to the primor-dial era, when polarities did not exist and man communicated directly and freely with gods. Hence it denotes the liminal roles of shamans, who attain the state of oneness or the whole through assuming asexuality or bisexuality. (Eliade 1952/1964: 168; Beattie & Middleton 1969: 224; Yu 1975: 333; Seo 1992 vol I: 168, 1992 vol. II: 150-151)

However, what is interesting is that more characteristically it in-volves the cross-dressing of the male shaman. Although, as Seo has said (1992 Vol II: 150-151), female Korean shamans also wear male clothes when possessed by male gods and spirits, and assume the masculine at-tributes during the ritual, in everyday life they are most often very femi-nine figures preferring to wear makeup and fashionable clothes. On the contrary, many male Korean shamans retain their feminine traits also outside the ritual context. Why then does this phenomenon occur, when the majority of human societies are male-dominated?

In Korea, while strong male dominance still prevails in mainstream society, female dominance is very apparent among the shamanistic community, not only quantitatively but also qualitatively. Eliade (Ibid.: 258) also briefly mentions that the widespread practice of transvestism among male shamans "is probably explained by an ideology derived from the archaic matriarchy." If shamanism is "a return to the primordial age" or what Gim Taegon calls the "archetype," then does it suggest that originally female hegemony existed in human society?

I will first briefly discuss the almost universal phenomenon of male dominance in human society, and the anthropological explanations for it. Then we will examine the theory of original female power which has been suggested by many feminist anthropologists. (Gillison 1980; Sanday 1981; Ortner and Whitehead 1982; Moore 1988)

In sum, this paper analyzes the phenomenon of transvestism in the context of Korean shamanism, to find out why it is usually the male shaman who dresses in women's clothes usually in, but also occasionally out of, the ritual context, and whether it is a reflection of female hegemony in the primeval era.

Transvestism in Shamanism

Transvestism is practised by shamans in many societies, ancient and modern. It was noticed by researchers among many Siberian and central Asian peoples such as the Chuckchee (Bogoras 1907: p448ff), the Kamchadal, the Koryaks, the Turkmens, the Kazakh, the Karakalpak, and Southern Asian and Oceanian peoples such as the Sea Dyak, the Ngadju Dyak of Borneo, etc. and also in Ramree Island off the coast of Burma. Among the Chukchee of north-eastern Siberia, male shamans dressed as women, did women's work and used the female language, which was said to symbolize their marriage with their guardian spirits. Across the Bering Strait in Alaska, Eskimo shaman Asatchaq would emulate birth when he took his *kikituk* effigy. Among the North American Indians, there existed a strong tradition of male transvestism called *berdache*. (Vitebsky 1995: 93) Among the Najavo, it is called *nadle*, which means "one who is transformed" or "the changing one," and when they became shamans, they were believed to be very powerful. The Mohave believed female shamans were more powerful than male shamans, and *berdache* stronger then either. In Korea many instances of transvestism among *baksu* (male shamans) have been reported. (Akiba 1950/1987: 168; Akamatsu & Akiba 1938 II:259; Seo I 1993: 168; 1992 II:150-151; Gim Geumhwa 1995; Jo Jaryong 1996a, 1996b; Hogarth 1998, 1999, 2003) As shown in Gim Geumhwha's "essays" (1995: 180) in *gut* (the Korean shamanistic ritual) the essential costume is *chima*, a long flowing traditional Korean woman's skirt, which both male and female shamans (generally called *mudang*) wear. During my field research, I have also noticed that in *gut*, the most essential costume of the *mudang* is *chima*, over which they wear various outer garments. Thus the shaman's transvestism characteristically involves the cross-dressing of the male shaman, and many researchers of shamanism have reported that the shaman's ritual costumes are sometimes feminine attire.

The shaman's costumes are important in shamanism, since they help "transform him before all eyes into a superhuman being," as Eliade (1951/1964: 168) has put it. Hence they may take the form of a skeleton, symbolizing the dead returning to this life through the shaman; they are sometimes decorated with feathers and other ornithological features representing a bird so that he/she could fly to the world of the spirits. [1] But why do male shamans wear women's clothes? And do they wear them only during the ritual, or also outside the ritual context?

Basilov (1996: 120-124) describes his encounter with an old Uzbek shaman called Taŝmat Kholmatov, who always wore female clothes and whose behaviour and mannerisms are considered feminine by his people. In the Korean context, Seo (1993: 168) describes many cases of *baksu*, whose voices and demeanours are feminine, and who indulge in feminine pursuits such as kitchen work, knitting and embroidery. According to him, there are some *baksu* who squat down like women when they urinate, and those who wear bras, panties, and outer female garments, and wear makeup. My field research supports his statement. Although it is usually during *gut* that they wear female clothes, I have seen them wear female clothes outside the ritual context. I have also heard of various acquaintances of *baksu* describing them as being "odd" even in their childhood, tying the jacket strings in the feminine way, i.e. the knot

---

1. For examples of feather decorations in shamanistic paraphernalia, see Figures 12.20, 12.52, 12.53, 12.54 in Part 2.

13. Transvestism in Shamanism: a Reflection of Female Hegemony in the Primeval Era?

213

to the right of the breast, etc. And also they often look and sound femi-nine, and occasionally wear makeup.

The most popular interpretation for the transvestism of the sha-mans would appear to be along the lines of Eliade (1951/1964: 352) who maintains that it arises from the shaman's need to "abolish polarities." According to him shamanism involves a return to the primordial era when the polarities such as god/human, man/woman did not exist. That is why among the Sea Dyak of Borneo, *manang*, who enjoy a high social standing, are usually sexless or impotent men. And also among the Ngad-ju Dyak of South Borneo, *balian* (shamaness) are often prostitutes, and *basir* hermaphrodite or impotent. Eliade interprets it as based on their need to incorporate both heaven (male) and earth (female), since they are regarded as intermediaries between the two. Similarly Middleton (1969: 224) claims that the asexuality of the shamans among the Lugbara sug-gests their liminal roles, representing their state of oneness or the whole, without the division of the sexes.

However, that does not fully explain why feminine apparels fea-ture importantly in shamanistic rituals, as in the Korean case, and why it is usually the male shamans who cross-dress, usually in, but also some-times out of, the ritual context. Could it possibly be that the reason is in the primordial era, women had hegemony in society? Before we tackle this question, I must briefly discuss various theories concerning male dominance and female power.

Male Dominance and Female Power

Male dominance and female subordination is a phenomenon which is prevalent in most human societies. The strong evidence exists in the ele-ments of cultural ideology, the informants' statements that explicitly de-value women, symbolic formulations of inferiority, and social-structural arrangements that exclude women from certain groups, roles or statuses. As Ortner (1974) claims, the search for a genuinely egalitarian, let alone matriarchal, cultures has proved futile, and male superiority is evident even among the matrilineal Crow.

Then why does male dominance exist almost universally? Many attempts have been made to explain the asymmetry between the sexes, mainly in terms of a universal and necessary cause. They range from the claim (Engels 1884/1972) that at some moment in history men "took" power away from women, to a more suggestive theory (Bettleheim 1964) that the cause is the male envy of female reproductive powers.

Another influential theory is put forward by anthropologist Mary Douglas (1966) through the concept of purity. In many traditional societies women are considered polluting because of childbirth and menstruation. Since pollution is dangerous, women are kept in subordination to protect society. The concept of pollution is also related to that of honour and shame in some societies, for example the Mediterranean societies. (Goodale 1980: 130-1) In those societies women have to preserve their purity, and their sexuality is controlled, since they carry the honour of their families. (Goddard in Caplan 1987) This conception is also directly linked to the preservation of the purity of the bloodline in patrilineal societies. Since patrilineal societies overwhelmingly outnumber matrilineal ones in human history, male dominance is an almost universal fact.

Ortner (1974) put forward a theory that "nature is to culture as female is to male," and as creators of culture, men are closer to culture and women are identified or symbolically associated with nature. Since culture's role is to control nature, it is superior, and likewise, women through their close association with nature, are also controlled and contained by men. Her formulation challenged some anthropologists like Forge (1972), who considers that the oppositions of male/female and nature/culture are better seen as complementary to each other rather than one single scale of superiority and inferiority, and had a powerful impact on social anthropology in the late 1970s and early 1980s.

Harris (1977: 81) argues that male dominance is a by product of warfare, which is "not the expression of human nature, but a response to reproductive and ecological pressures. Therefore, male supremacy is no more natural than warfare." He further maintains that male dominance is caused by an imbalance between protein supplies and population density.

In Confucian societies such as Korean society, male dominance is explained through the cosmological law governing the universe, which was developed by the Neo-Confucianists in Sung dynasty China in the 12th and 13th centuries. Neo-Confucianists believed that the human world and the cosmic order had to be in equilibrium, otherwise disaster would befall it. To be in complete harmony with the universe, human beings must observe the rules of the moral imperatives, which are commonly known as "*samgang* (the three basic bonds)" and "*oryun* (five moral rules in human relations)." *Samgang* meant that subject should obey sovereign, son father, and wife husband. "*Oryun*" decreed that there be

13. Transvestism in Shamanism: a Reflection of Female Hegemony in the Primeval Era?

215

loyalty between sovereign and subject, intimacy between father and son, distinction between husband and wife, order of priority between junior and senior, and trust between friends. Thus all human relationships were vertically structured; there were few horizontal relationships, even between friends, since they were either one's senior or junior. These rules emphasizing the hierarchical order of the world, which had a metaphysical basis, governed all human relationships, and underpinned the social matrix.

Correlated with the hierarchical order of society was the notion that each human being had to recognize his proper position in society and stay there. In cosmological terms, heaven (*yang*) dominated earth (*yin*) and correspondingly, male had precedence over female. This hierarchical order between the sexes was cosmologically sanctioned and was imperative for the proper functioning of the human order, which could be preserved only when passions were kept in check. To do this the Confucianists drew a sharp distinction between the man's "outer" or public sphere and the woman's "inner" or domestic sphere, and believed that the inner sphere is subordinated to the outer sphere. This asymmetry of the sexes was necessary to restrain sexual indulgence and selfishness which would lead to destruct the existing social order, and to establish the different function of husband and wife. In the Confucian view, the cosmological law thus accorded woman an inferior position. It was decreed that before marriage, a woman should obey her father, her husband after marriage, and her son after her husband's death (Known as "*sambu jongsa*" in Korean).

A detailed discussion of "which theory is the most plausible one" is beyond the scope of this paper, but whichever explanation one endorses, there is no doubt about the existence of male dominance in human society since the records began and even before that. Despite the efforts of some to improve women's position in society and the recent improvements in women's status, male dominance is still an undisputed fact of life. But the question that we may well ask is: "Is male dominance an inherent part of human society and did it exist in the primeval era of human history?"

Engels's claim (1884/1972) that at some moment in history men "took" power away from women, and Bettleheim's theory (1954) that the cause of male dominance is the male envy of female reproductive powers, suggest that women once held power. Many other scholars seem to agree that male dominance is not "an inherent quality of human sex-role plans" as Sanday (1981: 4) has put it. In fact many anthropological explanations for male dominance, including those that we examined earlier, suggest that it is a response to pressures that are most likely to have occurred relatively late in human social history.

The claim that women held power in early human societies has been made by many feminist anthropologists (Sanday 1981; Ortner and Whitehead 1982; Moore 1988). For example, Gillian Gillison explains the origin of male dominance in most contemporary societies through a myth of the Gimi of Papua New Guinea, which relates that the original wild woman was the keeper of the sacred flute, which represents the cosmic power, hidden under her bark-string skirt. One day her brother stole it from her. Man has since been fearful of losing it back to woman, so subjects woman to constant surveillance and restraint.

During my fieldwork in Korea in the early 1990s, Yi Jehwan, known in his circle as "the Scholar Shaman," also presented the view that "All cosmic power originated from woman."

Thus it could be said that male dominance, albeit widespread, may well not be always present in early human society, and is a later development in human history.

Female Predominance in Korean Shamanism

Korean society has long been Confucian-oriented, where men were honoured and women were considered subservient ("*namjon yeobi*" in Korean). Despite recent improvements in women's position in society, gender equality is a long way off, with the overwhelming majority of the members of the National Assembly being male, and a female head of state being still a distant dream. In almost every sector of the society, those holding power are invariably male, and male hegemony is very much in evidence.

What is interesting is that in shamanistic community the reverse is true. Female dominance is evident in the spirits, the shamans and their clients. Female *mudang* overwhelmingly outnumber their male compatriots, the male/female ratio being roughly 20:80[2]. It is a truism to say that most of their followers are women, men traditionally rejecting it as a "superstition." Hence *musok* has long been dubbed a "women's cult."

---

2. For a detailed discussion of this subject, see Hogarth 1998a:100.

13. Transvestism in Shamanism: a Reflection of Female Hegemony in the Primeval Era?

217

Although a majority of the important deities are depicted as male, female gods and spirits also feature prominently. The Mountain Spirit (Sansin), one of the most important gods in shamanism, is generally believed to be a male deity, but various scholars, such as Son (1947/1984), claim that Sansin was female in ancient times. In the shamanistic paintings, female deities are often depicted in the same size as the male ones, which testifies to a greater degree of gender equality in the shamanistic pantheon.

Female predominance is evident not only in quantitative terms, but also qualitatively as well. Many a female *mudang* is the main bread winner of a household. It may well be by default, i.e. in the absence of the men in their lives, since many *mudang* experience marriage break-ups and are single mothers bringing up their children on their own. Even when they are married, their husbands are often weak or unfortunate (often violent as well) people incapable of looking after the financial affairs of their families, and often rely on their wives for regular income. As breadwinners, they have much more power than ordinary housewives in mainstream Korean society. So a househusband that one comes across from time to time in the shamanistic community is not a laughing stock as he would be elsewhere, and carries no stigma. Within their community, there appears to be no prejudice against female *mudang*, who command as much respect as male, if they are considered gifted. As they age, they are shown due respect and consideration by younger *mudang*, both young and old, and often become matriarchal figures in their community. In the largest society of *mudang* in South Korea today, called Daehan Seunggong Gyeongsin Yeonhaphoe (The Spirit Worshippers Association for Victory over Communism), although the president and the vice presidents are male, most of the important committee members are female and they often hold sway. It seems to me that age, experience and knowledge, rather than gender, are deciding factors in commanding respect.

This female dominance is often interpreted as a degeneration of shamanism, i.e. women taking over what men discarded. Gim Taegon (1990) for example claims that in Sodo in the ancient times the leaders were male shamans with political, jurisdictional as well religious powers. According to him, over time, the leaders diverged into two; the male ones became kings in mainstream society while the female ones took over the religious aspect and went underground becoming *mudang* as we know them today. Lewis (1971/1989) presents a similar view that women took over shamanism after it was discarded by men.

However, shamanistic practices change their forms according to the type of society in which they are practised. Hence in hunting-gathering societies the ecstatic leaders are male, and travel to the realm of the spirits, while in settled agricultural societies, they tend to be female, and invite the spirits down to join them through possession.[3] And since shamanism was first introduced to the west after being "spotted by Russian travellers among the Tungus of Siberia in the late 17th century, people tend to regard the male shamans taking trips as the original form.

But we must remember that much existing evidence, such as rock engravings and paintings, suggests that shamanistic practices existed as early as the Palaeolithic Age, and possibly beyond that.[4] In that dawn of human history, could it be that human society was matriarchal and female had religio-political powers? Could the present female dominance in the Korean shamanistic community be a reflection of the social structure that once existed in that remote past?

In the absence of written documents and other concrete evidence, we cannot categorically say that it is the case. However, it is interesting that in *gut*, which is based on the concept of a return to the primordial era when polarities did not exist, the first thing the *mudang*, male or female, puts on is a woman's skirt, and that the widespread transvestism usually involves the male dressing in women's clothes. Those facts could be interpreted as suggesting that female hegemony may well have existed in the primeval era.

---

3. For details see Hogarth 1998b.

4. See Figures 1, 2, 3, 4, & 5 in Part 2.

13. Transvestism in Shamanism: a Reflection of Female Hegemony in the Primeval Era?

219

Part 14

GEOMANCY AND KOREAN SHAMANISM

Introduction

Geomancy, (風水: *pungsu* in Korean and *fengshui* in Chinese, literally meaning "wind and water" originated in ancient China, but over time became deeply rooted as a wide-spread popular folk belief in Korea. It premises that in the ground, although unseen, there exists "vital energy" called "*gi*" (translated by Maurice Freeman[1] as "cosmic breath") which affects the fortunes of a person/persons. In other words, the more *gi* a site contains, the better it is for people inhabiting it. Since *gi* is easily dispersed by wind and blocked by water, the direction of those two elements is paramount in its flow and settlement. Therefore the geographic conditions of a dwelling/work place or a town/village, such as the position of mountains, hills and rivers, which affect the flow of *gi*, are believed to be directly linked to the fortunes of its inhabitant(s). It is also believed that since *gi* is absorbed by the bones of the interred dead and transmitted to their living descendants, a gravesite likewise influences the fortunes of the descendants of its occupant. Over time it underwent further highly complex theoretical developments to become a quasi-scientific subject.

As a folk belief which has strongly influenced the lives of the

---

1. 1966, 1979.

Korean people, *pungsu* has naturally been incorporated into Korean shamanism (called *musok*) (Gim Taegon 1981). So Korean shamans, generally referred to as *mudang*, are frequently consulted by their clients about the auspiciousness of their new house/business site or the gravesites for their parents/grandparents.

However, although they have often been lumped together as superstitions by rationalized people, there is a vast difference between the techniques used to find an auspicious site between that of a professionally trained geomancer, most commonly called *jigwan* in Korea, and a Korean shaman generally referred to as *mudang*. The former uses a methodology which is based on the ancient Chinese cosmology called, *eumyang ohaeng* (the Theory of Yin/Yang and Five Elements)[2], and analyzes the data that he carefully collects through geographic survey. On the other hand, the latter relies on her/his sensory intuition and inspiration drawn directly from her/his tutelary spirits. This paper focuses on the Korean *mudang*'s methods of dealing with the issues concerning the location of house/business/grave sites. A detailed discussion of the methodology of *pungsu* is beyond the scope of this paper[3], but to discuss its similarities and dissimilarities with *musok* it is necessary first to examine briefly what classic *pungsu* is concerned with, and its influence on the Korean people through the ages.

Although *pungsu* has long been incorporated into Korean shamanism and the auspiciousness of a site for a house/office/grave is an important issue in *mudang*'s activities, it has not been dealt with in any depth in the studies of Korean shamanism so far. Seo Jeongbeom who published prolifically on *mudang* himself admits that *pungsu* is an area he has not explored so far; in fact in his extensive studies of Korean shamans published in five volumes as *Munyeo byeolgok* (Seo 1992-1993) *pungsu* hardly gets a mention. Yi Neunghwa's *Joseon musok go* (1927/1991), which minutely examines historical documents for any records of *musok*, however obliquely mentioned, rarely contains the word *pungsu*. Neither does it get more than a cursory mention in most other classic and more recent books dealing with Korean shamanism, such as

---

2. The Five Elements are metal, wood, water, fire and earth, and they are believed to form everything in the universe, and their interrelations decide the destiny of people and the turn of events.

3. For a detailed discussion of Korean geomancy, see Murayama (1931)1990; Choe Changjo 1984; Choe Gilseong 1989: m223-241; Choe Yeongju 1992.

Akamatsu & Akiba (1938), Son (1947/1984), Akiba (1950), Yu (1975), Choe (1978, 1989), Harvey (1979), Gim Taegon (1981), Cho Hung-youn (1983), Kendall (1985), Choi Chungmoo (1987), Hwang Rusi (1988), Ju (1992), etc. The books written by the Korean shamans in recent years do not frequently mention *pungsu*, either, but interestingly the word "*teo*" (meaning "site") appears fairly often. During my field research, I rarely came across the word, "*pungsu*" in *gongsu* (the messages sent from the gods and spirits via possessed *mudang*), whereas I often heard the word "*teo* (site)" as in '*jip teo* (house-site)," "*sanso teo* (gravesite)," "*gagye teo* (shop-site)" and that the position of a site was the cause of the recent misfortunes suffered by the sponsors of *gut*. Jo Jaryong (1996b) devotes most of his book, *Doggaebi Janggun Jo Jaryong* (*General Hobgoblin Jo Jaryong*) to the concept of "*teo*," which he views as a spiritual domain as well as material.

In this paper, I will analyze some case histories dealing with *pungsu* in *musok*, which include not only those that I collected during my fieldwork, but also those that appear in recently published books written about or even by Korean shamans (or ghost writers with their help) to give more objectivity. Those case histories will clearly reveal the methods used by the Korean shamans and how they differ from that of trained geomancers.

Geomancy in Korea

Geomancy, which is most commonly called *pungsu* or *pungsu jiriseol* in Korea, consists of *yanggi pungsu* (yang town-site geomancy), *yangtaek pungsu* (yang house-site geomancy) and *eumtaek pungsu* (yin grave-site geomancy). Geomancy is generally thought to have been introduced to Korea from China during the Three Kingdoms Period. Although there is no clear evidence, there are some records that suggest that similar practices existed during that period. [4]

It was mastered and further developed by Doseon, who became the royal advisor to the founder of the Goryeo dynasty, Wanggeom (King Taejo). Wanggeom's respect for Doseon was so great that he gave him the title of *guksa* (National Monk/Teacher). Although a devout Buddhist, Wanggeom was such a staunch follower of Doseon's *pungsu jiriseol*,

---

4. For some examples of such practices, see The Academy of Korean Studies, 1991. *Han-guk minjok dae baekgwa sajeon* (The Comprehensive Encyclopaedia of the Korean Nation) 23, pp 648-649.

that he moved the capital from Donggyeong (now Gyeongju) to Songak/ Songdo (now Gaeseong) which is located in the centre of the Korean peninsula as advised by Doseon. Moreover in *"hunyo sip jo* (ten important pieces of advice which must be heeded)" which is recorded in *Goryeosa* (*A History of Goryeo*), he instructs his descendants to consult Doseon when choosing sites for Buddhist temples (the second item). The fifth and eighth items are also concerned with *pungsu*.

It might well be that King Taejo's absolute belief in *pungsu jiriseol* was caused by his sense of insecurity, arising from the fact that he became king without having any royal blood. With the king as such an ardent believer of *pungsu*, it is no surprise it became very influential during this period. The great popularity of *pungsu jiriseol* during the Goryeo period (918-1392) can also be attributed to the unstable social conditions, exacerbated by frequent foreign invasions. The geomancy that was most prevalent during the Goryeo period was *yanggi/yangtaek pungsu*, i.e. that concerned with the sites of dwelling places of the living, rather than *eumtaek pungsu* which deals with the gravesites, since during that period the Buddhism being the national religion, in keeping with the Buddhist tradition cremation rather than burial was the norm,

The founder of the Joseon dynasty (1392-1910), Yi Seonggye, was in a similar situation as Wanggeom in that he was not descended from the royal line, but upturned his king to found a new dynasty. He moved his capital to Hanyang (now Seoul) which is deemed to be geomantically perfect, and built his capital according to the pusngu theory, which continued to be very popular. However, during the Joseon period greater emphasis was put on *eumtaek pungsu*, as a result of the importance of the *hyo* (filial piety) ideology that came to be considered as the supremest human virtue. There exist countless stories about auspicious gravesites bringing success and prosperity to the descendants, and misfortunes and disasters befalling those who buried their ascendants in inauspicious gravesites. *Jigwan*, a trained professional geomancer, was an indispensable person during the mortuary rites, as the future fortunes of a family depended on choosing an auspicious gravesite.

Today *pungsu* has lost much of its influence on the everyday lives of the people, but still maintains its relevance with some people. A *jigwan* is often employed to find an auspicious gravesite at a considerable fee. When something goes wrong after moving into a new house, starting a new business, or burying their parents/grandparents, people often won-der whether it is caused by the inauspicious site. When problems persist, many people still consult fortune-tellers, many, although not all, of them are *mudang*, and are often prepared to move house/gravesites immediately, if they are told that those sites are inauspicious, as we shall see in Case History 3. Now I will discuss how a *mudang*'s method differs from that of a *jigwan*.

Problems caused by inauspicious sites: *mudnag*'s diagnoses and solutions

The ultimate purpose of geomancy is to locate a spot with strong *gi*, which often translates as a warm, dry and bright site. This concept has long been incorporated into Korean shamanism, and *mudang* are frequently consulted by their clients about the auspiciousness of their prospective house or business sites before they move house or set up an office or factory.

However, there is a vast difference between the methods used by *jigwan* (trained geomancers) and *mudang*. The former undergo training and employs a "scientific" method in that they survey the geographic conditions and applies the data to the established theories to choose an auspicious site. The latter very rarely are trained in the traditional *pungsu* theories, although they may have a superficial knowledge of them, but rely on their intuition and also direct instructions from their tutelary spirits (Gim Geumhwa 1995: 58; Sim 1995; Jo 1996a, 1996b; Mun 2005).

There is also another fundamental difference between *pungsu* and *musok*; in *musok*, it is believed that a site not only has varying degrees of *gi* (or in some cases lack of it), but also is inhabited and governed by gods and spirits (Jo Jaryong 1996b: 64). Their names and domains are:

1) *teosin*: The most important god in overall charge of the site

2) *seongjusin*: resides in the central beam of the house supporting the roof (*daedeulbo* in Korean)

3) *jowangsin*: in the kitchen

4) *chiksin*: in the toilet.

Therefore for the well-being of the occupants of a site, the existence of good *gi* is not enough, but a harmony between its spirits (*teosin* in particular) and its occupants is also very important, hence the difference between methods used by *jigwan* and *mudang*. The former collects geographic data and analyses them according to the existing theory[5], while the latter presents a client's *saju* (the year, month, day, time of a person's birth which is believed to determine his/her destiny) to her/his tutelary spirits to get answers directly from them. The answers and solutions often come through *gongsu*, messages from the gods/spirits through the mouth of a possessed *mudang*. I shall present a few case histories:

Case History 1: A three-year-old boy's death (Hogarth 1998: 174-175)

On 28 September, 1993, I attended a *jinogi gut* (a *gut* for the dead) held most unusually[6] for a three-year-old boy, who had died after being run over by a car, nine days previously. A few days after the accident, his then pregnant 26 year-old-mother miscarried a boy foetus. It was revealed by a *mudang* during a divination session that the dead boy took his brother with him. Grief and terror gripped the grandparents; instead of two grandsons they would have had, they were left with none, and the dead boy's father (aged 31) being their only son, having a son and heir was vital to them. So they agreed to sponsor a *gut* to send the soul of their grandson safely to the other world, lest he would do any more harm to his living relatives. During the *gut*, the chief *mudang* sent a *gongsu* from the spirits that their misfortune was caused by the inauspicious house site, so they should move house as soon as possible.

Case History 2: A battered wife (Hogarth 1998: 176-177)

On 19 October, 1993, I was present at the *jaesu gut*[7] covertly sponsored by a battered wife (aged 43) of a modestly well-to-do timber merchant (aged 45). It was ostensibly held to pray for good luck for her family, particularly her eldest daughter (aged

---

5. I call *pungsu* a "quasi-science" as this theory is based on ancient Chinese cosmology, which is in essence a "belief system."

6. It is most unusual to perform a *jinogi gut* for a child, most being held to send the ascendants safely to the other world so that they can become benevolent ancestors bringing them luck. Children who die young are usually considered as "debtors/sinners," as they fail to repay their parents for the *gift of life* and upbringing. In traditional East Asian societies, they were often buried without elaborate ceremonies, normally given for the dead. (Jordan 1972; Wolf 1974; Hogarth 1998: 88)

7. A *gut* held to pray for good luck.

19) who was studying for her university entrance exams. But what prompted her to agree to sponsor a costly *gut* was that she also wanted to put a stop to her violent husband's frequent physical assault on her. During the *gut*, the chief *mudang*, possessed by her chief tutelary spirit, told her to move house, since the probable cause of her trouble was their inauspicious house site.

I have since then come across many similar cases of *mudang* advising their clients to move house or graves of their parents/grandparents, telling them their present house/grave sites were the direct cause of their problem, being inauspicious for them. But for objectivity, I will present some other similar case histories written in books by other authors including some *mudang* themselves.

According to Jo Jaryong, if clients heed the warning and move house, their lives can sometimes be saved:

Case History 3: The husband of one of Jo Jaryong's clients (Jo 1996b: 78-80; Mun 2005: 23-24)

A lady client came to consult Mr. Jo, since she was worried sick over her husband's promotion, and wondered whether his slow advancement was due to the inauspicious house site. When he put in the man's *saju*, his tutelary spirits told him that the husband's death was certain, if they did not move house immediately. Alarmed, she persuaded her husband to agree to move house hurriedly to the north of the River Han as advised by Mr. Jo. The whole process of their relocation took less than a fortnight. Three days after they moved into a new apartment, Seongsu Bridge[8], one of the largest bridges over the River Han, suddenly collapsed at the morning rush hour, killing many people. Since he drove through that bridge every morning to go to his office which was to the north of the River, he would certainly have been one of the casualties.

And if they ignore the warning, a disaster strikes:

---

8. Seongsu Daegyo (Large Bridge), which was built in October 1979, suddenly collapsed, on 21 October 1994, killing 32 and injuring 17 people, mostly commuters and students from the south to the north of the River Han.

Case History 4: Jo Jaryong's Politician Client (Mun 2005: 21-22)

A well-known politician visited Mr. Jo one day because he was suffering from ill health. Mr. Jo divined through his client's *saju* that the problem lay with the ancestral burial mountain (*seonsan*). He advised him to move the graves to another mountain, but being very busy with the presidential nomination, his client did not take action. Soon he fell down dead.

There is another important difference between *pungsu* and *musok* regarding a site. In *pungsu*, auspiciousness of a site is deemed to be geographic and therefore almost unvariable[9], so a professional *jigwan*'s services usually end with finding a good site for a house or a grave. On the other hand, in *musok*, it is not absolute (Jo 1996b: 37-39), and even a geomantically auspicious site can change into an inauspicious one and bring misfortunes to the occupants or their descendants, if unfortunate circumstances occur. The circumstances can change for various reasons:

1. A site itself can be affected by wandering malignant ghosts bearing grievances (called *japgwi*, *subi*, etc) hovering it, creating a dark cold atmosphere even though its geographical condition is warm and bright.

Case History 5: A squid restaurant that suddenly lost its customers (Mun 2005: 233-235)

It was once a very successful business, but suddenly customers stopped coming, and its owner who relied on it for livelihood was worried and consulted his neighbour, a *mudang* called Jo Geumsun. She found out that the problem was the wandering malignant ghost who stood by the door of the restaurant, creating a cold, dank, eerie atmosphere. She also correctly divined to his surprise that the husband of his wife's sister hanged himself after a heated argument over her affair with another man. Laden with grievances, the ghost of the cuckolded man stood by the door of his wife's brother-in-law's restaurant, keeping the customers away. Ms Jo recommended a *gut*, during which the ghost

---

9. Long-term changes in geographical conditions, such as rising sea level, shifting landscape, are not usually dealt with in traditional *pungsu*.

played havoc, so she recommended calling the wife's sister. When she came, the ghost borrowing the possessed **mudang**'s mouth called her all sorts unmentionable names and gave vivid descriptions of what she had done to those present, which would not normally be uttered in public. The woman, highly embarrassed and repentant, apologized profusely to the ghost/**mudang**, and Ms Jo managed to placate the ghost and send him safely to the other world. After the **gut**, the business regained its former glory.

Case History 6: Sex-crazed men whose bodies were invaded by a young man's ghost (Sim 1995: 162-167)

A couple with two children moved into their house seven years ago after years of hard work, saving and scrimping for it. Immediately afterwards the family was plagued with one problem after another. The husband became a nymphomaniac, demanding sex from his wife night and day, and wandering about outside at night with his penis exposed. Then he died suddenly of a heart attack. After that, their son, then aged 20, started behaving just like his father, and even tried to rape his own sister. So the woman came to ask Ms. Sim whether the cause was the inauspicious house site and she should relocate her family. Ms. Sim divined that the house site was fine, but it was caused by the ghost of a young man, whose lower half of the body lay buried under the house. After exorcising the young man's ghost and other malignant spirits, the son regained his normal self, and got married soon afterwards. The family had no further trouble.

2. Such malignant ghosts can also be brought into the house inadvertently by the owners through *moksin* (wood spirit) which resides in wood including furniture. So clients should consult their regular *mudang* before doing any house repairs, sticking nails or boring holes on wooden beams, buying a piece of wooden furniture or even moving the existing furniture around, lest any of these activities disturb and upset *moksin* (Jo 1996b: 65). *Mudang* sometimes attribute an inexplicable run of misfortunes in the family to the noxious *moksin* which was brought into the house unwittingly, and say it can affect the

events in the family members' immediate future.

3. Discord with *teosin* is another major reason for an auspicious site bringing bad luck to its occupants. In *musok* it is believed that an auspicious site is the one where a harmony between *teosin* and the occupants exists. But a discord can occur if the head of the family changes his occupation; for example, *teosin* can be in perfect harmony with him as a businessman, but not as a politician as we shall see in Case History 6. It is believed that misdemeanours of family members can also annoy *teosin*.

Case History 7: Jo Jrayong's client (Mun 2005: 13-16)

Jeong was a successful businessman, whose dearest wish was to run his company without the interference of the political powers. Although he was a devout Christian, who attended mass every Sunday, he visited Jo secretly whenever he had a difficult problem. He wanted to find out whether he would be elected a member of the National Assembly (Korean Parliament), having already obtained the support of his party. Borrowing Jo's mouth, his guardian spirits told them that the *gi* of Jeong's present house site was in perfect harmony with his *gi* as a businessman, but clashed with it as an aspiring politician, and recommended that he move house immediately to succeed in his new career. But because he was very attached to his house, having worked hard for years to buy it and logistical problems, Jeong ignored the advice of the spirits sent via Jo, and decided to stay in the same house. Although his election seemed to be a foregone conclusion, he failed to get elected. Three years later, he tried again and sought Jo's opinion, which remained the same. The problem according to the spirits was his house site, which is suitable for a businessman, but not for a politician. Jeong again chose not to heed the advice, and refused to move, and he again failed in the next election. At the third election, he compromised and instead of selling the house, let it out, and moved to an apartment that is considered auspicious. At that election he finally succeeded, but after achieving his goal, he moved back into his old house. Strangely enough, at the following election, despite the advantageous position as a serving member of the National Assembly, he failed to get re-elected.

4. Although ancestors' gravesites are geomantic auspicious, the ancestors can bring illness and other misfortune to their descendants, if the latter neglect them, instead of passing the beneficial *gi* that their bones collected through the good geographical conditions. In other words, the auspiciousness of a gravesite is not absolute, but can change. We shall see an example in Case 8 below.

Case History 8 (Yu Gang's Korean-American client: Mun 2005: 154-155)

A well-dressed middle-aged lady came to consult Yu Gang, who correctly divined that the problem was her husband who suddenly became paralysed from the waist down seven years ago. They met while studying at an American university, and thanks to their excellent brains and qualifications, got happily settled in the States. During the divination session, Mr. Yu was possessed by their ancestral spirits who upbraided her in an angry voice, "You despicable creatures! How dare you never visited our graves? Every time you came to Korea, you could have just shown your faces briefly to us. What use were those legs, if they could not carry him to our graves? Not even once for the past 30 long years? So we rendered them useless. Just consider yourselves lucky that he wasn't killed!" The grave sites were considered to be auspicious, but if the ancestors in them are not happy, they can apparently send punishment to their descendants.

As we saw in the above case histories, in Korean shamanism, unlike in conventional geomancy, the auspiciousness of a site is not a non-variable factor, but can change with different circumstances. A family can live in a house quite happily for years, but can suddenly suffer a run of bad luck. On the other hand, a geomantically bad site can be turned into a reasonably auspicious place, if a *gut* is held to placate *teosin*, or a person, who has stronger *gi* than *subi* or *japgwi* infesting the site or has a good rapport with the *teosin*, comes to inhabit it (Jo 1996b: 66). Jo Jaryong claims that even a house-site which has a water course (*sumaek*) running far beneath it which is supposed to be very inauspicious according to classic geomancy can be turned into a reasonable site and any illnesses cause by it can be controlled for 3-4 years, if a *gut* is held to supplicate the *teosin* (Jo 1996b: 59). Jo also gives descriptions of how he purchased a notoriously inauspicious site as his home/*sindang* (his business site with altar) years ago, when he was first starting out as a novice *mudang*, and turned it into a reasonable place after offering the gods and spirits a high-scale *gut* with a blood sacrifice of a large live ox (1996b: 37-39).

Conclusion

As we saw above, the basic principle of *pungsu*, i.e. an auspicious site is the one with plentiful *gi*, which makes it a bright and comfortable place to inhabit in life or death, has been embraced by *musok*. Although most *mudang* lack the professional training and knowledge of *jigwan*, and rely on their intuition and inspiration through their tutelary spirits, they instinctively know which is an auspicious site and which is not. However there is a philosophical/ethical dimension to the *pungsu* practised in *musok*; it is the notion that good people deserve good fortune. Therefore even an inauspicious site can be turned into an auspicious one, if the owner's *gi* is stronger than the site spirit's, or if he accrues merit, such as helping the poor or the suffering, or a *gut* is offered to suppress or chase away the malignant forces which cause misfortunes on the occupants and their descendant. Jo Jaryong (1996b: 275) sums it up very succinctly:

> According to an old saying connected with **pungsu**, auspicious grave sites are naturally allocated to filial sons and meritorious people. However, it's my view that however strong one's ancestors' **gi** is, if their descendants do not behave properly, its transmission to them is difficult. I think it is life's lesson that instructs us to be friendly to our neighbours, respect and serve our parents, and look after our ancestors by offering regular sacrifices.

Part 15

THE KOREAN SHAMANISTIC RITUAL AND PSYCHOANALYSIS

Introduction

This paper discusses similarities and differences between the principles and techniques used by modern psychoanalysts and Korean shamans (*mudang*) to cure patients, through examining two case histories, one Korean and the other one of Freud's patients. The Korean case is of a woman in her thirties, who started getting ill immediately after her cantankerous mother-in-law's death following a long sickness, and Freud's patient was suffering from delusions of jealousy about her faithful husband's imagined affair with a young woman. Interesting parallels can be drawn between them.

First, there is a need for a brief discussion of what psychoanalysis involves and what happens in the Korean shamanistic ritual, called *gut*. There are mainly two different types of psychoanalysis currently in use, namely psychoanalysis which takes long and frequent sessions of treatment, and psychoanalytic or psychodynamic therapy, which is a shorter version aimed at a specific purpose, involving less time and expense. The healing method used in the Korean shamanistic ritual (*gut*) resembles the second category, i.e. psychoanalytic therapy. It is interesting to note how uneducated Korean shamans were applying the same principles ages before the advent of the Freudian theories.

Psychoanalysis

Psychoanalysis, founded by Sigmund Freud (1856-1939) in Vienna in the 1890s, and further developed by Carl Jung (1875-1961), Melanie Klein (1882-1960), Anna Freud (1895-1982), Donald Winnicott (1896-1971), Jacque Lacan (1901-1981), Hyman Spotnitz (1908-2008), et al. has firmly established itself in mainstream medicine despite various critiques of its theories and efficacy over the years.

It is based on the premise that people repress feelings too painful or socially inappropriate into in the unconscious mind, which can cause neurotic disorders and symptoms, such as panic, phobias, convulsions, obsessions, compulsions and depression, sexual dysfunction, various relationship problems, a wide variety of personality disorders such as painful shyness, meanness, obnoxiousness, workaholism, hyperemotionality, hyeperfastidiousnesss, hypersedutiveness, etc. Freud (1900/1997, 1963/1973) posited that most of such thoughts and feelings were sexually orientated, which was subsequently refuted by some of his followers, including Carl Jung (1959; Jung and Kerényi 1942/1949), his initial ally, disciple and friend.

Many sophisticated theories have evolved from the early days of Freud, who himself developed his original theory further into the topographic theory which divides the mental apparatus into the systems of conscious, pre-conscious and unconscious, and then replacing it with the structural theory, according to which the human mind consists of "id," "ego" and "superego." Other theories, some of which were first suggested by Freud and refined and developed further by various others, include Ego Psychology (Kernberg 1975), Conflict Theory (Brenner 1982, 2006; Blackman 2003), Object Relations Theory (Spitz 1965; Mahler et al. 1975; Klein 1998; Sayers 2000), Self Psychology (Kohut 1979, 1982), Lacanian Psychoanalysis, Interpersonal Psychoanalysis (Sullivan 1953; Fromm-Reichmann 1960), Relational Psychoanalysis (Mitchell 1983), Intersubjective Psychoanalysis (Atwood and Stolorow 1984) and modern psychology which includes group therapy, developed by Hyman Spotnitz (1961, 1969) and his colleagues. Detailed critical analyses of those theories are beyond the scope of this paper, but what is relevant is that the basic principle of the existence of the "unconscious" and the important role it plays on people's mental lives has remained the same. The psychoanalyst identifies "the beast in men" hidden deep in his unconscious which causes mental health problems, using such methods as "free association," the interpretation of dreams and "parapraxes," etc, and through abreaction, attempts to solve the analysand's problem.

According to Freud (1963/1973: 289-290), an important difference between psychiatry and psychoanalysis is that while the former diagnoses and prognoses neurosis by investigating the patient's family history and his/her predisposition to it by hereditary transmission, the latter analyzes his/her unconscious and identifies the hidden repressed feelings and wishes, even unknown to the patient, which lie at the root of the problem. However, these days a distinction between the two seems to be somewhat blurred, the two terms being used to mean the same thing (Torrey 1986), or psychoanalytic methods being used in psychiatry. Because the patient often shows a strong resistance to exposing his or her repressed feelings, as we shall see later in the case of one of Freud's many short-term patients, the treatment requires a long period of regular sessions, demanding great financial and physical commitment of the analysand. Classical analysis usually requires three to five sessions of 50 minutes per week and on average may last 5.7 years (according to Wikipedia). For treatments for a specific purpose, such as Brief Psychodynamic Therapy (BPT), Brief Relational Therapy (BRT) and Time-Limited Dynamic Therapy (TLDT), 20-30 sessions or less are required. In most states of the USA, unlike Ontario and in Germany, classical psychoanalysis is not covered by health insurance, so costs involved could be negotiated. In the UK, psychodynamic therapy, not to mention lengthy psychoanalysis, is rarely on the NHS (National Health Service), patients being usually treated by clinical psychologists.

An important feature of classical psychoanalysis is that it is conducted on an individual basis, usually in private, the analyst sitting nearby but hidden from the view of the analysand who lies relaxed on a couch, so that the latter can freely talk to the former with minimal self-consciousness or embarrassment. Thus it is often described as a "talking cure." Although single-patient sessions remain the norm, recently the group therapy, developed by Spotnitz, and the play therapy for children are also used. Also studies have been done on cultural variations which come into play in therapy techniques (e.g. Thompson and Mullahy 1951).

Korean shamanism and the cure through *gut*

Evidence, such as petroglyphs and cave paintings, shows that shamanism has been in existence since at least the Palaeolithic Age, although the phenomenon that gave it its name was first introduced to the West in the 17th century by Russian travellers to Siberia. Various evidence, such as tomb murals and other archaeological finds (Hogarth 1999), suggests that shamanism has been an integral part of Korean culture from the ancient times.

There exists a poem (Yi Gyubo 1241-1242/1982) describing Korean shamanistic practices, in more or less the present form, which dates back to the 13th century, which clearly shows that even that early in Korean history shamanistic practices were already condemned by the government authorities who were mostly literati. The author of the poem, a senior government minister, celebrates the expulsion of his neighbour, a *mudang*, out of the capital. In that poem, he criticizes and laughs at the absurdity and irrationality of the shamanistic practices and the benighted multitude who were the clients of the *mudang*. However, historical records suggest that despite the strong official persecution, the government occasionally made use of *mudang*'s services. For example, there is occasional mention of *mudang* being recruited to pray for rain during long spells of drought and the healing and divination by them in Goryeosa (The History of the Goryeo Kingdom)[1], and during the Joseon dynasty, while it was officially persecuted, the government set up a health department called Seongsucheong and a charity hospital called Hwarinwon which employed *mudang* for curing illnesses (Yi Neunghwa 1927/1991; Hogarth 1999: 315-317).

In pre-modern Korea, before the advent of modern medicine and technology, the most important function of the *gut* was curing illnesses which were believed to be caused by malignant spirits (Yi Neunghwa 1927/1991; Akamatsu and Akiba 1938/1991; Akiba 1950/1987; Gim Taegon 1981; Hogarth 1998, 1999). The *gut* is essentially based on the principle of reciprocity (Hogarth 1998), in which various gods and spirits, both benevolent and malignant, are treated to good food, drink, entertainment and more recently gifts of money, so that they would bestow the same on its sponsors. The illness-causing malignant spirits are placated and treated to good things in life, binding them to Maussian (1950/1990)

---

1. For details see: Hogarth 1999: 297-300.

obligation to receive and reciprocate. If any of the gods and spirits bear grief and grievances themselves, they are dispersed by abreaction, i.e. bringing them out in the open and experiencing catharsis through tears. That is why interestingly the Korean shamanistic pantheon includes some historical characters and culture heroes who lived turbulent lives and met tragic ends (Hogarth 1998). Therefore, an indispensable feature of the *gut* is the copious tears shed by all those present, human or spiritual (Yi Neunghwa 1927/1991 ; (Akamatsu and Akiba 1938/1991; Akiba 1950/1987; Gim Taegon 1981; Hogarth 1998, 1999). Tears are misinterpreted by some (e.g. Gim Yeolgyu 1977) who claim that the *gut* is basically a sad mournful event, but they overlook the fact that tears are cathartic and help dissipate grief (Hogarth 1998: 84).

One of the lengthiest and the most important part of a *gut* is that dedicated to the sponsor's ancestors, in which the spirits of her/his agnatic kin make appearances through the possessed *mudang*(s). Just before the beginning of a *gut*, *mudang* has a short consultation session with the sponsor, and through various questions sort out the ancestors that played a significant part in his/her life before their death. Clothes for each ancestral spirit, usually in the form of a gift of a new set of clothes in his or her favourite colour and style, are provided by the sponsor, which are worn by *mudang* for each relevant part. When the ancestral spirits appear, they have a heart-to-heart talk directly with the sponsor, which can reveal hidden feelings of resentment, grievances, accusations, dissatisfaction, unfulfilled desires and wishes, etc, which were left unsaid before their death for various reasons such as social unacceptability or inappropriateness. This part dedicated to ancestral spirits, called "*josang puri*," mostly resembles the method used by psychoanalysis. It is a group therapy session when all the participants, living or dead, vent their repressed feelings, and experience catharsis through copious tears. Any discord, disagreement, or animosity is dissolved and the all the discordant parties are reconciled. Therefore reconciliation (*hwahae*) is a word that often crops up in *gut*.

Nowadays, however, *gut* are rarely performed for purely curing purposes, *mudang* advising their clients to go to hospital for somatic diseases, while undertaking a healing *gut* to cure inexplicable illnesses, which are beyond modern medicine. From my observation it would seem that what they cure effectively are psycho-somatic illnesses, as we shall see in a Korean case history later.

A *gut* is a party, in which all the participants, i.e. gods, spirits which include sponsors' ancestral spirits and wandering malignant ghosts, officiating *mudang* and spectators, have a good time. Even a most private *gut* involves a fair number of people, hence a community spirit is very much in evidence. The atmosphere of the *gut* is like that of any party, colourful, exuberant, intoxicatingly enjoyable to all those present: bright primary colours and loud music predominate, inhibitions being largely discarded. People talk, laugh and cry freely, and through abreaction experience catharsis. Performance is an inherent part of a *gut*, the sponsor(s) taking part in the psycho-drama, as well as the gods and spirits in the form of officiating *mudang* through possession. Schechner (1977, 1988; Schechner and Appel 1990) distinguishes ritual and performance, but *gut* does not easily fit in with his theory, being both ritual and performance. The enjoyment of dramatic performances produces endorphin in the brain, and has the same effect as taking anti-depressant.

As in psychoanalysis, in shamanism theoreticians and practitioners are the same people, hence there are almost as many theories as there are practitioners. In Korea, there are currently more than 135,000 practising *mudang* in South Korea (Hogarth 1998: 97), and therefore there are variations in *gut*, depending on the region and the group they belong to. Also they tend to go along with the times, and introduce various new gods and spirits, so small variations are endless. However, the basic principles of *gut* remain the same.

Psychoanalysis and *gut*
The principle underpinning these two seemingly vastly different methods of curing is surprisingly similar, although there are significant differences between them. We shall discuss similarities and differences by closely examining two cases, one a Korean case, and the other one of Freud's patient.

A Korean case:
A *gut* was sponsored by a 35-year-old woman, with the financial help of her mother, to send off her recently deceased mother-in-law's spirit to the other world. She had looked after the cantankerous old woman who had been an extremely difficult patient during her protracted terminal sickness. When she finally died, the daughter-in-law strangely started feeling very ill, having severe headaches and being unable to eat or sleep well,

despite her newly gained freedom from the gruelling daily routine of caring for a terminal patient on top of her already heavy workload as a wife and mother. As the doctors at the hospital could not find anything wrong with her, she was convinced that the spirits of her recently dead mother-in-law was causing her illness which would eventually kill her. So as a final resort, her mother took her to a *mudang*, who told them that her mother-in-law's newly departed restless spirit was indeed the cause of her illness, and that she would be cured if they held a *gut* to placate it.

A patient of Freud:
A well-preserved lady of 53 was brought to Freud for treatment by her son-in-law, a dashing officer who was on leave, because of her irrational behaviour, accusing her husband, the prosperous owner of a factory, of having an affair with a young female employee. Theirs having been a love match 30 years before, her husband had always been faithful to her, but it would seem that the imagined infidelity was more or less instigated by herself. About a year before, she confided to her maid that what would cause her the biggest pain would be for her husband to have an affair with a younger woman. The maid happened to harbour secret envy and antagonism towards one of her school friends who had done so much better in life than she had, having gained a responsible position in the lady's husband's factory through commercial training and vacancies that occurred through men being called to the military service. The next day the maid wrote her employer an anonymous letter in disguised handwriting informing her of her husband's affair with the girl in the factory, which never took place in reality. It triggered off her irrational neurotic behaviour, although both she and her husband knew what had happened and sacked the maid and kept the falsely accused girl. But whenever she saw or heard about the girl, she made herself so miserable that the happiness of the family was disturbed.

Prima facie, the above two cases have nothing in common, but the methodology of their curing processes is intriguingly similar. The Korean case was effectively cured by a *gut*, and the Freudian case was dealt with through two psychoanalytic sessions. Let us briefly examine what happened during their respective curing processes.

The Korean case:
The *gut* lasted about 12 hours with a short lunch break in the middle of

it. The usual array of important shamanistic gods appeared through the possessed *mudang*, and promised the patient that they would help her. There followed the spirits of her agnatic kin, the last of which was the climax of the *gut*, the confrontation between the patient and the spirit of her mother-in-law via the possessed *mudang*.

When "the mother-in-law" appeared, the mother of the patient leapt at the *mudang* who was possessed by the dead woman's spirit accusing her of unimaginable cruelty towards her daughter before dying. This kind of direct confrontation rarely occurs in reality, since in-laws are usually very civil to one another in Korean society, keeping a respectable distance between them. "The mother-in-law" apologized to the old woman profusely, and turning to "her daughter-in-law" and tenderly holding her hand said, "I was in so much pain I had to take it out on somebody, and unfortunately you had to bear the brunt, as you were always there for me. I realize now how much you must have suffered. Although I bullied you beyond endurance, I loved and cherished you more than anyone, apart from my own son. Please forgive me, and I promise I'll give you good fortune and happiness."

At this the younger woman started crying and said, "Oh, mother, I don't deserve your kind words. I am the one who caused your death, by wishing everyday you'd die and relieve me of my suffering. How could I have such wicked thoughts? I'm indeed the most unfilial wretch that ever lived."

"The mother-in-law" said, "I do understand how you, such a gentle dutiful woman, must have felt to have such extreme thoughts. No, no, you are not to blame; it was my fault for having made your life a living hell." The younger woman threw herself in the "mother-in-law"/ possessed *mudang*'s arms and the two of them cried their eyes out. The mother of the patient joined in, and all three wept until their eyes became all red and swollen. Then it was time for "the mother-in-law" to depart the scene.

It would appear then that the young woman was projecting her "guilty" wish for her mother-in-law's death on the older woman's spirit, i.e. the latter wanted to kill her through spite. As a woman who had been brought up with the conception that filial piety is the supreme human virtue (Yi 1926/1990: 484; Lee Kwang Kyu 1975: Choe Gilseong 1981), this idea must have been most abhorrent, so she must have repressed it and hidden it in her unconscious mind, which was causing the inexplicable illness in her. After being reassured by the person causing her guilty complex that it was an understandable feeling under the circumstances, her gratitude and relief released her from the burden of guilt and eventually cured her illness.

After the *gut*, both the young woman and her mother told me (the author of this paper) that they felt as though a great weight had been lifted from their heart (*gaseum-i siwonhada*), and a few days later the *mudang* in charge told me the woman was completely cured.

Freud's psychoanalytic session

The patient lay on the now famous couch looking at the ceiling, with Freud sitting next to her, out of her view and listening. She at first told him the background story, and whatever was in her mind. Gradually Freud would delve into her unconscious mind, digging out the repressed feelings, through such methods as free association, interpretation of dreams, etc. What Freud found, despite the patient's initial resistance was that the woman harboured a strong love of a sexual nature for her handsome son-in-law, the very man who brought her to Freud, and was in effect projecting her guilty feelings on her innocent husband. Her repression of her socially unacceptable love for her dashing son-in-law was such that she wanted to discontinue her treatment by Freud only after a couple of sessions, claiming she was already feeling better. According to Freud's analysis, at the basis of the projection of her "inappropriate" love for her son-in-law on her husband lay the possibility that her affectionate faithful husband failed to give her full sexual gratification. Freud admits he could not get to the bottom of this problem, as the lady was quite adamant that she felt much better and was sure that her absurd delusions of jealousy would never return. It is possible that her realization after a couple of sessions that her delusions were in fact a projection of her "guilt" on her faithful husband, effectively made her realize the absurdity of her delusions. Freud interprets her refusal to carry on with any further sessions as her resistance to exposing her repressed "guilty feelings."

The above two cases have commonalities in that the healers identify the cause of their physical and neurotic symptoms, and through abreaction, attempt to cure the patient. In both cases, the healers merely provide the patient with an opportunity to discover their repressed feelings, buried deep in their unconscious mind, and the latter through abreaction is made to feel better.

Conclusion

E. Fuller Torrey (1986: 210) claims that psychotherapists (including psychoanalysts), and "witchdoctors" (broadly referring to indigenous healers including shamans) are "cultural variations of the same people." So psychotherapists in the States are "simply the indigenous therapists of the dominant American culture" (ibid.: 232). By that remark, he does not condemn them both as having "no scientific basis," as the article by an unidentified writer in Wikipedia states (Under Psychoanalysis, subheading Scientific Criticism, third paragraph). On the contrary, he emphasizes that "Recognition of this fact should not downgrade psychiatrists; rather it should upgrade witchdoctors."[2] (ibid.: 232) He is right in that what the psychoanalyst calls "the beast within man" is analogous to what the *mudang* calls "the malignant spirit." Torrey's view is also shared by some Korean psychiatrists, most notably Dr. Rhi Bou-yong (Yi Buyeong), MD (1970, 1977, 1978, 1983: 413-414).

However, the *mudang*'s techniques differ from those of the psychoanalyst in that the healing is carried out through impromptu drama skilfully instigated by them, in which the repressed feelings of guilt, pain, wishes, etc. are identified and revealed, and antagonistic parties involved are reconciled. In Schechner's terms (1977, 1988), *gut* is both ritual and performance, and in *gut*, this dramatic performance is enhanced by the addition of what people enjoy in life, such as good food, drink, music, and colourful costumes and decors, which produces endorphin in the brains of the participants and acts as anti-depressants. Being spontaneous, highly entertaining and enjoyable as well as achieving abreaction and catharsis through tears, their method can produce a dramatic success. But it must be emphasized that most modern Korean *mudang* are enlightened and well informed through popular media such as TV, and can quite often differentiate somatic diseases from psycho-somatic ones, although occasional failures have been reported.

---

2. Here is a good example of why the information contained in Wikipedia should not be directly cited, but approached with care.

Part 16

REVIVAL OF ONCE-LOST CULTURAL HERITGE: FROM SUBVERSION TO CULTURAL NATIONALISM

Introduction

As a cult of the traditionally "subservient" women and dispossessed men, Korean shamanism has always contained elements of subversion. Socially inappropriate or politically incorrect ideas or behaviours in mainstream Korean society were often displayed freely in Korean shamanistic rituals, called *gut*, in pre-modern Korea, further strengthening official persecution. Historical personages and culture heroes who fell victim to the socio-political injustice of the establishment were deified, featuring prominently in the Korean shamanistic pantheon (Hogarth 1998, 1999). The community *gut* often contained a dramatic part at the end, which like many folk performances provided a "safety valve" (Gluckman 1963) for the downtrodden masses. The folk drama, as well as giving entertainment, provided an opportunity for the underprivileged masses publicly to air their resentment of the exploitive ruling classes (*yangban*), poking fun at their human frailties, thus obliquely suggesting equality of all human beings. To appeal to the aesthetic/artistic sense of the uneducated masses, it was often crude, direct and vulgar. What is interesting is that educated and sophisticated *yangban* not only closed their eyes to such activities, but also actively encouraged them, being fully aware that such occasional venting of the lower classes' pent-up discontentment ironically helped maintain the highly unfair hierarchical social system.

However, during the transitional period of Korean history, which saw the sudden collapse of the old social order and the introduction of different Western-orientated aesthetic and artistic tastes, such rituals or performances lost their appeal and were gradually being neglected or forgotten by the people. Many disappeared during the Japanese colonial period, since they lost much of poignancy, the exploiters being no longer the *yangban*, but foreign invaders. After liberation, Korean people were preoccupied with building a new nation in the bewildering new modern world, and such performances were becoming insignificant to the point of being almost lost. Community *gut*, which often included such dramas at the end, were performed infrequently, most *gut* being performed by individuals to pray for themselves and their close family members. However, in the 1970s as Korea was beginning to emerge as an industrialized modern nation-state following the success of President Park Chung Hee's economic development projects, there began a movement to revive such performances by people including some social elites. The 1980s were the age of globalization in Korea, but paradoxically also saw an increase in such movements, which led to the official recognition of many near-lost traditional cultural heritage.

Two of the best examples are *Hahoe tal chum/tal nori* (the Hahoe Mask Dance/Drama) and *Nami Janggun daeje/sadangje* (General Nami's Shrine Ritual). The Hahoe Mask Dance/Drama was once a part of a community *gut* called, Hahoe *byeolsin gut*, but is now separately performed, and has been established as one of today's best loved folk performances in Korea, drawing large audiences, and was named Important Intangible Cultural Treasure No. 69 by the government in 1980. The masks dating back to the Goryeo period were placed in the National Museum as National Treasure No 121 in 1964. General Nami's Shrine Ritual was officially designated as Intangible Cultural Treasure No. 20 in 1982 with the title of *Nami Janggun daeje* (The Great Ritual of General Nami).

I will analyze these two rituals/performances to divulge the reasons for their revival and its implications in today's globalizing Korean society. But since beauty is an important factor in all religious rituals, I will first discuss the dynamics of beauty in religion. By "beauty" I mean all aspects of aesthetics, visual and spiritual.

Religion and Beauty

John Keats' much quoted phrase in *Ode on a Grecian Urn*, "Beauty is truth, truth beauty" is well reflected in religion, which is in essence a pursuit of truth. Places of worship are decorated according to the prevailing concept of beauty, which helps draw people to the religion. So the best way to learn the concept of beauty of a particular people is to visit their places of worship. *Gut*, as a "religious ritual"[1], reflects the traditional Korean concept of beauty in every aspect.

Among the reasons for the revival and popularity of shamanistic rituals and performances, an important factor is "beauty," people being attracted to them because they think that they are beautiful. It is a truism that the concept of beauty is highly individual, and moreover prone to change according to the prevailing fashion. One of the reasons why these performances were being neglected for such a long period was that the Korean people's concept of beauty was undergoing great changes during the period of social upheaval, foreign invasions, and the sudden influx of Western culture. Their revival then suggests that the Korean people are rediscovering the beauty of their traditional heritage, of which shamanism is an important part. I would venture to call it "cultural nationalism." But first, there is a need to present definitions of nation, nationalism and cultural nationalism.

Definition of nation, nationalism and cultural nationalism

"Nation" is notoriously difficult to define, since they have a multiplicity of meanings.[2] It can be loosely described as a "political community of people who have much commonality." But the concept of the nation as a "political community" poses problems, since it is not a community in the traditional sense of the word, lacking close personal interrelations among its members. Hence Anderson (1983/91: 6) defines the nation as "an imagined political community – and imagined as both inherently limited

---

1. There is controversy surrounding whether Korean shamanism is a religion or not (For detailed discussion see Hogarth 1998: 24). However even those who argue *musok* is not an organized religion agrees that *gut* is undoubtedly a religious ritual.

2. Hugh Seton-Watson (1977: 5), a recognized authority on the subject, remarks: "Thus I am driven to the conclusion that no 'scientific definition' of the nation can be devised; yet the phenomenon has existed and exists."

and sovereign."[3] Renan (1947-61: 892) makes a similar remark; "*Or l'essence d'une nation est que tous les individus aient beaucoup de chose en commun, et aussi que tous aient oublié bien des choses* (The essence of a nation is that all the individuals have much in common, and also that all of them have forgotten many things)."[4] Gellner (1964: 69) expresses a similar view more bluntly: "Nationalism is not the awakening of nations to self-consciousness: it invents nations where they do not exist."

However negative and complex various scholars' views on the nation may be, it is undeniable that nationalism has exerted a great influence on the modern world. Today its hold on people everywhere is quite evident. It is all the more surprising to learn that the general use of the term is only a recent phenomenon.[5] During the course of the 20th century, the destinies of people were changed by it, and innumerable people have even lost their lives for its cause. Thus Nairn (1977: 359) wryly remarks: "'Nationalism' is the pathology of modern developmental history, as inescapable as 'neurosis' in the individual, with much the same essential ambiguity attaching to it, a similar built-in capacity for descent into dementia, rooted in the dilemmas of helplessness thrust upon most of the world (the equivalent of infantilism for societies) and largely incurable."

Gellner (1983: 1) provides a more generalized definition: it is "a political principle, which holds that the political and the national unit should be congruent." Thus "nationalist sentiment is the feeling of anger aroused by the violation of the principle, or the feeling of satisfaction aroused by its fulfilment."

Nationalism is then a principle of political legitimacy. Therefore, nationalist sentiment is most disturbed if the political unit is ruled by rulers who belong to a nation other than that of the ruled. Typical situations are the colonization or subordination of one nation by another.

Cultural nationalism is the nationalist sentiment towards one's culture. Before defining "cultural nationalism," it is necessary to find a suitable definition of "culture," which has a variety of meanings. In the

---

3. By this definition, he emphasizes the artificiality and ambiguity of the nation. According to him, it is not a "community" in the strict sense of the word, but only an "imagined community," since its members cannot possibly know one another.

4. Renan further supplies historical evidence which clearly suggests that the boundaries of nations become blurred if you closely examine the historical events of the past.

5. Kemiläinen (1964: 10,33) points out that the term "nationalism" was not generally used until the end of the 19th century.

anthropological sense, it means "a system of ideas and signs and associations and ways of behaving and communicating (Gellner 1983: 7)."

Cultural nationalism then may be defined as an ideology that not only the political and the national unit should be congruent, but the members of a national unit should also share the same system of ideas, signs, associations, and ways of behaving and communicating.

The Revival of Ethnicity in Contemporary Societies

At the turn of the 20th century, many tribal and agrarian peoples were undergoing great social changes in the aftermath of the colonization by the industrialized western nation-states. Since they immediately observed the benefits of the industrialization, such as improved health through advanced medicine, an easier lifestyle with the highly developed western technology, what they sought was to become like their colonial masters. In other words, their modernization equated with westernization. Thus the millenarian movements, called the "cargo cults," which swept through Melanesia in the early 20th century, were greatly influenced by the European preoccupation with materialism. (Worsley 1957)

After the two great world wars, many tribal peoples were grouped as a "nation," which then became an independent modern nation-state. There swiftly followed modernization or more precisely westernization. They adopted a parliamentary system based on western democracy, a modern market economy and an education system similar to that of advanced industrialized nation-states.

By the 1950s, industry and commerce dominated the world, and the rapid development in science, technology and communications, resulting in easier travel and contact with other cultures, seemed to suggest the dissolution of cultural boundaries and the creation of a single homogeneous global culture. Liberals and the cosmopolitan idealists predicted, "as mankind moved from a primitive, tribal stage of social organization towards large-scale industrial societies, the various primordial ties of religion, language, ethnicity and race which divided it would gradually but inexorably lose their hold and disappear. The great forces of trade and industry would bind continents together and erase internal barriers and differences. Ancient customs and traditions would become obsolete and the myths of common ancestry would be recognized for what they were and consigned to the museum of mankind's memory (Smith 1981: 2)."

However, what has actually been happening is not congruent with the predictions of the liberals. Today the cosmopolitan ideals and rationalistic expectations have withered (Smith 1981: 1). Instead, ethnic ties and sentiments of nationalism have been revitalized. The recent ethnic conflicts in the former Yugoslavia and Rwanda have thrown into relief the modern renaissance of ethnic solidarity and sentiment, which is often aggressive and fanatical.

Anthropologists and ethnographers studying rapidly modernizing, or more specifically westernizing, societies, have often remarked on the revival of ancient or traditional rituals or customs by the people, including sometimes the sophisticated elite of the society, as a way of asserting their national identity and expressing their cultural nationalism. (Lewis 1971/89: 141; Bloch 1986; Smith 1981; Lan 1985; Pentikäinen 1997: 97-98) Maurice Bloch (1986) has shown how the ancient custom of circumcision took on various meanings according to the changing social conditions in Madagascar. The custom, which was considered "barbaric" in the early days of colonization of the island, became a vehicle for their cultural nationalism later on. In Japan, there has been a movement to "discover" long-forgotten ancient customs or traditional objects, with the slogan "One Traditional Item per Village" in a given time. (Gim Gwangeok in private conversation) We shall see that a similar phenomenon has been happening in Korea.

This revival of ethnicity and nationalist feelings are not only confined to the Third World countries, but also in many advanced industrialized nation-states with heterogeneous populations and cultures. Since the Second World War, the world has witnessed a revival of ethnicity and nationalistic aspirations among the Bretons, Basques, Scots, Welsh, Cornish, Flemish Quebecois, Catalans, Kurds, Ibo, Somali, to name but a few.

Smith (1981) analyzes the underlying causes for the revival of ethnicity in the modern world by examining the development of a sense of history, which first arose in 18th century Europe. This 'historicist' vision involves both a rejection of the materialism and impersonal political system of modern nation-states, and a quest for spiritual regeneration in historical communities. He argues that the cause of this dissatisfaction is the rise of the "scientific state," the "peculiarly western type of state." This and the impersonal modern urban lifestyle have generated a highly charged romantic nationalism, and revived the ancient ethnic bonds, whose extinction liberals and socialists predicted with the advancement of science and industry. Ethnic nationalism can alleviate the sense of estrangement and exclusion, which is the main reason why the ethnic revival is continuing to flourish not only in Africa, Asia, but also in Europe and North America.

Ecstatic cults, in various forms, have suffered gravely by the introduction of Christianity, which deprecates them as "demonic," as testified by numerous missionaries' and western travellers' accounts (e.g. Bishop 1898/1970). During the colonial periods, they remained largely in the "primitive" backwaters of the society, being kept alive by the "ignorant" rural community.

However, when circumstances call for a desperate measure, the hitherto marginalized traditional religious phenomenon can take on a new significance. For example, in the 1960s and 1970s, among the Zezuru in Southern Rhodesia, the ZANLA guerrillas fighting for independence against the white regime received the traditional spirit mediums' approval and assistance, which helped them gain the support and assistance of the peasants. The young guerrillas were legitimated as the returning ancestors by traditional spirit mediums, by observing the ritual rules set by them (Lan 1985). In a less deliberate and self-conscious way, among the Kaffa of south-western Ethiopia, the *ego* (spirit) cult serves as a vehicle for Kaffa cultural nationalism (Lewis 1971/89: 129-131).

Likewise, in Korea, shamanism, which has never ceased to play an important part in the people's lives despite a long history of severe official persecution, is being reappraised as a uniquely Korean religio-cultural heritage. One scholar (Gim Taegon 1972) goes as far as to maintain that shamanism is "the source of the Korean people's spiritual energy." But as in the case of other revived ancient rituals and customs, the main reason for its revival is cultural nationalism, rather than rediscovered religiosity.

The Hahoe Mask Dance/Drama (Hahoe *tal chum/tal nori*)

The Hahoe *byeolsin gut* is particularly famous for its drama. It is different from an ordinary *gut* drama in that it consists mainly of dancing and is not performed by *mudang,* but villagers, and masks are worn. In the old days the players were serfs and were called *gwangdae*, or clowns. Nowadays the mask dance/drama is frequently detached from the *byeolsin gut* and performed separately for entertainment, having lost any religiosity attached to it.

The mask dance is a popular form of folk art in Korea, and there are numerous varieties. However, the Hahoe Mask Dance/Drama is unique in many ways. First of all, being originally part of a religious ritual, scrupulous religious codes of conduct were observed, and therefore all the 20 or so players were men, women being considered unclean. Today, any religiosity attached to it having vanished, it is for pure entertainment, and there are more fmale participants, and sometimes even one or two small children can be spotted among the players, especially drummers.

Secondly, the expenses of the *gut* and the mask dance were paid by all the villagers, including the land-owning *yangban*, who were the objects of ridicule in the play. The oppressed farmers, who were mere serfs, were allowed to relax and eliminate the stress and tension during the performance, by poking fun at their masters, who not only closed their eyes to it, but also actively encouraged it. However, the *yangban* would not dream of attending such a gathering, dismissing it as vulgar and beneath their dignity. Nowadays they are frequently performed by voluntary enthusiasts in the area without pay, and managed by a non-profit preservation society, called *Hahoe byeolsin gut tal nori bojonhoe*.

Thirdly, while the other mask dances were performed in certain designated places the Hahoe Mask Dance/Drama was performed in the front yard of a sponsor's house. One or two acts were performed in each yard, before they moved on to the next one. Therefore, an act is called a madang (literally meaning "front yard"). Today it is performed in a specially purpose-built arena.

Last, but not least, at the other mask dances, which are mainly folk dances to entertain people, masks being made of cheap disposable materials such as paper, cardboard and gourd are burned after each performance, whereas the Hahoe masks were elaborately made of good-quality wood and kept for a long time. They used to be considered sacred with an attached warning that anyone who touched them would die a violent death, and kept in a holy place until the next performance. Therefore the masks have been well preserved accurately keeping their original forms. In the National Museum, Hahoe masks dating back to the Goryeo period designated National Treasure No. 121 can be seen. The masks themselves are considered to be superb objects d'arts. There were originally twelve in all, but only nine have survived. They depict different characters so vividly and realistically that even today passing through the area faces resembling the masks can sometimes be detected among the villagers. They are also carved in such a way to convey different emotions and idiosyncrasies of each character, depending on the angle they are seen. For example, when it looks up, the mask looks smiling and cheerful, showing the *yang* or bright side of the character, and when it looks down, it looks sinister or mournful, showing the *yin* or dark side.

There is a sad legend attached to the creator of the masks, Master Heo, who was commanded to keep himself cleansed of all pollution, and made to work in a sacred place. A 17-year-old maiden of the Uiseong Kim clan harboured a secret love for him, and not seeing him around the village for a long time, traced him to his place of work, and out of curiosity peeped through a hole made in the rice paper window of his workroom. At that moment Master Heo fell down dead, vomiting blood. He had finished making all the other masks except the chin of *Imae tal* (The Village Idiot mask), which is said to be why it has no chin. Heart broken, the girl hanged herself, and became the Village Guardian Spirit for whom this *gut* was performed.

The masks in the order of appearance are:

1) *Gakssi tal* (The bride mask): It has very small eyes and a tiny mouth indicating as a bride she should not see or talk much. It is made up for the wedding, i.e. a white powdered face and three round circles of red rouge on its cheeks and brow. It is supposed to be the Village Guardian Spirit, who is believed to be the spirit of the tragic Maiden Kim, or a local woman who was widowed at 15.

2) *Choraengi tal* (The flippant shallow servant mask): It has a tiny lopsided brown face with buck teeth to show his low birth and flippant stupidity. It is thought to be a representation of a private servant who was depicted as a lopsided half mute to indicate he had no freedom of speech. (Bak Jintae 1990: 88). Its distorted small face also shows that however hastily he meddles into things, he is shallow and stupid because of his lack of educational and social opportunities.

3) *Baekjeong tal* (The butcher mask): It has a coarse lined brown face which can show both the good and evil sides of his character.

4) *Halmi tal* (The granny mask): It has a tiny wizened brown face

to show the hard life this old woman has had since she was widowed at 15. It has a pathetic expression and a big mouth which is ever ready to take in food and pour out her lamentations about her sad life.

5) *Bunye tal* (The painted harlot mask): This young courtesan has a heavily made-up seductive face with coquettish eyes and a smiling mouth which attract men.

6) *Pagyeseung tal* (The fallen Buddhist monk mask): It has a greasy grinning face to show his lascivious side.

7) *Imae tal* (The village idiot): It has a happy-go-lucky face which instantly shows that he is a half wit. For reasons stated earlier, this is the only mask without a chin.

8) *Yangban tal* (The nobleman mask): It is considered to be a true masterpiece in artistic terms, simultaneously showing the dignity of this high-ranking government official of noble birth, and his greed, vanity and pettiness.

9) *Seonbi tal* (The scholar mask): A *seonbi* was a scholar who did not yet hold a government post, and supposedly spent their time studying the Chinese classics or writing poetry, but in reality most *seonbi* were only human. In the play, Seonbi is severely satirized together with Yangban, his social compatriot.

There are seven parts in all:

1) *Mudong madang* (Riding on shoulders): Entrance of the Village Guardian Spirit, represented by Gakssi, riding on a man's shoulders, and collection of donations from the audience.

2) *Juji madang* (two fighting "lions"): Purification by two ferocious fighting creatures. Enter a male and female *juji*, who are generally believed to be "lions" (but look nothing like them) and fight, the female triumphing and climbing over the male in the end. Enter Choraengi who makes the audience laugh with his flippant behaviour.

3) *Baekjeong madang* (Butcher): Butcher enters and kills an ox, and tries to sell its testicles, but no one buys it. This part may be a residue of blood sacrifices in *gut* in by-gone days.

4) *Halmi madang* (Granny): Lamentations of the old woman who was widowed at age 15 only three days after the wedding.

5) *Jung madang*: (the fallen Buddhist monk): Bunye, the painted harlot, enters and urinates by the roadside. The passing Buddhist monk sees her, and aroused by the smell of the urine yields to the carnal temptation and carries her off into the bush. Choraengi witnesses it, and tells Imae.

6) *Yangban/Seonbi madang*: Enter Yangban accompanied by his servant Choraengi, and Seonbi by his mistress Bunye, and they stand far away from each other. Bunye flits between the two, coquettishly massaging their shoulders, etc. Choraengi suggests a formal introduction, and while they are bowing to each other on the floor, he sits on the head of Yangban, a highly improper gesture by a servant which causes laughter among the audience. To impress Bunye, Yangban and Seonbi argue, each claiming their social superiority over the other, but both see the futility of their argument after Choraengi meddles into it. The servant's vulgar flippancy eventually reconciles the two warring aristocrats and they all dance together. Halmi tries to chip in, but after a brief initial rejection of her by Seonbi, they all dance together. Enter Baekjeong (the butcher), carrying the ox testicles, and claims they are good for virility, and Yangban and Seonbi fight over them, each claiming he wanted to buy them first. Enter Imae, the village idiot, and shouts the tax collector is coming, upon which all exit in haste.

7) Hollye madang and choya (The wedding ceremony and the first night): This part is to appease the Village Guardian Spirit, represented by Gakssi. The groom is played by Seonbi, with Yangban officiating. Gakssi makes a ceremonial bow all the way to the floor twice while the groom does it once. After the brief ceremony, a wedding night scene is enacted on a straw mat. It is also a kind of fertility rite. It was commonly believed that if a childless couple made love on the mat, they would have a son.

The characters, dialogues and actions in the play are imbued with religiosity (Pak 1999), but the detailed analysis of the mask dance/drama from that perspective is beyond the scope of this paper. What is relevant to our current discussion is that even a cursory look at the dance clearly shows the subversiveness of the lower classes who through exposing the human weaknesses of the ruling classes and even religious practitioners suggest the equality of all human beings regardless of their birth, education or social status. In the *Yangban/Seonbi madang*, the lowly servant Choraengi actually puts his bum on Yangban's head.

The Hahoe Mask Dance/Drama was last performed in 1928, and revived in the 1970s by a group of enthusiasts with the help of the memories of Yi Changhui (1913-1996) who played the role of Gakssi in the last performance. After participating in the National Folk Festival, it attracted the attention of folklore scholars whose academic research into it subsequently led the government to designate it as Important Intangible Cultural Treasure No. 69 in 1980.

General Nami's Shrine Ritual (*Nami Janggun Daeje/Sadangje*)

Nami Janggun Daeje on the other hand is a full shamanistic ritual, dedicated to a distinguished historical personage, who despite his high birth and illustrious career, fell victim to the intrigue of his political enemies who were jealous of his achievements.

General Nami was born in 1441, as a grandson of Nam Hui, one of King Taejong's sons-in-law. On top of his military skills, he possessed excellent literary talent, which helped him pass the *mugwa* (national examinations for selection of the military officials) with distinction in 1458, and held a series of high government posts. He was hailed as a national hero after quashing Yi Siae's Rebellion and vanquishing the foreign invaders in the north. However, his distinguished career made some political enemies among his jealous contemporaries, who falsely accused him of treason. He was wrongly convicted and put to cruel death in 1468.

Legend has it that he had paranormal powers which enabled him to see malignant ghosts and chase them away while alive. After death, he was deified, and several shrines dedicated to him were built in Seoul, where both Confucian sacrifices and shamanistic rituals were regularly offered. It came to an end temporarily but was revived in the 1980s by a group of folklore scholars, and was finally designated Intangible Cultural Treasure No. 20.

Today a large-scale *gut* in the classic Seoul area *gut* format is performed regularly, attended by the local government district officials and a large crowd of residents and tourists, who are each treated to a bowl of noodles adding to the festive atmosphere. The ritual has expanded to include colourful street processions headed by a man dressed as General Nami on horseback.

Conclusion: Conflict, reconciliation and harmony

As we saw in the Hohoe Mask Dance and General Nami's Shrine Ritual, the essence of the shamanistic ritual is resolving the ever-present conflict in human society, and achieving harmony through reconciliation. In the former, warring Yangban and Seonbi are reconciled and dance happily with their social inferiors, Bunye, Choraengi, and even poor, old and ugly Halmi, suggesting equality and harmony among all people regardless of status, education, age, gender or physical beauty. The harmonious dance also suggests the acceptance of the strict hierarchical social system by the oppressed, however unfair they may find it to be, thus helping maintain stability in a highly unfair situation. In the latter, the presence of the male government officials suggests the reconciliation of the establishment and its victim, General Nami, and harmonious co-existence of all.

Likewise, while the revival of the shamanistic rituals and perfor-mances in Korea is essentially a protest against cultural colonization by the west, it also implies a hope for harmonious co-existence of Korean traditional and globalized cultures.

Hahoe Masks 1: Gakssi (The Bride)

- Closed eyes and mouth – a bride should not see or talk much.
- Made up for the wedding – white powdered face and three circles of red rouge on the cheeks and forehead.
- The Village Guardian Spirit: believed to be the tragic Maiden of the Uiseong Kim Clan, or a local lady who got widowed at age 15.

Hahoe Masks 2: Choraengi (The Flippant Servant)

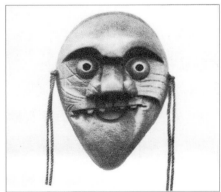

- A tiny lopsided brown face with buck teeth to show his low birth and flippant stupidity.
- His distorted small face indicates that however hastily he meddles into things, he is shallow and stupid because of his lack of educational and social opportunities.

Hahoe Masks 3: Baekjeong (the Butcher)

· A coarse brown face which can show both the good and evil sides of his character.
· When it looks up, he looks jovial, and when it looks down he looks sinister and cruel.

Hahoe Masks 4: Halmi (The Granny)

· A tiny wizened face to show the hard life this old woman has had; widowed at 15 only three days after the wedding, etc.
· A pathetic expression and a big mouth which is ever ready to take in food and pour out lamentations about her hard life.

Hahoe Masks 5: Bunye (The Painted Courtesan)

· A heavily made up seductive oval face with coquettish eyes and a smiling mouth to attract men

Hahoe Masks 6: Jung (The Fallen Buddhist Monk)

· A greasy leering face to show his lascivious side.

Hahoe Masks 7: Imae (The Village Idiot)

· A happy-go-lucky grinning face which instantly shows that he is a half wit.
· The only mask without a chin.

Hahoe Masks 8: Yangban (The Nobleman)

· Considered to be a true masterpiece in artistic terms
· It simultaneously shows the dignity of this high-ranking government official of noble birth, and his greed, vanity and pettiness.

Hahoe Masks 9: Seonbi (The Scholar)

- Younger than Yangban, he does not yet hold a government post.
- Supposed to be spending his time studying the Chinese classics, but in reality he is only human.
- It shows his competitive and argumentative character.

Hahoe Mask Dance/Drama 1: *Mudong madang*

- Entrance of the Village Guardian Spirit, represented by Gakssi (the Bride) riding on a man's shoulders.
- Collection of money from the audience.

Hahoe Mask Dance/Drama 2: *juji madang*

· Two fighting *juji* ('lions').
· Purification by two ferocious fighting creatures, a male and a female. – The female triumphs over the male.
· Enter Choraengi and makes the audience laugh with his flippant behaviour and remarks.

Hahoe Mask Dance/Drama 3: Paekchŏng *madang* (the Butcher)

· The Butcher kills an ox, and tries to sell its testicles, but nobody buy it.
· A residue of blood sacrifice in *gut* in the by-gone age?

Hahoe Mask Dance/Drama 4: Halmi *madang* (the Granny)

· Lamentations of the old woman who was widowed at 15, only three days after her wedding.

Hahoe Mask Dance/Drama 5. Jung *madang* (the Fallen Buddhist Monk)

- Bunye, the Painted Courtesan enters and urinates.
- The passing monk sees her, and aroused by the small of the urine yields to the carnal temptation and carried her off into the bush.
- Choraengi witnesses it and tells Imae.

Hahoe Mask Dance/Drama 6. Yangban/Seonbi *madang* (the Nobleman/the Scholar)

· Antagonism between Yangban and Seonbi.
· Choraengi suggests a formal introduction, and while they are bowing to each other he sits on Yangban's head.
· They argue each claiming their social and scholarly superiority over the other. Bunye flits between the two.
· Enter Baekchong, carrying the ox testicles, and claims they are good for virility, and Yangban and Seonbi fight over them.
· After Choraengi chips in and makes flippant remarks, they realize the futility of their argument, and decide to have a dance.
· Halmi chips it, but Seonbi pushes her away, but eventually all dance happily together.
· Enter Imae and shouts the tax collector is coming, upon which all exit in haste.

Hahoe Mask Dance/Drama 7: *Hollye/choya madang* (the Wedding and the First Night)

· Supposed to appease the Village Guardian Spirit. The groom is played by Seonbi with Yangban officiating.
· After a brief ceremony, a wedding night scene is enacted on a straw mat.
· A kind of fertility rite. It was commonly believed that if a childless couple made love on the mate, they would have a son.

General Nami's Shrine Ritual I

· General Nami:
  -born in 1441, as a grandson of Nam Hui, one of King Taejong's sons-in-law
  -passed *mugwa* with distinction in 1458.
  -hailed as a national hero after quashing Yi Siae's Rebellion and vanquishing foreign
   invaders in the north.
  -fell victim to his political enemies who falsely accused him of treason
  -put to cruel death in 1468.
  -after death became a shamanistic deity.
  -believed to have had paranormal abilities to see malignant ghosts and chase them
   away.

General Nam Yi's Shrine Ritual II

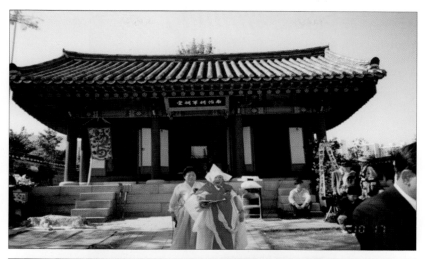

· There are several shrines dedicated to him in Seoul, where both Confucian and shamanistic rituals were regularly offered.
· This one is the largest and situated in Yongsan.

General Nami's Shrine Ritual III

- A large-scale *gut* in the classic Seoul area *gut* format is performed regularly, attended by the local government district officials and a large crowd of residents and tourists. – a bowl of noodle soup for all.
- The ritual has recently been expanded to include a colourful street processions headed by a man dressed a General Nami on horseback.

GLOSSARY

baksu (mudang)	박수	male shaman
bangsaengje	방생제 (放生祭)	'liberating life' ritual in Buddhism, in which fish or turtles are released into the sea or the river, for merit-making
Bari Gongju	바리 공주 (公主)	Abandoned Princess
beopsa	법사 (法師)	A euphemism for a male 'shaman,' who usually recites the Buddhist Scriptures for exorcizing the evil spirits
bosal	보살 (菩薩)	Bodhisattva. A popular term of address for a female *mudang* and/or fortune-teller
Bugun	부군 (府君)	Village Guardian Spirit

bujeong	부정 (不淨)	pollution
Bulsa Halmeoni	불사 (佛師) 할머니	Buddhist Guru Grandmother
buri	부리	root
Byeolsang	별상	spirits of the tragic kings
byeolshin gut	별신굿	a community *gut*
byeong/uhwan gut	병/우환 (病/憂患) 굿	A healing *gut*
Changbu	창부 (唱夫)	The Performer Spirit
cheon	천 (天)	heaven, sky
cheon-gun/in	천군/인 (天君/人)	heavenly spirit/man
Chilseong	칠성 (七星)	The Seven Stars (Spirit)
chima/jeogori	치마/저고리	traditional Korean ladies' top and skirt
Chuseok	추석 (秋夕)	harvest Moon Festival
daedong gut	대동 굿	a community *gut*
Daehan Gyeongshin Yeonhaphoe	대한 경신 연합회 (大漢 敬神 聯合會)	The Korean Spirits Worshippers' Association
daeju	대주 (大主)	the male head of the *gut* sponsoring family
Dan'gun	단군 (檀君)	The mythological progenitor of the Korean nation
dari	다리	bridge
ddeok	떡	rice cake

dokgaebi	도깨비	mischievous 'hobgoblin'
(dok)gyeong	독경 (讀經)	reciting Buddhist/Taoist Scriptures for exorcizing evil spirits
dongbeop	동법	malignant spirits that exists in wood stone and earth
doryeong	도령	a young unmarried man
dosa	도사 (道師)	an enlightened one in Taoism
dwitjeon	뒷전	final part of a *gut*, in which all the sundry ghosts are fed
eop	업	karma
eum	음 (陰)	yin; the negative, dark or female elements in nature
eunhye	은혜 (恩惠)	favours, benefits, kindness, grace, obligations
gamang	가망	invitation of spirits
gangshinmu	강신무 (降神巫)	god-descended shaman
gi	기 (氣)	Ccosmic breath or energy
giju	기주	female sponsor
gisaeng	기생 (妓生)	entertainer (geisha)
geollip	걸립	wandering ghosts
geori	거리	Material, stuff, subject, part or act in *gut*
geungnak	극락 (極樂)	Buddhist (Lotus) paradise

gongju	공주 (公主)	princess
gosa	고사	simple ritual offering to household gods
-gun	-군 (君)	prince, lord
gunung	군웅 (軍雄)	spirits of war heroes
gut	굿	A shamanistic ritual
gyeja/gija	계자 (啓者)/기자	a preferred term of address of *mudang*
halmeoni	할머니	grandmother
han	한	Unsatisfied longing or unresolved grudges/grief
Hogu	호구	The spirits of the young women, who were forcibly taken by the Mongols
hwangje	황제 (皇帝)	Emperor
hwaraengi	화랭이	male shaman
hyodo	효도 (孝道)	Filial piety, or more accurately *pietas* (Latin)
indari	인 (人) 다리	'human bridge,' dying of close relatives of a prospective *mudang*
jaebi/aksa	재비/악사 (樂士)	musicians in *gut*
jaesu	재수 (財數)	Luck, good fortune
Janggun	장군 (將軍)	The General (Spirit)
japgwi	잡귀 (雜鬼)	Sundry ghosts
je	제 (祭)	A ritual

jeja	제자 (弟者)	Disciple, a euphemism for *mudang*
jetga	젯가 (祭家)	A good-sponsoring family
jesa	제사 (祭祀)	Domestic ancestral ritual
Jeseok	제석 (帝釋)	The Buddha Emperor (Spirit)
jinjeok gut	진적 굿	A *mudang*'s annual offering to her/his tutelary spirits
jinogi gut	진오기 굿	Gut for the dead
jip	집	House
Jishin	지신 (地神)	The Earth Spirit, the Site Spirit
josang	조상 (祖上)	Ancestors
maengin/mangin	맹인 (盲人)/망인	Blind-man
maji	마지 (摩旨)	Offering rice in a Buddhist temple or a *mudang* shrine. Can also mean 'welcoming'
malmi	말미 ()	'final tail,' the recitation of the Ballad of Pari Gonju in *jinogi gut*
malmun	말문	'word gate,' a neophyte's first message from the spirits
malmyeong	말령	Spirits of a victim of an untimely death
Manmyeong	만명	The spirit of General Gim Yushin's mother.

manshin	만신 (萬神)	A respectful term for a female *mudang*
michin gut	미친 굿	Gut for curing insanity
miko (Jp)		Female medium
mok	목 (木)	Wood
mudang	무당 (巫堂)	General term for all shamans and quasi-shamans
muga	무가 (巫歌)	Shaman song
muggyeok	무격 (巫覡)	Male and female mudang
mun	문 (門)	Door
munyeo	무녀 (巫女)	Female *mudang*
Musok Bojon-hoe	무속 보존회 (巫俗 保存會)	Musok Preservation Society, the name of the institute run by Bak Ino for training neophyte *mudang*
musok-in	무속인 (巫俗人)	Musok person/people
myeongdo/myeongdu	명도/명두 (明圖/明斗?)	Convex brass mirror
naerim/shin gut	내림/신 (神) 굿	Mudang's initiation ritual
nal	날	Day
nam	남 (男)	Male, man
namjon yeobi	남존여비 (男尊女卑)	Honoured men, subservient women
neok	넋	Soul

neok geonjigi gut	넋건지기 굿	Gut for a drowned person
nori	놀이	'play,' a part of a gut
obanggi	오방기 (五方旗)	Flags representing the five directions
Obang Shin-jang	오방신장 (五方神將)	Five Directional General Spirit
osaek cheon	오색 (五色) 천	Ficw differently coloured pieces of clot, which symbolize 'sundry ghosts'
pansu	판수 (判數?)	Blind fortunes-teller
piri	피리	Small pipe
pungeo-je	풍어제 (風魚祭)	Community gut to pray for a good catch of fish
puri	풀이	Dispelling, exorcism
Sagu-je	사구제 (四九祭)	Buddhist ritual held on the 49th day after a person's death
saje	사제	Death Messenger
sal	살	Arrow, sudden death
sal puri	살 풀이	exorcism to remove sal
sam	삼 (三)	three

Samjae Pallan	삼재 팔난 (三災 八難)	Literally 'three disasters' and 'eight hardships.' In Buddhism, 'the Three Disasters' are flood, fire and gales. Alternatively they refer to was, pestilence and famine. 'The Eight Hardships' consist of hunger, thirst, cold, heat, water, fire, knife and war. (*Sae urimal keun sajeon* 1992)
samil chiseong	삼일 치성 (三日 致誠)	simple sacrifice offered on the third day after a *gut*
Sambul/Samshin	삼불/삼신 (三佛/三神)	Three Buddhas/Three Spirits (Birth Spirits)
Samseong	삼성 (三聖/三星)	Holy Trinity or Three Stars
Samseong	삼성	Death Messenger who takes people to the other world by sudden death, hence more feared than Saje
Samu-je	삼우제 (三虞祭)	gravesite sacrifice offered on the third day after a funeral
Sanshin	산신 (山神)	the Mountain Spirit
seseummu	세습무 (世襲巫)	hereditary *mudang*
shik	식 (式)	ceremony
shin	신 (神)	spirit, god
sinbyeong	신병 (神病)	possession sickness
shindang	신당 (神堂)	*mudang*'s shrine

shinnada	신(神)나다	to get excited, elated
shiwang	시왕 (十王)	the Ten Lords of the Under-world
so	소 (小)	small, little
soju	소주	strong distilled liquor (alcohol content 20-35%) made from rice, millet and other grains
Seokjeon-je	석전제 (釋奠祭)	sacrificial offerings to Confucius and his disciples
Seonang	서낭/성황 (城隍?)	village tutelary spirit
Seonggyuing-wan	성균관 (成均館)	the National Confucian Academy
Seongju	성주 (城主)	Housesite Spirit
soseul gut	솟을 굿	'soaring' *gut*, part of *naer-im gut*
ssal	쌀	raw rice
ssi	씨 (氏)	lineage
ssikkim gut	씻김굿	'cleansing' *gut*, mortuary *gut*
subi	수비	ghosts of people who died unnatural deaths
sumang gut	수망 (水亡) 굿	*gut* for the drowned
taryeong	타령 (打令/妥靈?)	ballad
Teoju Daegam	터주 대감 ()	Housesite Spirit
wang	왕 (王)	king

Yaksa Yeorae	약사 여래 (藥師 如來)	'Pharmacist Buddha'; Manla (the Supreme Physician)
Yaksa Bosal	약사 보살 (藥師 菩薩)	'Pharmacist Bodhisattva'
yang	양 (陽)	the positive, bright, male element
yangban	양반 (兩班)	old Korean nobility, consisting of civil and military classes
yeo	여 (女)	female, woman
yeokhak	역학 (易學)	fortune-telling based on Chinese cosmology and sometimes statistics
Yeokshin	역신 (疫神)	the Plague Spirit
yeombul	염불 (念佛)	reciting the Buddhist Scriptures
Yeomna Dae-wang	염라 대왕 (閻羅 大王)	the king of the underworld, Yama (God of Death); Skr. Dharmapāla/Dharmarãja
Yeondeunghoe	연등회 (燃燈會)	a 'shamanistic' Buddhist festival held on the first full moon day during Shilla and Goryo
yeongsan	영산 (靈散?)	ghosts of victims of vilent death
Yesu jaengi	예수 쟁이	Jesus lackey
yong	용 (龍)	dragon
Yonggungdang	용궁당 (龍宮堂)	the Dragon Palace Shrine

Yonggung gut	용궁 (龍宮) 굿	shamanistic term for bang-saeng-je
Yongwang	용왕 (龍王)	the Dragon King
yunhoe	윤회 (輪廻)	the Eternal cycle of Death and Rebirth in Buddhism

REFERENCES

Ahern, Emily M. 1973. The Cult of the Dead in a Chinese Village. Stanford: Stanford University Press.

Akamatsu, Chijo & Akiba, Takashi. 1937 (Book I) & 1938 (Book II)/1991. *Chōsen fuzoku no kenkyū*. Tōkyō: Osaka Yagō Shoten. Korean trans. by Sim Useong, *Hang-uk musok-ui yeon-gu* (*A Study of Korean Shamanism*). Seoul: Dongmunseon.

Akiba, Takashi. 1950/1987. *Chōsen fuzoku no genchi kenkyū*. Nara: Yōtokusha. Korean trans. by Choe Gilseong, *Joseon musok-ui hyeonji yeon-gu* (*A Field Research on Korean Shamanism*). Daegu: Gyemyeong University Press.

——— 1953/1993. *Joseon minsok ji*. Korean trans. by Sim Useong. Seoul: Dongmunseon.

Anderson, Benedict. 1983/1991. *Imagined Communities*. Rev. ed. London:Verso.

Atwood, George E and Robert D Stolorow. 1984. *Structures of Subjectivity: Exploration in Psychoanalytic Phenomenology*. Hillsdale, NJ: Analytic Press.

Aung, M H. 1962. *Folk Elements in Burmese Buddhism*. Oxford: Oxford University Press.

Babcock, Barbara A (ed). 1978. *The Reversible World: Symbolic Inversion in Art and Society*. Ithaca, New York: Cornell University Press.

Bak, Ino. 1990. *Jeontong Hanyang gut geori* (*Traditional Seoul Gut Procedures*). Seoul: Samdo Chulpansa.

Bak Jintae. 1990. *Talnori-ui giwon-gwa gujo* (*The Origin and Structure of the Masked Dance Drama*). Seoul: Saemunsa.

Banton, Michael (ed). 1966. *Anthropological Approaches to the Study of Religion*. London: Tavistock Publications.

Basilov, V N (1996) Vestiges of Transvestism in Central-Asian Shamanism. In Diózegi, Vilmos & Hoppál, Miháy (eds.), *Shamanism in Siberia: selected reprints*. Budapest: Akadémiai Kiadó.

Bauman, Richard (ed). 1992. *Folklore, Cultural Performances, and Popular Entertain-nment: A Communications-Centered Handbook.* New York: Oxford University Press.

Beattie, John & Middleton, John (Eds). 1969. *Spirit Mediumship and Society in Africa.* London: Routledge & Kegan Paul.

Belshaw, Cyril S. 1965. *Traditional Exchange and Modern Markets.* Englewood Cliffs, New Jersey: Prentice Hall.

Bettleheim, Bruno. 1954. *Symbolic Wounds: Puberty Rites and the Envious Male.* London: Thames & Hudson.

Bishop, Isabella Bird. 1897/ 1970. *Korea and Her Neighbours.* Seoul: Yonsei University Press.

Blacker, Carmen. 1975. *The Catalpa Bow.* London: George Allen and Unwin.

Blackman, Jerome. 2003. *101 Defenses: How the Mind Shields Itself.* New York: Routledge.

Blau, Peter Michael. 1964. *Exchange and Power in Social Life.* New York: John Wiley & Sons.

Bloch, Maurice. 1986. 'From Blessing to Violence.' In *Current Anthropologist.* 27:4.

Bloch, Maurice, & Parry, Jonathan (eds). 1982. *Death and Regeneration of Life.* Cambridge: University Press.

Bogoras, Waldemar. 1907. *The Jesup North Pacific Expedition, Vol. 11, The Chuckchee.* New York and Leiden.

Bourguignon, Erica (ed). 1968. 'World distribution and Patterns of Possession Steates.' In Raymond Prince (ed), *Trance and Possession States: 3-34.* Montreal: R.M. Buckley Memorial Society.

——— 1973. Religion, *Altered States of Consciousness and Social Change.* Colombus: Ohio State University Press.

——— 1976. *Possession.* San Francisco: Chandler & Sharp Publishers.

——— 1979. *Psychological Anthropology: An Introduction to Human Nature and Cultural Differences.* New York: Holt, Rinehart and Winston.

Brenner, Charles. 1982. *Mind in Conflict.* Madison: International University Press.

——— 2006. *Psychoanalysis or Mind and Meaning.* New York: Psychoanalytic Quarterly, Incorporated.

Caillois, Roger. 1979. *Man, Play and Games.* New York: Schocken.

Caplan, P. 1987. *The Cultural Construction of Sexuality.* New York: Tavistock.

Carrithers, M. 1983. *The Forest Monks of Sri Lanka: An Anthropological and Historical Study.* Delhi: Oxford University Press.

Chijun, Murayama. 1931/1990. *Joseon-ui pungsu (Korean Geomancy).* Korean Trans. (1990) by Choe, Gilseong. Seoul: Mineumsa.

Cho, Hung-youn (Jo, Heungyun). 1983. *Han-guk-ui mu* (*The Korean Mu*), Seoul: Jeongeumsa.

—— 1984. 'Problems in the Study of Korean Shamanism.' In *Shamanism in Eurasia II*, ed. by Mihály Hoppál. Götingen.

—— 1990. *Mu-wa minjok munhwa* (*Shamanism and Folk Culture*). Seoul: Minjok Munhwasa.

—— 1992. 'Le Chamanisme au début de la Dynastie Chosŏn.' In *Cahiers d'Extrême-Asie, 6: Special Issue, Korean Shamanism*. Paris: L'école Française d'Êxrême Orient.

—— 1993. 'Sara nameum gajokdeul-gwa mangja-ui jakbeol-gwa janchi (A Farewell and Feast between the Dead and the Living Family Members).' In *Seoul Jinogi Gut, Han-guk-ui Gut 20*. Seoul Yeolhwadang.

—— 1994. 'Han-guk Dan-gun sinang-ui siltae.' In Yun, Iheum et al. *Dan-gun geuihae-wa jaryo* (*Understanding Dan-gun and Research Data*). Seoul: Seoul National University Press.

Choe, Byeongheon. 1994. 'Goryeo sidae Dan-gun sinhwa jeonseung munheon-ui geomto (A Study of Documents on the Dan-gun Myth from the Goryeo Period).' In Yun, Ihum et al. *Dan-gun, geu ihae-wa jaryo* (*Understanding Dan-gun and Research Data*). Seoul: Seoul National University Press.

Choe, Changjo. 1984. *Han-guk-ui pungsu sasang* (*The Ideology of Geomancy in Korea*). Seoul: Mineumsa.

Choe, Gilseong. 1969. 'Han-guk mosok-ui ekstasi byeoncheon go (A Discourse on the Metamorphosis of Korean Shamanism).' In *Asea yeon-gu*, Vol. XII, No. 2, pp 49-64. Seoul: Goryeo Daehakgyo Asea Munje Yeon-guso.

—— 1978. *Han-guk musok-ui yeon-gu* (*A Research on Korean Shamanism*). Seoul: Asea Munhwasa.

—— 1981a. *Han-guk-ui mudang* (*The Korean Shaman*). Seoul: Yeolhwadang.

—— 1981b. *Han-guk musok non* (*Essays on Korean Shamanism*). Seoul: Hyeongseol Chulpansa.

—— 1989. *Han-guk min-gan sinang-ui yeongu* (*A Research on Korean Folk Beliefs*). Daegu : Gyemyeong University Press.

—— 1992. *Han-guk musok ji* (*A Record of Korean Shamanism*), 2 vols. Seoul: Asea Munhwasa.

Choe, Gwangsik. 1994. *Godae Han-guk-ui gukga-wa jesa* (*The Nation and Ritual of Ancient Korean*). Seoul: Han-gilsa.

Choe Jaeseok. 1982/1990. *Han-guk gajok yeon-gu* (*A Study of the Korean Family*). Rev. 5th ed. Seoul: Iljisa.

Choe Namseon. 1988. 'Dan-gun keup (및) ki yeon-gu (Dan-gun and its study).' In Lee

Ki-baik (ed), *Dan-gun sinhwa nonjip* (*Essays on the Dan-gun Myth*). Seoul: Saemunsa.

Choe, Un-gwon. 1990. *Gwisin iyagi* (*Ghost Stories*). Seoul: Boseong Chulpansa.

Choe, Yeongju. 1992. *Sin Han-guk pungsu* (*New Korean Geomancy*). Seoul: Donghak-sa.

Choi, Chungmoo (Choe Jungmu). 1987. *The Competence of Korean Shamans as Performers of Folklore*. Ph.D thesis. Indiana University.

———— 1991. 'Nami. Chae, and Oksun: Superstar Shamans in Korea.' In Heinze, Ruth-Inge (ed), *Shamans of the 20th Century*. New York: Irvington Publishers.

Choi, Joon-sik (Choe, Junsik). 1996. 'Koreans' View of Life and Death: The Traditional Interpretation and a New Understanding.' In *Korea Journal*, Vol 36 No.2, Summer, pp 5-25.

Clark, Charles Allen. *1932/1961*. *Religions of Old Korea*. Seoul: The Christian Literature Society of Korea.

Covell, Alan Carter. 1986. *Folk Art and Magic: Shamanism in Korea*. New Jersey & Seoul: Hollym.

Cozin, M. 1987. 'Won Buddhism: The Origin and Growth of a New Korean Religion.' In L. Kendall & G. Dix (eds), *Religion and Ritual in Korean Society*. Berkeley: University of California Press.

Crapanzano, Vincent & Garrison, Vivian (Eds). 1977. *Case Studies in Spirit Possession*. New York: Wiley.

De Rios, Marlene Dobkin. 1992. *Amazon Healer: The life and Times of an Urban Shaman*. Bridport: Prism Press.

Derrett, J. D. M. 1979. Spirit Possession and the Gerasene Demoniac, in *Man* 13, 2.

Deuchler, Martina. 1977. 'The Tradition: Women during the Yi dynasty . In *Virtues in Conflict: Tradition and the Korean Woman Today*, ed. By Sandra Mattielli. Seoul: Royal Asiatic Society.

Diószegi, Vilmos, & Hoppál, Mihály (eds). *1978/1996*. *Shamanism in Siberia*. Budapest: Akadémiai Kiadó.

Dix, Griffin M. 1980. 'The Place of the Almanac in Korean Folk Religion.' In *Journal of Korean Studies 2*.

Douglas, Mary. 1966/1991. *Purity and Danger*. London: Routledge.

Drury, Nevill. 1989. *The Elements of Shamanism*. Shaftesbury: Element.

Dundes, Alan. 1980. *Interpreting Folklore*. Bloomington: Indiana University Press.

Durkheim, Emile. 1915/1966. *The Elementary Forms of the Religious Life*. English trans by Karen E Fields. New York: Free Press.

Edsman, Carl Martin (ed). 1967. *Studies in Shamanism*. Stockholm: Almqvist & Wiksell.

Eliade, Mircea. 1951/1964. *Le Chamanisme et les techniques archaiques de l'extase*. English trans. by Willard R. Trask, as *Shamanism: Archaic Techniques of Ecstasy*. London: Arkana.

Engels, Fiedrich. 1884/1972. *The Origin of the Family, Private Property and the State*. New York: Pathfinder.

Epstein. Lawrence and Wenbin, Peng. 1998. 'Ritual, Ethnicity, and Generational Identity.' In Melvyn C. Goldstein & Matthew T. Kapstein (eds), *Buddhism in Contemporary Tibet: Religious Revival and Cultural Identity*. Berkeley: University of California Press.

Evans-Pritchard, Edward Evan. 1976. *Witchcraft, Oracles and Magic Among the Azande*. Oxford: Oxford University Press.

Firth, Raymond. 1967. 'Individual Fantasy and Social Norms: Séances with Spirit Mediums.' In *Tikopia Ritual and Belief*. London: George Allen and Unwin.

——— 1969. 'Introduction.' In J Beattie & J Middleton (eds), *Spirit Mediumship and Society on Africa*. London: Routledge and Kegan Paul.

Fortes, Meyer. 1957. *The Web of Kinship Among the Tallensi*. Oxford: Oxford University Press.

Frazer, J G. 1890/1963. *The Golden Bough*. New York: Macmillan.

Freedman, Maurice. 1966. *Chinese Lineage and Society*. London: Athlone Press.

——— 1967. *Rites and Duties of Chinese Marriage*. London: G. Bell and Sons Ltd.

——— 1979. 'Ancestor Worship: Two Facets of the Chinese Case.' In *The Study of Chinese Society: Essays by Maurice Freedman*, ed. by G W Skinner. Stanford: Stanford University Press.

Freud, Sigmund. 1913. *Totem and Tabu*. Vienna: Hugo Heller. English trans. as *Totem and Taboo, by James Strachey*. London: Cohen & West Ltd.

——— 1963/1973. *Introductory Lectures on Psychoanalysis (1915-1917)*. Reprint of the English translation by James Strachey first published by the Hogarth Press in 1963. Penguin Books.

——— 1900/1997. *The Interpretation of Dreams*. English translation by A A Brill, with Introduction by Stephen Wilson. Wordsworth Classics of World Literature.

Fromm-Reichmann, Frieda. 1960. *Principles of Intensive Psychotherapy*. Chicago: University of Chicago Press.

Fromm-Reichmann, Frieda. 1960. *Principles of Intensive Psychotherapy*. Chicago: University of Chicago Press.

Furst, P T (Ed). 1972. *Flesh of the Gods: The Ritual Use of Hallucinogens*. New York.

Gang, Muhak. *Han-gukin-ui bburi (The Koran People's Roots)*. Seoul: Geumgang Seowon.

Geertz, Clifford. 1966. 'Religion as a Cultural System.' In M. Banton (ed), *Anthropo-*

logical Approaches for the Study of Religion. London.

—— 1966/1973. 'Person, Time and Conduct in Bali.' In C. Geertz (ed), *The Interpretation of Cultures.* New York: Basic Books.

—— 1973. *The Interpretation of Cultures.* New York: Basic Books.

—— 1980. *Negara: the theatre State in 19th Century Bali.* Princeton: Princeton University Press.

Gellner, Ernest. 1964. *Thoughts and Change.* London: Weidenfeld and Nicholson.

—— 1983. *Nations and Nationalism.* Oxford: Oxford University Press.

Gifford, Daniel L. 1892. 'Ancestor Worship as Practiced in Korea.' In *The Korea Repository 1: 169-76.*

Gilbert, R. 1984. 'How to Recognize a Shaman Among Other Religious Specialists?' In Hoppal, M (ed), *Shamanism in Eurasia.* Göttengen: Herodot.

Gillison, Gillian. 1980. 'Images of Nature in Gimi Thought.' In Carol MacCormack and Marilyn Strathern (eds), *Nature, Culture and Gender.* Cambridge: Cambridge University Press.

Gim, Busik. (1145)1984. *Samguk sagi (A History of the Three Kingdoms).* Modern Korean version, trans. by Gim, Jonggwon. Seoul: Myeongmundang.

Gim Gwangeok. 1989. *Jeongchijeok damnon gijero-ui minjung munhwa undong: sahoegeuk-euroseo-ui madanggeuk (Popular Cultural Movement as a Political Discourse: the Yard Play as the Social Drama).* Seoul: the Korean Cultural Anthropological Society.

Gim Geumhwa. 1995. *Bok-eun nanugo han-eun pusige (Let's Share Good Luck and Disperse Grievances).* Seoul: Doseochulpan Pureunsup.

Gim, Heonseon. 1994. *Han-guk-ui changse sinhwa (Korean Creation Myths).* Seoul: Doseo Chulpan Gilbeot.

Gim, Huisu, et al. 2003. *Sin-gwa mannaneun saramdeul (People who meet with Spirits).* Seoul: Gutdei Sinmum.

Gim, Hyeokje and Han, Jungsu. 1981. *Gwan hong sang jerye dae sajeon (A Comprehensive Dictionary of the Korean Rites of Passage).* Seoul: Myeongmundang.

Gim, Inhoe. 1985. 'Suyongpo sumang gut-gwa musok-e seo ui jugeum-ui uimi (The *Gut* for the Drowned in Suyongpo and the Meaning of Death in *Gut*).' In *Hwanghae-do Jinogi Gut, Han-guk-ui Gut 4.* Seoul: Yeolhwadang.

—— 1987. *Han-guk musok sasang yeon-gu (A Study of Korean Mu Ideology).* Seoul: Jipmoondang.

—— 1993. 'Gut-eseo-ui jugeum-ui gyoyukjeok uimi (An Educational Meaning of Death in Gut). In *Hwanghae-do jinogi gut, Han-guk-ui gut 17.* Seoul: Yeolhwadang.

Gim, Jongdeok. 1989. Hanyang seon geori (Seoul Area Gut Procedures). Seoul: Min-san Chulpansa.

Gim Maesun. 1819/1989. *Yeolyang sesigi*. In *Dongguk Sesigi*. Trans. into modern Korean with annotations by Choe Daerim. Seoul: Hongsin Chulpansa.

Gim Seongwon (ed.) 1987. *Han-guk-ui sesi pungsok (Seasonal Customs of Korea)*. Seoul: Myeongmundang.

Gim, Taegon. 1972. 'The Influence of Shamanism on the Living Pattern of People in Contemporary Korea.' In Gim Taegon (ed), *The Modern Meaning of Shamanism*. Seoul.

—— 1981. *Hanguk musok yeon-gu (A Study of Korean Shamanism)*. Seoul: Jipmoondang.

—— 1990. 'Sodo-ui jonggyo minsokhakjeok jomyeong (The Spotlight on the Religion and Folklore of Sodo).' In *Mahan/Baeke Munhwa* vol. 12. Seoul.

—— 1991. *Hanguk-ui musok (Korean Shamanism)*. Seoul.

Gim, Takgyu & Seong, Byeongui (eds). 1982. *Han-guk minsok yeon-gu nonmunseon (Selected Essays on Korean Folklore Studies)*. Seoul: Iljogak.

Gim, Yeolgyu. 1977. *Han-guk sinhwa-wa musok yeon-gu (A Study of Korean Mythology and Shamanism)*. Seoul: Iljogak.

Gim Yeongsang. 1989. *Seoul 600 nyeon (Seoul 600 Years)*. Seoul: Han-guk Ilbosa Chulpan-guk.

Gluckman, Max. 1963. *Order and Rebellion in Tribal Africa: Collected Essays*. London: Cohen & West.

Gombrich, R F. 1971. *Precept and Practice: Traditional Buddhism in the Rural Highlands of Ceylon*. Oxford: Clarendon Press.

Gomm, R. 1975. 'Bargaining from Weakness: Spirit Possession on the South Kenyan Coast.' In *Man* (NS) 19 Dec.

Goodale, Jane C. 1980. 'Gender, Sexuality and Marriage: a Kaulong Model of Nature and Culture.' In C MacCormack & M Strathern (eds), *Nature, Culture and and Gender*, pp 119-42. Cambridge: Cambridge University Press.

Gray, Andrew. 1997. *The Last Shaman: Change in an Amazonian Community*. Oxford: Berghahn Books.

Grayson, James Huntley. 1985. *Early Buddhism and Christianity in Korea*. Leiden: E.J. Brill.

—— 1989. *Korea: A Religious History*. Oxford: Clarendon Press.

Gusan Seunim (The Venerable Monk Gusan). 1985. *The Way of Korean Zen*. English trans. by Martine Pages and ed. by Stephen Batchelor. New York & Tokyo: Weatherhill.

Halifax, Joan. 1982. *Shaman: The Wounded Healer*. New York: Crossroad.

Han Chungsu (compiled) under the supervision of Gim Hyeokje. 1981. *Sin gu gwan-*

honsangje daejeo (New and Old: A Canon of Rites of Passage). Seoul Myeong-mundang.

Han, Woo-keun (Han Ugeun). 1970. *Han-guk tongsa*. Seoul: Euryu Munhwasa. English translation by Lee Kyung-shik (Yi Gyeongsik), ed. by Grafton K Mintz as *The History of Korea*. Seoul: Eul Yu Munhwasa.

Han-guk Jonggyo Sahoe Yeon-guso (Research Institute for Korean Religion and Society). 1993. *Han-guk Jonggyo Yeon-gam (The Yearbook of Korean Religions)*. Seoul: Halimweon.

Harner, Michael J (ed). 1973. *Hallucinogens and Shamanism*. New York: Oxford University Press.

———— 1980. *The Way of the Shaman: A Guide to Power and Healing*. San Francisco: Harper & Row.

Harris, Marvin. 1974. *Cows, Pigs, Wars, and Witches*. New York: Vintage Books/Random House.

———— 1977. *Cannibals and Kings*. New York: Vintage Books/Random House.

Harva, Uno. 1938. *Dir religiösen Vorstellungen der altaischen Völker*. Helsinki (FFC LII, 125).

Harvey, Yongsook Kim. 1979. *Six Korean Women: The Socialization of Shamans*. St. Paul and New York: West Publishing.

Heinze, Ruth-Inge. 1991. *Shamans of the 20th Century*. New York: Irvington Publishers.

Hines, Donald M. 1993. *Magic in the Mountains: The Yakima Shamans: Power & Practice*. Issaquah: Great Eagle Publishing.

Hobsbawm, Eric & Ranger, Terence (eds). 1983. *The Invention of Tradition*. Cambridge: Cambridge University Press.

Hogarth, Hyun-key Kim. 1995. *Reciprocity, Status and the Korean Shamanistic Ritual*. A PhD thesis in social anthropology at the University of Kent at Canterbury.

———— 1998a. *Kut: Happiness Through Reciprocity*. Budapest: Akadémiai Kiadó.

———— 1998b. '"Trance" and "Possession Trance" in the Perspective of Korean Shamanism.' In Keith Howard (ed.), *Korean Shamanism, Revivals, Survaval, and Change*. Seoul; The Royal Asiatic Society, Korea Branch Seoul Press.

———— 1999. *Korean Shamansim and Cultural Nationalism*. Seoul: Jimoondang.

———— 2002. *Syncretism of Buddhism and Shamanism in Korea*. Edison & Seoul: Jimoondang.

———— 2012. 'South Korea's Sunshine Policy, Reciprocity and Nationhood.' In *Perspectives on Global Development and Technology* vol. 11, pp 99-111. Leiden · Boston: Brill.

Hong, Seokmo. 1849?/1989. 'Dongguk Sesigi.' In *Dongguk Sesigi*, translated into modern Korean with annotations by Choe Taerim. Seoul: Hongsin Chulpansa.

Hong, Queen Hyegyeonggung Hongssi. (1795) 1993. *Hanjungnok*, compiled by Bak Dongu. Seoul: Jeongmoksa.

Hoppál, Mihály (ed). 1984. *Shamanism in Eurasia*, 2 vols. Göttingen: Herodot.

Hoppál, Mihály & Juha Pentikäinen (eds). 1992. *Northern Religions and Shamanism*. Budapest: Akaprint.

Hoppál, Mihály & Otto von Sadovszky (eds). 1989. *Shamanism, Past and Present*, 2 vols. Budapest: Ethnographic Institute.

Hori, Ichiro. 1968. *Folk Religion in Japan: Continuity and Change*. Eng trans, by Kitagawa, J. and Miller, A. Chicago: Chicago University Press.

Howard, Keith. 2002. 'Shaman Music, Drumming, and Into the "New Age".' In *Shaman*, Volume 10 Numbers 1 & 2 Spring/Autumn2002. Budapest: Molnar & Kelemen Oriental Publishers.

Htin Aung, M. 1962. *Folk Elements in Burmese Buddhism*. Oxford: Oxford University Press.

Hulbert, Homer B. 1906/1970. *The Passing of Korea*. Seoul: Yonsei University Press.

Hultkranz, Åke. 1978/96. 'Ecological and Phenomenological Aspects of Shamanism.' In Vilmos Diószegi & Mihály Hoppál eds, *Shamanism in Siberia*. Budapest: Académiai Kiadó.

Hwang Rusi. 1985a. 'Jae cheheom-eul tonghan jugeum-eui ihae – dari gut-ui gujo-wa geu gineung (Understanding Death through Indirect Experience – The Structure and Function of dari gut).' In *Pyeongan-do dari gut, Hanguk-ui gut 5*. Seoul: Yeolhwadang.

—— 1985b. 'Jeolje-doen han puri-ui mihak – sangjingjeok uirye-roseo uissitggim gut (Aesthetics of Dispersion of Frustrated Han – ssitgim gut as a Symbolic Ritual).' In *Jeolla-do ssitggim gut, Hanguk-ui Gut 6*. Seoul:Yeolhwadang.

—— 1988. *Han-guk in-ui gut-gwa mudang (The Korean People's Shamanistic Rituals and Shamans)*. Seoul: Muneumsa.

Hyde, Maggie and McGuinness, Michael. 1992. *Jung for Beginners*. Cambridge: Icon Books.

Hyeon, Yongjun. 1985. 'Jejudo-ui bada – salm-ui teojeon, jugeum-ui jari geurigo gut han madang (The Sea of Jejudo – Site for Life, Death and A Round of Gut).' In *Jejudo muhon Gut, Han-guk-ui Gut 7*. Seoul: Yeolhwadang.

—— 1986. *Jejudo musok yeongu (A Study of Shamanism in Jejudo)*. Seoul: Jipmoon-dang

Im Donggwon. 1971. *Han-guk minsokhak non-go (A Discourse on Korean Folklore)*. Seoul: Jipmoondang.

Im Hyojae. 1992. *Han-guk godae munhwa-ui heurum (The Flow of Ancient Korean Culture)*. Seoul: Jipmoondang.

Im Seokjae. 1985. 'Iseung-gwa jeoseung-eul innun shinhwa-ui segye – Hamgyeong-do musok-ui seonggyeok (The World of Myths Connecting This World and the Other World – A Characteristic of Hamgyeong-do Musok).' In *Hamgyeong-do mangmuk gut, Han-guk-ui Gut 8*. Seoul: Yeolhwadang.

Iryeon. 13th century (1281?). *Samguk yusa (The Memorabilia of the Three Kingdoms)*. 1987 Modern Korean trans. by Bak Seongbong & Go Gyeongsik. Seoul: Seomun Munhwasa.

Janelli, Roger L & Dawnhee Yim Janelli. 1982. *Ancestor Worship and Korean Society*. Stanford: Stanford University Press.

Jang Cheolsu. 1995. *Hang-uk-ui gwanhonsangje (The Korean Rites of Passage)*. Seoul: Jipmoondang.

Jang, Hogeun. 2000. *Han-guk mugyo: Choe Nameok Hoejang-gwa Daehan Seunggong Gyeongsin Yeonhaphoe 30-nyeon baljachwi (Korean Shamanism: Chairman Choe Nameok and Tracing the 30-year History of Daehan Seuggong Gyeongsin Yeonhaphoe)*. Seoul: Chulpansidae.

Jang, Sugeun. 1964. 'Han-guk-ui sindang hyeongtae go (A Discourse on the Korean Shamanistic Shrine Shapes)' In *Minjok munhwa yeon'gu*, Vol 1. Research Institute of Korean Studies, Korea University.

———— 1974. 'Min-gan sinang (Folk Beliefs).' In Yi Duhyeon, Jang, Sugeun & Lee, Kwang Kyu (Yi Gwanggyu) (eds), *Han-guk minsokhak gaeseol, (An Introduction to Korean Folklore)*. Seoul: Minjung Seogwan.

———— 1978. 'Musok.' In *Han-guk minsok jonghap josa bogoseo (A Comprehensive Report on Korean Folkloristic Research)*, vol. Gyeonggi-do (pp 106 - 130).

Jang, Sugeun and Choe Gilseong. 1967. *Gyeonggi-do jiyeok musok (Gyeonggi-do Area Shamanism)*.

Jang, Hogeun. 2000. *Han-guk mugyo: Choe Nameok Hoejang-gwa Daehan Seunggong Gyeongsin Yeonhaphoe 30-nyeon baljachwi (Korean Shamanism: Chairman Choe Nameok and Tracing the 30-year History of Daehan Seunggong Gyeongsin Yeonhaphoe)*. Seoul: Chulpansidae.

———— 1996b. *Dokggaebi Janggun Jo Jaryong (General Hobgoblin Jo Jaryong)*. Seoul: Doseo Chulpan Gwanggaeto.

Jang, Ujin. 1989. *Joseon saram-ui giwon (The Origin of the Korean People)*. (North Korea: Sahoe Gwahak Chulpansa.

Jeong Byeongho 1989. 'Gutpan-e pyohyeon doen han-gwa sinmyeong. Tongyeong Ogwi saenam gut-ui guseong-gwa chum-ui gineung (Grievances and Elation Expressed in Gut. The Composition of Tongyeong Mortuary Gut and the Function of Dance).' In *Han-guk-ui Gut 14*. Seoul: Yeolhwadang.

Jeong Yonghun. 1995. *Dan-gun-gwa geundae han-guk minjok undong (Dan-gun and* the Modern Korean Nationalstic Movement). Seoul: The Academy of Korean Studies.

Jo, Jaryong (Jo Yongjin). 1996a. *Sin-eul seontaekhan namja (The Man Who Chose the Spirits)*. Seoul: Baeksong.

———— 1996b. *Dokggaebi Janggun Jo Jaryong (General Hobgoblin Jo Jaryong)*. Seoul: Doseochulpan Gwanggaeto.

Joralemon, Donald & Douglas Sharon. 1993. *Sorcery and Shamanism: Curanderos and Clients in Northern Peru*. Salt Lake City: University of Utah Press.

Jordan, David K. 1972. *Gods, Ghosts and Ancestors: Folk Religion in a Taiwanese Village*. Berkeley: University of California Press.

Ju Ganghyeon. 1992. *Gut-ui sahoesa (The Social History of Gut)*. Seoul: Ungjin Publishing Co.

Jung, Carl Gustav. 1959. *The Archetypes and the Collective Unconscious*. English trans, by R F C Hull. Princeton: Princeton University Press.

Jung, Carl Gustav, & Kerényi, Károly (Karl. Carl). 1942/1949/1969. *Essays on a Science of Mythology*. Princeton: Princeton University Press.

Kemiläinen, Aira. 1964. *Nationalism: Problems Concerning the Word, the Concept and Classification*. Jyväskylä: Kustantajat.

Kendall, Laurel. 1985. *Shamans, Housewives and Other Restless Spirits*. Honolulu: University of Hawaii Press.

———— 1988. *The Life and Hard Times of a Korean Shaman*. Honolulu: University of Hawaii Press.

Kendall, Laurel & Dix, Griffin (eds). 1987. *Religion and Ritual in Korean Society*. Berkeley: University of California Press.

Kernberg, Otto F. 1975. *Borderline Conditions and Pathological Narcissism*. New York: Jason Aronson Inc.

Klein, Melanie. 1998. *Love, Guilt and Reparation: And other works 1921-1945 (The Writings of Melanie Klein)*. London: Vintage.

Kleinman, Arthur. 1980. *Patients and Healers in the Context of Culture*. Berkeley: University of California Press.

Kohut, Heinz. 1979. *The Psychology of the Self*. New York: International University Press.

———— 1982. *The Analysis of the Self: A Systematic Approach to Treatment of Narcissistic Personality Disorder*. New York: International University Press.

Korea Research Institute for Religion and Society. 1995 Vol 1. *Jonggyo yeon-gam (The Yearbook of Korean Religions)*. Seoul: Korea Hallimwon.

Lan, David. 1985. *Guns and Rain*. London: James Currey.

Lebra, William P. 1966. *Okinawan Religion: Belief, Ritual and Social Structure*. Honolulu: University of Hawaii Press.

———— (ed). 1976. *Culture-bound Syndromes, Ethnopsychiatry and Alternate Therapies*. Honolulu: University of Hawaii Press.

Lee, Hyun Song (Yi Hyeonsong). 1996. 'Change in Funeral Customs in Contemporary Korea.' In *Korea Journal*, Vol 36, No.2, Summer, pp 49-60.

Lee, Ki-baik (Yi Gibaek). 1967/1994. *Han-guksa sin ron (A New History of Korea)*, rev. ed. Seoul: Iljogak.

———— 1988. 'Dan-gun sinhwa-ui munjejeom (Problems of the Dan-gun Myth).' In Lee Ki-baik (ed), *Dan-gun sinhwa nonjip (Essays on the Dan-gun Myth)*. Seoul: aemunsa.

Lee, Ki-baik (Yi Gibaek), Eckert, et al. 1990. *Korea Old and New: A History*. Seoul: Iljogak for the Korea Institute, Harvard University.

Lee, Kwang Kyu (Yi Gwanggyu). 1975. *Han-guk gajok-ui gujo bunseok (Analysis of the Korean Family Structure)*. Seoul: Iljisa.

———— 1984. 'Family and Religion in Traditional and Contemporary Korea.' In *SENRI Ethnological Studies 11*.

Lee, Peter H (ed.). 1993. *Sourcebook of Korean Civilization*. New York: Columbia University Press.

Lehtisalo , T. 1937. 'Der Tod unde die Wiedergeburt des künftingen Schamanen.'In *JSFO*, XLVIII, fasc. 3 1-34.

Lévi-Strauss, Claude. 1975&1979/1983. *The Way of the Masks*. Originally pub. as La Voix des Masques. Part I in 1975 by Edition d'Art Albert Skira, Geneva & Part II in 1979 by Librarie Plon, Paris. English trans. by Sylvia Modelski in 1982. London: Jonathan Cape.

Lewis, G. 1980. *Day of Shining Red*. Cambridge: Cambridge University Press.

Lewis, I M. 1971/1989. *Ecstatic Religion: An Anthropological Study of Spirit Possession and Shamanism*. London: Routledge.

———— 1984. 'What is a Shaman?' In Hoppal, M (ed), *Shamanism in Eurasia*. Göttingen: Herodot.

Loeb. E. M. 1924. 'The Shaman of Niue.' In *American Anthropologist 26*.

Lowie. Robert H. 1963. *Indians on the Plains, American Museum Science Books 4*. New York.

Lubbock, Sir John. 1865/2005. *Prehistoric Times as Illustrated by Ancient Remains, and the Manners and Customs of Modern Savages*. London: Elibron Classics. Adamant Media Corporation.

MacCormack, Carol & Strathern, Marilyn (eds). 1980. *Nature, Culture and Gender*. Cambridge: Cambridge University Press.

McCann, David R, John Middleton & Edward Shultz (eds). 1979. *Studies on Korea in*

Transition. Honolulu: University of Hawaii Press.

McClain, Carol Shepherd (ed). 1989. *Women as Healers*. New Brunswick and London: Rutgers University Press.

Mahler, Margaret S, Fred Pine & Anni Bergman. 1975. *The Psychological Birth of the Human Infant: Symbiosis and Individuation*. New York: Basic Books.

Mason, David A. 1999. *Spirit of the Mountains: Korea's San-Shin and Traditions of Mountain-Worship*. Seoul: Hollym.

Mattielli, Sandra (ed). 1977. *Virtues in Conflict: Tradition and the Korean Woman Today*. Seoul: Royal Asiatic Society, Korea Branch.

Mauss, Marcel. 1950/1990. *The Gift The Forms and reason for Exchange in Archaic Societies*. English Trans. by W. D. Hall. London: Routledge.

Metcalf, Peter and Huntington, Richard. 1991. *Celebrations of Death. The Anthropology of Mortuary Ritual*. 2nd ed. Cambridge: Cambridge University Press.

Merkur, Dan. 1992. *Becoming Half Hidden: Shamanism and Initiation Among the Inuit*. New York & London: Garland Publishing.

Messing, S. 1958. 'Group Therapy and Social Status in the Zar Cult of Ethiopia.' In *American Anthropologist 60*.

Minsok Hakhoe (Folklore Society). 1994. *Han-guk minsokhak-ui ihae (Understanding Korean Folklore)*. Seoul: Munhak Academy.

Mischel, W. & F. 1958. 'Psychological Aspects of Spirit Possession.' In *American Anthropologist 60*.

Mitchell, Stephen A and Jay R Greenberg. 1983. *Object Relations in Psychoanalytic Theory*. Cambridge, MA: Harvard Univerwisty Pres.

Moore, Henrietta. 1988. *Feminism and Anthropology*. Cambridge: Polity Press.

Mun Gyeonghyeon. 1985. 'Dan-gun sinhwa-ui sin gochal (A new Study of the Dangun Myth).' In *Gyonam sahak*, I.

Mun, Jaehyeon. 2005. *In-gandeul-eun sin-eul mannaji mot haetta (Humans could not meet the Spirits)*. Seoul: Cheonghak Chulpansa.

Murayama, Chijun. 1932/1990. *Chōsen no fugeki (Korean Geomancy)*. Keijo: Chōsen Sōtokufu. Korean trans, by Choe, Gilseong as Joseon-ui pungsu (Korean Geomancy). Seoul: Mineumsa.

Nairn, Tom. 1977. *The Break-up of Britain*. London: New Left Books.

Nam, Doyeong. 1960. *Guksa jeongseol (A Detailed History of Korea)*. Seoul: Donga Chulpansa.

No Taedon. 1994. 'Go Joseon-ui byoncheon.' In Yun, Iheum et al. *Dan-gun, geu ihaewa jaryo (Understanding Dan-gun and Research Data)*. Seoul: Seoul National University Press.

O, Hyeonggeun. 1978/1995. *Bulgyo-ui yeonghon-gwa yunhoe gwan (The Buddhist*

View of the Soul and Samsara). Rev. ed. Seoul: Saeteo.

Obeysekere, Gananath. 1963. 'The Great Tradition and the Little in the Perspective of Sinhalese Buddhism.' In *Journal of Asian Studies*, XXII 2: 139-153.

—— 1968. 'Theodicy, Sin and Salvation in Sociology of Buddhism.' In E R Leach (ed), *Dialectic m Practical Religion*. Cambridge: Cambridge University Press.

Orent, Amnon. 11969. 'Lineage Structure and the Supernatural: the Kaffa of southwest Ethiopia.' Unpublished PhD thesis, Boston University.

Ortner, Sherry B (Sherry Ortner Paul). 1974. 'Is female to male as nature is to culture?' In M. Z. Rosaldo & L. Lamphere (eds.), *Woman, Culture, and Society*. Stanford: Stanford University Press.

—— 1978. *Sherpas Through Their Rituals*. Cambridge: Cambridge University Press.

—— 1989. *High Religion: A Cultural and Political History of Sherpa Buddhism*. Princeton: Princeton University Press.

Ortner, Sherry B & Whitehead, Harriet (eds). 1981. *Sexual Meanings The Cultural Construction of Gender and Sexuality*. Cambridge: Cambridge University Press.

Pentikäinen, J. 1995. 'The Revival of Shamanism in the Contemporary North.' In Kim Taegon and Hoppál, M (eds), *Shamanism in Performing Arts*. Budapest: Akadémiai Kiadó, Bibliotheca Shamananistica, Vol. 1, 263-272.

Potter, Jack M. 1974. 'Cantonese Shamanism.' In A P Wolf (ed), *Religion and Ritual in Chinese Society*. Stanford: Stanford University Press.

Radcliffe-Brown, A R. 1952. Structure and Function in Primitive Society. London: Cohen & West.

Radin, Paul. 1937. *Primitive Religion*. New York.

Ramstedt, G. J. 1949. *Studies in Korean Etymology*. Helsinki.

Rasmussen, Knud Johan Victor. 1929. *The Intellectual Culture of the Iglulik Eskimos*. Copenhagen: Nordisk Forlag.

Renan, Ernest. 1947-61. 'Qu'est-ce qu'une nation?' In *Oeuvres Complètes*, pp 887-906. Paris: Calmann-Lévy.

Rhi, Bou-yong (Yi, Buyeong). 1970. 'Saryeong-ui musokjeok chiryo e daehan bunseok simnihakjeok gochal (A Psychoanalytic Study of the Shasmanistic Cure by the Spirits of the Dead).' In *Choegeun uihak (Latest Medicine)*, 13: 1 (pp 75 -90). Seoul.

—— 1977. 'Psychological Problems among Korean Women.' In S Mattielli (ed), *Virtues in Conflict*. Seoul: Royal Asiatic Society, Korea Branch .

—— 1978. *Bunseok simnihak (Psychoanalysis)*. Seoul: Iljogak.

—— 1983. *Ireobeorin geurimja (Lost Shadows)*. Seoul: Jeongusa.

—— 1985. 'Jugeun ja-wa sanja-ui daehwa (A Dialogue Between the Dead and the Living).' In *Jejudo muhon gut, Han-guk-ui gut 7*. Seoul: Yeolhwadang.

Rogers, Spencer L. 1982. *The Shaman*. Springfield: Charles C Thomas Publishers.

Rosaldo, Michelle Z & Louise Lamphere (eds). 1974. *Women, Culture and Society*. Stanford: Stanford University Press.

Rouget, Gilbert. 1980/1985. *La Musique et la transe*. Paris: Gallimard. Trans. into English and rev. by Brunhilde Biebuyck as Music and Trance: A Theory of the Relations between Music and Possession. Chicago: University of Chicago Press.

Sanday, Peggy. 1981. *Female Power and Male Dominance On the Origins of Sexual Inequality*. Cambridge: Cambridge University Press.

Sayers, Janet. 2000. *Kleinians: Psychoanalysis Inside Out*. Cambridge: Polity Press.

Schechner, Richard. 1977. *Essays on Performance Theory*. New York: Drama Book Specialists.

—— 1988. *Performance Theory*. London: Routledge.

Schechner, Richard & Appel, Willa, (eds). 1990. *By Means of Performance*. Cambridge: Cambridge University Press.

Seo, Daeseok. 1989. 'Musok-e natanan segye gwan (The World View Represented in Musok).' In *Tongyeong ogwi saenam gut, Han-guk-ui gut 14*. Seoul: Yeolhwadang.

Seo, Jeongbeom. 1992. *Munyeo byeolgok, Vol. I Nabi sonyeo-ui sarang iyagi (A Love Story of the Butterfly Girl)*. Seoul:Hannara.

—— 1992. *Munyeo byeolgok, Vol. II Uri sarang iseung eseo jeoseung euro (Our Love from This World To the Next)*. Seoul: Hannara.

—— 1992. *Munyeo byeolgok, Vol. III Saetani-wa jilgeobari*. Seoul: Hannara.

—— 1993. *Munyeo byeolgok, Vol. IV Chosani-wa madeuri*. Seoul: Hannara.

—— 1993. *Munyeo byeolgok, Vol. V Buri-wa mugguri*. Seoul: Hannara.

Seo, Yeongdae. 1994. 'Dan-gun gwan-gye munheon jaryo yeon-gu (A Study of Dan-gun-related documents).' In Yun, Iheum et al. *Dan-gun, geu ihae-wa jaryo (Understanding Dan-gun and Research Data)*. Seoul: Seoul National University Press.

Service, Elman. 1962. *Primitive Social Organization: an Evolutionary Perspective*. New York: Random House.

Seton-Watson, Hugh. 1977. *Nations and States: An Enquiry into the Origins of Nations and the Policies of Nationalism*. Boulder, Colo.: Westview Press.

Sim Jinsong. 1995. *Shin-i seontaekhan yeoja (A Woman Chosen by the Spirits)*. Seoul: Doseo Chulpan Baeksong.

Sin, Chaeho. 1948/1983. *Juseok Joseon sanggosa (An Annotated Ancient History of Korea)*. Seoul: Danjae Sin Chaeho Seonsaeng Ginyeom Saeophoe.

Sin Gicheol & Sin, Yeongcheol. 1989/1992. *Sae urimal keun sajeon (A New Comprehensive Korean Dictionary)*, I & II. Seoul: Samseong Publishing Co.

Sin, Taeung. 1989. *Han-guk gwisin yeon-gu (A Study of Korean Ghosts)*. Seoul: Doseo Chulpan Rogos.

Shirokogoroff, S M. 1935. *Psychomental Complex of the Tungus*. London: Kegan Paul, Trench, Trubner.

Silverman, Julian. 1967. 'Shamans and Acute Schizophrenia.' In *American Anthropologist 69*.

Siikala, Anna-Leena. 1978. *The Rite Technique of the Siberian Shaman*. Helsinki: Suomalainen Tiedeakatemia Academia Scientiarum Fennica.

Sin, Myeonggi. 2001. *Mudang Naeryeok (The Origin of Mudang)*. Seoul: Minsokwon.

Smith, Anthony D. 1981. *The Ethnic Revival. Cambridge: Cambridge University Press*.

Son, Jintae. 1947/1984. *Monsok non-go (A Study of Folklore)*. Seoul: Daewang Munhwasa.

Southwold, Melford E. 1983. *Buddhism in Life: The Anthropological Study of Religion and the Sinhalese Practice of Buddhism*. Manchester: Manchester University Press.

Spiro, Melford E. 1967/ 1974. *Burmese Supernaturalism*. Expanded ed. Philadelphia: Institute for the Study of Human Issues.

—— 1971. *Buddhism and Society: A Great Tradition and Its Burmese Vicissitudes*. London: George Alien & Unwin.

Spitz, René Árpád. 1965. *The First Year of Life: a Psychoanalytic Study of Normal and Deviant Development of Object Relations*. New York: International University Press.

Spotnitz, Hyman. 1961. *The Couch and the Circle: A Story of Group Psychotherapy*. New York: Alfred A. Knopf Inc.

—— 1969. *Modern Psychoanalysis of the Schizophrenic Patient: Theory of the Technique*. New York: Grune & Stratton.

Sternberg, Leo. 1925. 'Divine Election in Primitive Religion.' In *Congrés Internaional des Americanistes, Compte-Rendu de la XXIe session*, Pt 2 (1924), pp 472-512. Göteborg.

Sullivan, Harry Stack. 1953. *The Interpersonal Theory of Psychiatry*. New York & London: W W Norton.

Tambiah, S J. 1970. *Buddhism and the Spirit Cults in Northeast Thailand*. Cambridge: Cambridge University Presss.

—— 1984. *The Buddhist Saints of the Forest and the Cult of Amulets: A Study in Charisma, Hagiography, Sectarianism, and millennial Buddhism*. Cambridge: Cambridge University Press.

Terwiel. B J. 1975/1984. *Monks and Magic: An Analysis of Religious Ceremonies in Central Thailand*. London: Curzon press.

Thompson, Clara Mable & Patrick Mullahy. 1951. *Psychoanalysis: Evolution and Development*. Third ed. New York: Hermitage House.

Torrey, E. Fuller. 1986. *Witchdoctors and Psychiatrists: The Common Roots of Psychotherapy and Its Future*. New York: Harper & Row.

Turner, Victor. 1967. *The Forest of Symbols. Aspect of Ndembu Ritual*. Ithaca and London: Cornell University Press.

———— 1969. *The Ritual Process. Structure and Anti-Structure*. New York: Aldine de Gruyter.

Underhill, Ruth. 1965. *Red Man's Religion*. Chicago: University of Chicago Press.

Van Gennep, Arnold. 1909/1960. *The Rites of Passage*. London: Routledge & Kegan Paul.

Vitebsky, Piers. 1995. *The Shaman*. London: Macmillan.

Voigt, V. 1984. 'Shaman—Person or Word?' In Hoppal, M (ed), *Shamanism in Eurasia*. Göttingen: Herodot.

Weber, Max. 1922. *The Sociology of Religion*. London: Methuen & Co.

———— 1948. *From Max Weber: Essays in Sociology*. Trans. & ed with an introduction by H H Gerth & C. Wright Mills. London: Routledge.

Wilson, Peter J. 1967. 'Status Ambiguity and Spirit Possession.' In *Man 2*.

Winkelman, Michael James. 1992. *Shamans, Priests and Witches: A Cross-Cultural Study of Magico-Religious Practitioners*. Arizona State University Anthropological Research Papers No. 44.

Wolf, Arthur P (ed). 1974. *Religion Ritual in Chinese Society*. Stanford: Stanford University Press.

Worsley, Peter. 1957. *The Trumpet Shall Sound*. London: Paladin.

Yang, C. K. 1961/1967. *Religion in Chinese Society*. Berkeley: University of California Press.

Yi Gangryeol. 1989. *Minsok-gwa chukje (Folklore and Festival)*. Seoul: Doseochulpan Wonbanggak.

Yi Gyubo. 1241?/1982. *Dongguk Yi Sangguk jip (Anthology of Eastern Country Minister Yi's Writings)*. Seoul: Myeongmundang.

Yi, Neunghwa. 1927/ 1990. *Joseon yeosok go (A Discourse on Korean Women's Ways)*. Modern Korean version, trans. by Gim Sangeok. Seoul: Dongmunseon.

———— 1927/1991. *Joseon musok go (A Discourse on Korean Shamanism)*. Modern Korean version, trans. by Yi Jaegon. Seoul: Dongmunseon.

Yi Pilyeong. 1994. 'Dan-gun yeon-gusa (A History of Dan-gun Studies).' In Yun, Iheum et al. *Dan-gun, geu ihae-wa jaryo (Understanding Dan-gun and Research Data)*. Seoul: Seoul National University Press.

Yi Ulho. 1994. 'Dan-gun seolhwa-ui gibon gwaje (The Basic Task in the Dan-gun Myth

Study)' In Yi Unbong (ed), *Dan-gun sinhwa-ui yeon-gu (A Study of the Dan-gun Myth)*. Seoul: Onnuri.

Yim, Suk-jay (Im Seokjae). 1970. 'Han-guk musok yeon-gu seoseol, (Introduction to Korean musok).' In *Journal of Asian Women* 9:73-90, 161-217. Seoul.

Yu, Chai-shin & Guisso, R (eds). 1988. *Shamanism: the Spirit World of Korea*. Berkeley: University of California Press.

Yu Deukgong. 18th century/1989. *Gyeongdo japgi*. In Dongguk Sesigi. Modern Korean Trans. with annotations by Choe Daerim. Seoul: Hongsin Chulpansa.

Yu, Dongsik. 1975. *Han-guk mugyo-ui yeoksa-wa gujo (The History and Structure of Korean Mu Religion)*. Seoul: Yonsei University Press.

Yun, Iheum. 1988. 'Jonggyo in-gu josa bangbeom non gaebal-gwa han-guk in-ui jonggyo seonghyang (Development of Methodology in Religious Population Research and the Religious Trend of the Korean People.' In *Han-guk jonggyo yeon-gu*, Vol. II. Seoul: Jipmoondang.

Yun, Iheum et al. 1994. 'Dan-gun sinhwa-wa han minjok-ui yeoksa (The Dan-gun Myth and a History of the Korean People).' In Yun, Iheum et al. *Dan-gun, geu ihae-wa jaryo (Understanding Dan-gun and Research Data)*. Seoul: Seoul National University Press.

Yun, Naehyeon. 1986. *Han-guk godaesa sin ron (A new Discourse on Ancient Korean History)*. Seoul: Iljisa.

—— 1992. 'Gojoseon-ui gukga gujo (The State Structure of Gojoseon).' In *Gyeorye Munhwa 6*, Seoul: Gyeorye Munhwa Yeon-guweon.

—— 1993. 'Gojoseon-ui jonggyo-wa geu sasang (Religion and Ideology of Gojoseon).' In *Dongyanghak (Asian Studies) 23*. Seoul.

SOURCES OF THE PROVERBS CITED:

1. *The Concise Oxford Dictionary of Proverbs*, by John Simpson. 1982. Oxford: Oxford University Press.

2. *Maxims and Proverbs of Old Korea*, by Tae Hung Ha (Ha Taeheung). 1970. Seoul: Yonsei University Press.

3. *Proverbs, East and West*, compiled by Kim Yong-cheol. 1991. Seoul & New Jersey: Hollym International Corp.

4. *Sokdam (Proverbs) 3000*. 1988. Seoul: Gyohaksa.

OTHER REFERENCE BOOKS CONSULTED:

1. *Encyclopedia of Cultural Anthropology*, ed. by David Levinson, and Melvin Ember, 1996, New York: Henry Holt.

2. *Encyclopedia of Social and Cultural Anthropology*, ed. by Alan Barnard and Jonathan

Spencer. 1996. London: Routeledge.

3. *MacMillan Dictionary of Anthropology*, by Chasrlotte Seymour-Smith. 1986. London: MacMillan Press.

4. *Han-guk minjok munhwa dae baekgwa sajeon (The Encyclopedia of Korean National Culture)*, compiled by the Academy of Korean Studies.

5. *The Hutchinson Encyclopedia* (Tenth Edition). 1992. London: Helion.

6. *The New World Comprehensive Korean-English Dictionary*. 1979. Seoul: Sisa Yeongeosa.

7. *The Oxford Encyclopedic English Dictionary*, ed. by Joyce Hawkins and & Robert Allen. 1991. Oxford: Clarendon Press.

8. *Bibeop hanja (A Secret Method of Learning Chinese Characters)*, compiled by Gang Junghui under the supervision of Jeong, Juyeong, 1985, Seoul: Hakil Chulpansa.

9. *Sae urimal keun sajeon (A New Comprehensive Korean Dictionary)*, I & II, compiled by Sin, Gicheol & Sin, Yongcheol. 1989/1992. Seoul: Samseong (Samseong) Chulpansa.

10. *Han-guk inmyeong dae sajeon (The Encyclopaedia of Prominent Korean People)*, compiled by Yi Huiseung, Bak Jonghong, Yi Sangbaek, Baek Cheol, Han Takgeun and Jeong Byeonguk. 1995. Seoul: Sin-gu Munhwasa.

11. *Han-guksa dae sajeon (The Encyclopaedia of Korean History)*, compiled by Yu Hongryeol. 1996. Seoul: Goryeo Chulpansa.

12. Wikipedia, the free encyclopaedia on the internet.

Dr. Hyun-key Kim Hogarth

Dr. Hyun-key Kim Hogarth is a Korean-born British anthropologist, and a fellow of the Royal Anthropological Institute. She received her MA and PhD in social anthropology from the University of Kent at Canterbury, UK. She conducted extensive fieldwork among the Korean shamans for her PhD in 1993-1994, and has maintained her interest in them. She has published four one author books on Korean folk religions, entitled, *Kut Happiness through Reciprocity* (1998), *Korean Shamanism and Cultural Nationalism* (1999), *Syncretism of Buddhism and Shamanism in Korea* (2002), and *Gut, The Korean Shamanistic Ritual* (2009) and also co-authored *Tasks and Times* (2004) with ex-Foreign Minister Lee Tong Won. Many of her papers/articles on Korean society and culture also appear in various academic book, journals and magazines. She is currently working on three more book projects.

She was born and brought up in Seoul, Korea, and educated at Kyunggi Girls' High School, and Ewha Women's University, graduating with a BA in English Language and Literature. She became a British citizen in 1968 on her marriage to a British diplomat who passed away in 2003. She has two grown-up children, and lives in Canterbury, England.